Deaf Lives in Contrast

Deaf Lives in Contrast

Two Women's Stories

Mary V. Rivers and Dvora Shurman

GALLAUDET UNIVERSITY PRESS
Washington, D.C.

Gallaudet University Press

Deaf Lives

A Series Edited by Brenda Jo Brueggemann

Gallaudet University Press

Washington, D.C. 20002

© 2008 by Gallaudet University

Published in 2008

Printed in the United States of America

Library of Congress Cataloging-in-Publication Data

Rivers, Mary V.
  Deaf lives in contrast : two women's stories / Mary V. Rivers and Dvora
Shurman.
     p. cm. — (Deaf lives)
  Includes bibliographical references.
  ISBN 978-1-56368-394-7 (alk. paper)
  1. Rivers, Mary V.   2. Deaf parents—United States—Biography.
  3. Shurman, Dvora.   4. Children of deaf parents—Biography.   5. Deaf—
  Family relationships—United States—Case studies.   6. Deaf—Family
  relationships—Case studies.   I. Shurman, Dvora.   II. Title.
  HQ759.912.R58 2008
  306.874092′2—dc22
  [B]   2008026075

∞ The paper used in this publication meets the minimum requirements for
American National Standard for Information Sciences—Permanence of Paper
for Printed Library Materials, ANSI Z39.48-1984.

Contents

Silent World
Mary V. Rivers   I

Between Two Worlds
Dvora Shurman   IOI

Deaf Lives in Contrast

Silent World

Mary V. Rivers

To all my loved ones:
My dear husband Bruce
Monty, Darrell, Clay, Patricia, and Bruce Jr.

Preface

I remember clearly sitting in the doctor's office and hearing her tell me that my little boy could not hear anything, that he was deaf. I also remember hearing her say that she could do nothing to help him. This was a great shock to me, and it made me very angry. How could she be so cruel, to interfere with the happy life my husband and three handsome little boys led? Monty was three, Darrell was two, and Clay was only fourteen months old. Clay was a healthy looking baby. He had a round face and very alert green eyes and a reddish curl of hair on the top of his head. He was an adorable baby. They were all very handsome little boys. Now this doctor was telling me that Clay was deaf. I couldn't believe this was happening to me. I had read about it happening to other people, but not to me.

Clay's deafness was invisible, and I knew nothing about his silent world. I imagined it was like living in a large glass bubble, seeing everything and hearing nothing. I felt like he lived in one world and I lived in another.

From that point on, instead of being resentful, I realized that I must study his every movement in order to try and understand what each meant. I had to face reality, because Clay's deafness was mine to conquer with much strength and courage. I prayed to God to please show me the way. I knew nothing of this deaf world and it scared me.

Acknowledgments

I would like to thank Miss Leela Middleton for her help, encouragement, guidance, sympathy, and understanding in helping me with this manuscript. Miss Middleton is a retired teacher who taught first grade for forty-five years at the Many Elementary School in Many, Louisiana. Over the years, she taught 1,700 first-grade children, including my husband Bruce H. Rivers Sr. I would like to thank Ivey Pittle Wallace, editor of Gallaudet University Press, for giving me hope and encouraging me not to give up trying to get my manuscript published. I would like to thank Professor Brenda Brueggemann for all her hard work in helping me to get my story published.

I want to thank my husband, Bruce, for his patience while I spent long hours in front of my computer, and my children for believing in me and encouraging me to write this story.

Chapter 1. My Beginnings

I was born on a windy March day in 1933, to Cajun parents. For those of you who are not familiar with the term, Cajuns are a group of people in southern Louisiana and Texas who are descendants of French Canadian settlers, who were called Acadians. The Acadian region included New Brunswick and Nova Scotia. The term "Cajun" came from "Acadian." Cajuns maintain a unique culture that has many Acadian French characteristics. Today most Cajuns speak both English and French, but there are still some old timers who speak only French. Neither one of my parents could speak English. Like many people in our area, we spoke only Cajun French. My mother's name was Marie Octavie Devillier, and my father's name was Marcel Fontenot.

I was the youngest of eight children: five girls and three boys. The oldest was Vorence. We called him Slim because he was a tall man. I regret to say that Slim passed away in 2002. That leaves my other two brothers, Lawrence and Jean. My oldest sister is Gladyes, followed by Murdis, Gert, and Rose. They named me Mary Virgin Fontenot. Everyone in the family called me Vir until Bruce's Aunt Zula started calling me Mary. She said that I looked more like a Mary, and I have been going by the name of Mary ever since.

My father was involved in bootlegging, making and selling illegal homemade whiskey. That was common in the late 1930s. Times were hard, and one day he just walked out, leaving behind his wife, a new baby, and one son dying with pneumonia in a crib. I guess you could say we were dirt poor. The house I was born in had huge cracks, and my mother stuffed the cracks with an old catalog sheets to keep the March wind out. We did not own a car, so we had to walk to the store, church, school, and any other place we wanted to go. We had no electricity, so my sisters did their schoolwork by a kerosene lamp. We had no running water, just a pump on a deep well. We didn't have a telephone. We only had an outdoor toilet. Although we were poor, what I resented most was not having a father at home. The other little girls I played with had fathers, so why didn't I have a father at home? I really don't know how much I was affected by not having a father at home.

My little brother finally got better. I remember my dad coming to the house once in a while, and sometimes he would have a large bag of groceries with him. He would bring sugar, coffee, flour, and syrup. The syrup was called Johnny Fair, and we put it on biscuits. During these visits, my dad would beg my mother to take him back. She told him, "You left when I needed you, I don't need you now." She never did take him back.

My mother had a lot of pride. She took in washing and ironing to help make ends meet. She was a hard-working woman. She parched coffee beans in a big black pot on the stove. Then, she would grind the beans in a grinder we had on the wall. Many times I came home from school to smell the freshly parched coffee. It sure did smell good. Slim took care of the crops and kept us from starving to death. Later on he joined the Civilian Conservation Corps so that he could send some money home. Lawrence, my next oldest brother, managed somehow to get some money together and opened a small restaurant.

Mom spoke only a little English, just what she had picked up from the kids. My sisters taught her how to sign her name. She couldn't read. She didn't have schooling because her father was very ill when she was growing up, and she had to stay home to help with the crops. In spite of not being able to read or write she was very intelligent, and she knew a lot about money. She raised a big, beautiful garden, so we always had plenty of fresh vegetables. I can remember the butterbeans climbing on the fence. She raised big pumpkins and tomatoes, okra, cucumbers, and mustard green.

Mom also raised the biggest hogs I have ever seen. Sometimes my brother Jean and I would ride on their backs. Mom kept them in a pen, and I used to watch them waddle in the mud. She didn't kill and butcher the pigs herself, but hired someone else to do it. First they took a sharp knife and stuck it in the pig's throat, then they dipped the pig in scalding hot water. Finally they laid the pig on a piece of plywood, scraped all the hair off, and cut the meat up. My mother used this meat to make our own bacon and sausage. We had a small barn in the back yard. She strung some wire way up high and had coals burning on the dirt floor below. She strung the sausage over the wire. Sometimes I had to go stoke the fire, to keep the coals from going out. The aroma would make anyone hungry. Since we didn't have electricity or a refrigerator, she kept the bacon and sausage in large crock pots, about four feet tall, and salted the meat down to preserve it for awhile.

My mom was usually working in the garden when I came in from school. She wore an old-fashioned bonnet to keep the sun out of her face. One day I was hungry for a chocolate cake. I must have been around ten or twelve years old. Mom was hoeing the garden. I opened the kitchen window, which faced the garden, and hollered in French, "Mom, I want to bake a cake, how do I start?"

She hollered back, "Get a large bowl and break two eggs."

"What else?"

"One stick of butter. Two cups of flour, a little milk, two cups of sugar, a little salt, a little baking powder, and a little vanilla flavor." I melted chocolate and sugar and butter for the frosting. I made the best chocolate cake anyone could ask for. I was proud of my first cake and Mom was surprised at how good my cake turned out.

Mom sewed very well. She could make anything, even coats that looked store-bought. She found great pleasure in sewing for her girls. She made cute dresses for me to wear to school. I remember one in particular, a red dress with white polka-dots. It had big ruffled "butterfly" sleeves, and she made a pinafore to go with it. I wore it with a white blouse. Like most Cajun people, we were Catholics, and my mother believed in going to church on Sundays, taking us kids along. If she saw someone in church wearing a dress that she liked, she could cut a pattern out of old newspapers and make herself a dress just like it.

I started school in Mamou, Louisiana, in 1939. I couldn't speak or understand English. Mom only spoke French, and until I started school, French had been my only language.

I had beautiful, long, black hair that hung way down my back. When I didn't understand what my teacher, Mrs. Sable, wrote on the black board, or if I didn't understand what she was saying, she would get very angry and pull my hair. Her face would turn very red and as she pulled hair, she would say, "I can't do nothing with that little thing." In those days, speaking French in school was very much discouraged. Mrs. Sable pulled my hair so much that one day I felt something trickle down my leg. I was so embarrassed—I had wet in my pants. I told my mother what happened and she became very angry. Mom went and talked to the principal about it, but I don't really remember if Mrs. Sable stopped pulling my hair after that incident.

Mrs. Sable also kept a thick wooden paddle, about five feet long with holes at one end, in her desk drawer. If any of us misbehaved, she would call us up to her desk. She made us hold our hands out, palms up, and hit us several times until our hands turned bright red! That really did hurt! Needless to say, I failed the first grade. When school started again in the fall, I decided to go to a different teacher's room. My new class was overcrowded, and one day the teachers came around looking for students to move into other rooms. I sat low in my chair, hoping that they wouldn't put me back in Mrs. Sable's class, but she picked me to go back in her room. I guess I was finally learning English, because Mrs. Sable treated me very differently the second year.

While I was in grade school we had no electricity. We didn't have a radio either. For entertainment, we had a very old black Victrola that sat on a table. To make the turntable move, someone had to turn the handle, and if the handle was turned too much it would unwind and hit the person turning it. We had a stack of Blue Bird records, including some by Jimmy Davis, who became governor of Louisiana in 1944. We had his most famous record, "You Are My Sunshine." I did my homework by the light of a kerosene lamp. Sometimes, when my sister-in-law was visiting, I would ask her to call out my spelling words so I would know them the next day.

My father had married again and was living in Ville Platte, Louisiana, a town about twelve miles from Mamou. My mother found a house she wanted to buy, a two-bedroom frame house on a nice corner lot, but first she had to come up with a $700 down payment. We all worked hard to help her come up with the money. I was about fourteen or fifteen years old, my sisters and I picked cotton to help my mother come up with her down payment. We would get up very early in the morning, around 4:30. When I woke up, I could smell the French toast my mom was cooking for us to bring to the cotton field. We all picked cotton until about nine in the morning, and then we would sit at the end of a cotton row and eat our French toast. (That is, if the aunts didn't find it first!)

To pick cotton, I dragged a large burlap sack on a strap around my shoulder. We began picking at the beginning of the row, taking the big white fluffy cotton from the bushes. Sometimes, early in the morning, the cotton balls would be heavy and wet with dew. When I first started picking cotton, the farmers were paying seventy-five cents for a hundred pounds. Later they were paying one dollar and fifty cents, or even up to two dollars, for that same hundred pounds.

Mom finally saved enough money to buy the house. She was so proud of that little house. It was on a nice corner lot with shade trees. The front door opened into the living room, and straight ahead was a large kitchen. There were two bedrooms and a bathroom on the left, just off of the kitchen. We gradually fixed up the house, adding a porch in back and another small bedroom. We had electricity put in, then running water, and finally a real bathtub and indoor toilet. That little house was our mansion.

Today I realize that my mother depended on me for some things after I started school and learned to read and write. She depended on me to read incoming letters and explain to her (in French) what they said. She would charge little things at a nearby lumberyard, Deville's Lumber Co. Sometimes she bought paint or nails, and once a new light fixture for the living room. She would ask me to check the sales slip for errors. She could count money in French as well as I can count in English. No one cheated her out of a penny without her noticing. Every penny counted.

My mother was a strong-willed person, and I undoubtedly inherited some of her characteristics, such as the desire to better myself and the ability to set a goal and work very hard to accomplish it. Her goal was to raise her girls right, provide for all of her children, and improve our small house in any way she could to make a home for us. In spite of all the hardships she faced while raising a family alone, she had a great sense of humor. I miss her terribly.

My older sisters Rose and Gert finished high school and left home. I grew up to be a teenager who loved to dance—I think all French people love music and dancing. Back in those days, mothers escorted their daughters to dances. They sat on benches along the walls so they could keep an eye on their daughters. My mother was pretty strict with us. When I got a little older, she finally agreed to let me go to dances with a friend who was a little older than me. We used to ride a school bus to the dances in a nearby town called Basile. My best friend and I used to love to steal each other's "boyfriends."

One night when I was sixteen years old, we were sitting at a table at the dance hall when I saw three GIs walk in. One was tall, with a dark complexion, and very handsome in his Air Force uniform. I nudged my girlfriend and said, "See that tall one? He is mine. You just as well keep your hands off of him!" I just had to meet him.

I got up, walked past him, and said, "Hi, Sergeant." He wasn't even a sergeant, only a corporal, but I didn't know one rank from another. We started talking, but he didn't ask me to dance. Finally I asked, "Don't you dance, Sergeant?"

He said, "I don't know how to dance but I sure would like to take you home."

"I bet you would."

"I came here on a bus, and I am going home on a bus," he told me.

"Well, can I walk you to the bus?" he asked.

"Yes, it's parked right out front."

Me, at sixteen.

So he walked me to the bus, removed his dog tags, put them around my neck, and kissed me. He said, "Some day I'll come back and make you my wife." I thought, boy, has he got a line. I figured I'd never see him again. About a week later I went to the post office and there was a letter from Cpl. Bruce H. Rivers, A.F., Bergstrom Air Force Base in Austin, Texas. I couldn't believe it! This handsome, young, good-looking soldier had written me a letter.

Bruce told me that he was from north Louisiana, a small town called Many. He was a sharecropper's son and one of nine children. His family raised cotton, corn, peas, and vegetables on halves—they kept half of what they raised and the other half went to the landowner.

Bruce did not own a pair of shoes until he was five years old. His parents bought shoes only for the children who were in school. One day, Bruce stood on the old wooden porch, barefoot and wearing an old pair of faded overalls, watching his father hitch the horses to the wagon. Mr. Rivers was going to town to sell the cotton, so Bruce said to him, "Pa Pa, if you have enough money, bring me back a pair of shoes."

"Well, if I have any money left over, I'll do that, Bruce," his father answered. After selling the cotton at the gin, Mr. Rivers went in a store and saw a display of shoes on a table with a sign: "25 cents." He brought back a pair of shiny black high-top leather shoes that buttoned to the top. They were little girl's shoes, but Bruce was so proud of his first pair of shoes, he didn't even care.

The Rivers family lived about seven miles from town. On Saturdays each child got twenty-five cents to go to town to see a movie. The movie cost twelve cents. After the movie, they spent the rest of the money on a short loaf of white bread to eat on the way back home. White bread was a luxury back then—they ate cornbread and biscuits at home.

The boys got into scrapes at school. Mrs. Little was Bruce's teacher, and her son was named Tobby. He was well-dressed and he made fun of Bruce's overalls and biscuit lunch. One day Bruce punched Tobby and they went rolling down a hill in the school yard. Tobby got a nose bleed and his nice clothes got all dirty. Mrs. Little suspended Bruce for three days. Bruce's father decided to go see the principal. When the principal asked Bruce what the fight was about, Bruce answered, "I got tired of him making fun of my clothes and my lunch."

One day Bruce and his brothers got in a scrabble at school. The principal made them walk all around the school yard, about 200 yards, each carrying a piece of firewood over their shoulder and one piece of firewood under their arm. Mr. Rivers was really angry when he found out about their punishment, and he rode the bus to school the next morning. He strolled into the principal's office and the principal said, "Now, Tom, take it easy."

Tom started chasing the principal around the desk, howling, "If you ever do that to my kids again, I'll whip your ass."

All the principal could say was, "Take it easy, Tom." From what I heard, the principal got the message. Bruce and his brothers never had to carry firewood on their shoulders again as a punishment.

The children were given soup cards that allowed them to eat in the cafeteria. It was part of a program started by our old governor, Huey P. Long, so that poor children could get a hot meal. One day when Bruce was in the eighth grade, Mrs. Little asked him to pass out the soup cards. Some of the other boys were standing around the classroom, and Mrs. Little got upset because the class was disrupted. She spanked Bruce along with the other boys, using a thick wooden paddle about five feet long. The paddle had a handle at one end and holes at the other end. Bruce protested, "You told me to pass out the soup cards!" Bruce went to his desk and cleaned out his books and laid them on Mrs. Little's desk.

"What are you doing?" she asked.

He replied, "I am leaving, you need these books worse than I do." He walked out of the classroom and back to the farm.

His parents really needed help on the farm so they didn't encourage Bruce to go back to school. He got up at five in the morning and plowed the cotton fields. Bruce laid the plows down just before he turned seventeen in order to join the Army Air Corps. He didn't have a pair of dress shoes, so he borrowed his brother Woodrow's cowboy boots and rode a bus to Barksdale Air Force Base in Shreveport, Louisiana. He was sworn in on June 13, 1946. His father didn't know that Bruce had joined the Army Air Corps, and when he found out he threatened to get Bruce out. Bruce said, "You can get me out now, but when I am of age I will join again." Bruce took his basic training at San Antonio, Texas. On the train ride there he thought, "I will never see Mama and Pa Pa again."

At the end of the letter, Bruce told me that he would like to see me again. I couldn't believe that he was interested in me, a poor little Cajun girl. I wrote back to him right away, and from then on we started corresponding.

Chapter 2. Marriage and a Family

I was sixteen years old when I met Bruce. I was growing restless in school, tired of being poor and not having pretty store-bought clothes like other girls my age. They came to school wearing pretty cashmere sweaters. It made me conscious of my home-made clothes, although they were very well made and looked nice. I completed the eighth grade and didn't go back in the fall. I guess I just wanted to move on to more exciting things in life, so I moved in with my sister Rose and brother-in-law Acey in Eunice, another small town about twelve miles from Mamou. I found a job working as a waitress. Waiting tables wasn't so bad. I had good meals and the tips were good.

One night while I was working, I turned around and found Bruce Rivers sitting at the end of the counter. He had gotten a leave without my knowing. Every time I walked past him, Bruce whispered, "Ask your boss if you can take off early and go out with me for the rest of the evening."

Finally I asked my boss for the rest of the evening off. My boss replied, "You can have the rest of the evening off and don't bother to come back." I lost my job right there and it was Bruce's fault! He should have waited until I got off work, or at least let me know that he was coming. I was very upset and I told him that I didn't want to go out anymore. I walked back very fast to my sister's house. Bruce followed me the whole way. Finally I turned around and said, "You caused me to lose my job, what more do you want? Leave me alone!" What could he say? I didn't go out with him that night.

Bruce returned to Bergstrom Air Force Base. We continued to correspond, and later he was shipped to Japan and Korea. I dated other boys, and Rose would say about each one, "He is nice, but I like Bruce better." Deep down I knew I liked Bruce better too, but I was afraid to admit it, maybe even afraid of falling in love. I got a job at Reese's Variety Store across the street from the restaurant where I had been working. I went to the restaurant during my breaks.

One day, the manager asked me if I would like to come back to work. I told him yes, because I made more money there with my tips than at the variety store. I worked at that restaurant until I was seventeen years old.

After leaving the restaurant, I decided to enroll in a beauty school. I worked during the day selling hosiery and went to beauty school at night. I learned to give manicures. Some customers even asked for that cute little brunette girl. It made me feel good that the customers liked me. For a while it worked out fine, but I was really pushing myself and I began to feel tired. Finally I decided to see a doctor. He said that I was working too hard and ordered complete rest for a while. I obeyed his orders and went back home to my mother, who was living alone now. After three years of working, my old familiar bedroom never looked so good to me. My big, white four-poster bed was still waiting for me.

One Saturday morning in March, I was still in bed with curlers in my hair, just enjoying being lazy, when I heard someone knocking on the front door. My mother let the caller in. There stood Bruce right inside my bedroom, and me with curlers in my hair. "Let's get married!" he said. I was so surprised all I could think to say was, "Well, let me wake up first." It seemed strange to me that I fell in love with a military man, but was it? When I was very young, I used to say that when I grew up I wanted to travel and see the whole world. I knew there was more to life than this little town where I grew up, and I wanted to see it.

Bruce was only on a three-day pass, which presented a problem. Bruce was not a Catholic, and the priest would not marry us on such a short notice. He said he needed a four-month advance notice, so that the wedding notice could be published in the Sunday bulletin. We talked to a couple of different priests, but got the same negative answer each time. Bruce said, "I don't know or suppose your mother would let you get married by a justice of the peace?"

I loved Bruce so much that I couldn't bear the thought of him going back to Bergstrom without me, so I asked my mother. "Could we, mama? We'll have our marriage blessed in church someday, I promise."

On March 29, 1952, we were married by the justice of the peace in Mamou, Louisiana. I wore a simple white tailored suit, with a white hat and white gloves. Bruce wore his dress uniform. My oldest sister, Gladyes, was our witness, and Bruce's brother, Eirtis, was the best man. I thought Bruce looked very handsome. My mother bought a cake and made a pitcher of lemonade. I hugged my mom good-bye and we headed toward Bergstrom Air Force Base in Austin, Texas, where Bruce was stationed. Since my family didn't have a car, I had never been out of the state of Louisiana. I was fascinated with the ride to Austin and took in the scenery while Bruce drove.

Bruce, twenty, and me, sixteen.

We found a small house near the base. I loved to keep it neat. We even planted flowers on each side of the sidewalk in front. We were very happy.

My Three Boys

On June 12, 1953, our first child was born in Austin, Texas. We named him Monty Raymond Rivers, and he was a beautiful healthy baby with a full head of black hair. At that time, doctors didn't allow husbands to be in the labor room with the wives, so I was in labor for about ten hours with no one to share the pain. During my labor, I actually thought that I was dying. After I went home, I think Bruce brought his whole outfit to see the baby. It was quite a picture—a tiny baby lying in the middle of our big bed surrounded by a dozen Army aviators. When Monty was only six weeks old, we transferred to Sandia Base in Albuquerque, New Mexico. We got a house on the base this time. It was nice. We had a living room, kitchen, three bedrooms, and one bath.

I couldn't believe the size of the mountains. I was so taken with them, they looked so huge and mysterious. I kept asking Bruce, "What if the rocks start falling down on the car?"

Bruce just laughed and said, "It is not likely that they will fall." I feel sure that he was laughing at me, too. I thought the country and mountains were beautiful. We enjoyed our new baby, and we enjoyed living on Sandia Base. We met some friends and did some sight-seeing together.

About one month after Monty was born, I had a bout of morning sickness. I thought, "Oh no, not again!" I went to the doctor, and he confirmed my suspicions. I was pregnant again! Eleven months later we had our second baby, another boy. I had a good pregnancy and a very fast delivery. This baby had blue eyes and blond hair, a big contrast to our first baby. We named him Darrell Gene Rivers. Gene was the name of one of Bruce's brothers. When we left the Sandia Base Hospital, the nurse said, "See you next year."

"Not if I can help it," I replied.

Fifteen months later I was right back in the maternity ward. Same bed, same doctor. The doctor told me the baby was due in July. It was so hot that summer and I was so tired of being pregnant. I was really getting tired of wearing maternity clothes. Bruce was a Staff Sergeant and our money was pretty tight.

One night I kept running to the bathroom, and I finally decided that I must be in labor. It was about a thirty-mile drive to the Sandia Base Hospital. I woke Bruce up and told him it was time to go to the hospital. My neighbor Beth across the street had agreed to come and stay with Monty and Darrell while I went to have this baby. I called Beth and told her that it was time for me to go to the hospital. She came right over. When we got to the hospital, the nurse kept asking me all kinds of questions. "How far apart are your pains?" She just kept asking me questions.

I was having strong contractions by then. Finally I said, "Lady, this is my third baby and you better do something fast." She put me in a labor room instead of taking me straight to delivery.

I felt the baby coming and I screamed. A nurse came running in. She threw her hands up and cried, "Oh God, she is having the baby all by herself." Bruce had gone down to the parking lot to get my suitcase. When he returned, the doctor came out of delivery and told him, "You have a fine baby boy."

My third baby was born in just the short amount of time it took Bruce to run down to the parking lot and then back into the hospital, maybe ten minutes at the most. He was born on September 6, 1955. He was a beautiful baby. He had a round face and a lot of reddish-colored hair. We named him Clayton Lee Rivers. His middle name, Lee, was after Bruce's Uncle Lee, who was married to Aunt Zula. We called him Clay for short. I read an article in the newspaper about a man named Clay and I thought, "What a beautiful name," so we named him Clay.

My neighbor was keeping Monty and Darrell while I was in the hospital. Monty was two now, and Darrell was just fifteen and a half months old, and now I had a new baby. I had a bit of time to relax in the hospital. While I rested, I thought to myself, *how in the world will I manage three babies?* They let me go home after three days in the hospital. I will never forget the sight of my babies when I got back home. They were standing together, looking out of the screen door, while I got out of the car. Darrell's diaper was hanging loose on one side and about to fall off. *Dear God, help me*, I thought. I had three babies now and the oldest was only two years old. The guys in Bruce's outfit pitched in and bought a playpen for Clayton. That playpen was a godsend, since I had two others to chase after all day. Clay was a good baby. He would lie in the playpen for hours, so content and quiet. My friends would say, "He is the best baby: you never hear him cry." I soon had three very handsome little boys. I enjoyed dressing Monty and Darrell alike, and a lot of people would ask me if they were twins. Sometimes, to save the trouble of explaining that they were only eleven months apart, I would say yes. I found a routine for taking care of my three babies, but I was a very busy little mom.

Darrell and Monty with Ti Pi.

My Babies and Me

When Clay was three months old, Bruce was transferred to Greenville Air Force Base in South Carolina. We found a small house right off the base. We had only been there a short time when Bruce announced that he had been given orders to transfer to Chatereaux, France. I was surprised, but then I had always known that he would get overseas orders sooner or later.

At that time, the housing situation in France was poor, and there wouldn't be anywhere for all of us to live. Bruce said that as soon as he could, he would put in for a transfer for Germany, and that we could join him there. In the meantime I had to go back to Louisiana, near my mother's house, and find a place for my babies and me to live. We weren't able to find a house right in town; however, my cousin had a really nice house outside of town that we could use. This nice house was in the middle of a cotton patch. Railroad tracks ran in front of the house. The boys had lots of room to play, but it was a lonely time for me. Every night, after I went to bed, I could hear that train coming down the tracks, *clack, clack, clack*. I would hear it starting when it was a long way down the tracks, until finally it passed right in front of the house. I don't think any thing sounds so lonely as the sound of a train coming in from far away, especially if you are already lonely. Sometimes I would bury my face in the pillow and have a good cry. I missed Bruce terribly.

Every night, after I put my boys to bed, I'd sit at the dining room table and write Bruce a letter. One night I had my head down, writing Bruce a letter, and when I raised my head I saw my reflection in those glass doors. It really scared me. Another time I was startled by a loud noise on the back porch. It turned out that some darn cat had jumped on some overturned wash tubs. I guess I was jumpy, being alone with my boys in that house, the nearest neighbor about one block away. After the cat scared me, I decided that I was going to find a house in town, closer to my mother. I finally managed to find a small wooden house on a corner with a fenced in backyard. I was really happy that it had a fenced-in yard for the boys to play.

One day we went to visit my mother. She had left a can of paint on the back porch. While I was talking to my mom, the boys somehow got the can of paint open, and they smeared paint everywhere. I threw myself across the bed and had a good cry. Mom helped me clean up the mess. That night I wrote Bruce a letter and told him that I just had to come meet him. The boys were driving me crazy. I asked him to try and hurry the transfer to Germany.

Chapter 3. Clay

When Clay was about a year old, I decided to visit my in-laws in Many. I thought that the change would do us all some good. Their farmhouse was set way back from the road and the boys had plenty of space to play. They played with little cars under the trees. Monty would hold a long stick over his shoulder and pretend that it was a rifle. Mrs. Rivers said, "He walks like he is six feet tall." They got so dirty. Mrs. Rivers would say, "Let them play, we will bathe them later. They are having such a good time."

Mr. Rivers would sneak up behind the boys and make a loud scary whistling noise. I thought he was trying to scare them. None of the boys ever seemed scared by it, and Clay would keep right on playing like nothing had happened. At first I thought Clay was ignoring

Clay at six months with me.

Mr. Rivers, and I didn't think much of it. We had a nice visit and we drove back to Mamou.

Later on I brought Clay to the barber shop for a haircut. His hair had a reddish highlight and it turned into a big curl on top. The barber talked to Clay as he cut his hair. I was sitting down, watching Clay and the barber. After a while the barber turned to me and asked, "Can your little boy hear?"

What sort of question was that? "Of course he can hear," I responded. He was a beautiful, healthy, active baby boy. True he wasn't talking yet, but he was only fourteen months old. He had time to talk. He laughed very loud and cried very loud and made noises like all babies do at fourteen months old. I wasn't worried about Clay not talking. He would talk when he got ready to talk. Some babies learn to talk faster than others. Why was that barber asking me if he can hear? I had enough to worry about. Why was he trying to scare me like that?

As the days went on, the barber's question kept going through my mind. "Can your little boy hear? Can your little boy hear?" It was like one of the old Bluebird records I used to listen to when I was little—sometimes the record would get stuck and repeat the same verse over and over. It was really nagging me. I started to observe Clay more closely. He certainly was an active baby, and he had fun playing with Monty and Darrell. I remembered how he would never cry in his playpen, and how my friends would remark what a good baby Clay was. They commented, "I never hear him cry." I wondered, is it possible he didn't cry because he couldn't hear himself cry? What if Clay can't hear? No. That is not possible. Things like that happen to other people, but not to me.

Fort Polk Army Base was only sixty-five miles away from Mamou. I decided to drive down there and see a doctor so I could have peace of mind. One morning I asked Mom to keep Monty and Darrell. I didn't tell her where I was going. I got up real early and dressed myself and Clay and headed toward Ft. Polk Medical Center. I felt sure my baby could hear, and soon I would be convinced of this and relieved. How little I knew. The doctor examined Clay and then ran a lot of different tests on him, even though he was too young for an accurate hearing test. The doctor tested Clay in a sound-proof room, using an audiometer, a device that uses simple vibrations at various frequencies and intensities to measure hearing. Even though it's not possible to test an infant's hearing directly, tests like the one with the audiometer let doctors measure alterations in brain waves and other bodily responses. Of course, this was all new to me at the time, and I didn't know what to expect. Finally, the doctor called me into his office. I remember him saying, "I guess there is no easy way to break the news to anyone. We believe your little boy has congenital deafness."

"What is he saying?" I thought to myself, "What does he mean?"

He explained to me that he believed Clay was deaf since birth, what was called congenital deafness. While the doctor was trying to explain all the medical terms to me, I got cold. I felt like someone looking in, maybe looking at a movie. Suddenly, I was brought back to reality and I felt like I was going to faint. I laid my head on the doctor's desk and sobbed. I was shaking all over. I couldn't believe this was happening to me and my beautiful baby. My thoughts turned to Bruce, and I heard the doctor say, "What's wrong?"

"My husband is in France," I sobbed. "You just told me my little boy cannot hear and you sit there and ask me what's wrong?" *How can I handle this all alone?* I wondered. I wanted my husband with me.

As I drove home, my head nearly burst with all my thoughts. *Dear God, I have to tell Bruce our little boy cannot hear. Our little boy is deaf. Our little boy will have to live in a silent world all his own for the rest of his life. He will never hear his mother or father calling him. He will never hear his brothers' or sister's voices. He will never hear his teacher, his friends, his wife and his own children, his baby crying or laughing. He will never hear the birds singing early in the morning, the sound of raindrops on the roof. The whistle of wind blowing, the thunder, the croaking of frogs after the rain. He will never hear a rooster crowing early in the morning. He will never hear the sound of music, the television, a radio, the alarm clock going off. He will never hear a cat mewing or a dog barking. My handsome little Clay will never hear any of the simplest things in his life. Things and sounds that we hearing people take for granted, my son will never hear. By some unfortunate mistake of nature, my perfect little boy will never hear.*

It's only human, in a situation like this, to ask, "Dear God, why me? Why my little boy? Why not someone else's little boy?" It's human to wonder if God put a few deaf people on earth, a few blind people and a few crippled people, to make us all a little more appreciative. But do we become more appreciative? No, we do not. We take it all for granted. We believe that the Lord is going to make us all perfect human beings. We feel He owes it to us. We are so wrapped up in ourselves, so self-centered, that we forget that what the Lord gives us today, He can take it away tomorrow.

As with any shock, I don't believe the full impact of the situation hit me right away. I thought, "This can't be happening to me." I had heard and read about things like this happening to other people. I never thought it would happen to me! I learned it can happen to anyone, even to me, to my family. When something like this happens to you, you have to try to accept it and learn to live with it, one day at a time. You have to gather all your strength, all your courage, all your determination to face reality. The only way you can do that is to pray to God to help you. You have to face it. You have to realize that it is not something you can treat, not something like mumps or chicken pox or measles that will go away in a few weeks. It is not a disease. It is not contagious. It is a permanent condition. It's something you will be living with for the rest of your life. The sooner you face up to it, the better off you'll be, and the faster you can start getting on with your life.

Dear God, I have to tell Bruce our little boy cannot hear. How do I write something like that in a letter? Well, as much as it hurt, there was only one way to write it—"Our beautiful little Clay cannot hear." I knew it had to be done. So I sat down and wrote my letter to Bruce.

Bruce was just as shocked when he received my letter as I had been in that doctor's office. There was nothing that he could do to advance the transfer to Germany. All I could do now was wait. I drove back to Mamou, and I had to tell my mom that Clay was deaf. I told her that I went to Fort Polk to see a doctor, and that he told me that Clay had been deaf since birth. My mom said that she sort of suspected that he couldn't hear but didn't know how to tell me. Next I had to go back to Many to tell Bruce's parents. I waited until they were both in the same room and I said, "There is something that I have to tell you. I took Clay to the doctor in Fort Polk. After doing some tests on Clay, he told me that Clay has been deaf since birth." His mother went to pieces just as I had done. She threw herself across the bed and cried. I was so sorry to have to tell her such bad news—it was bad enough that we had not seen Bruce in almost a year. Mr. Rivers said that he'd suspected something was wrong but he didn't know exactly what it was. That was why he had made those scary noises behind the boys! He had been trying to find out if Clay could hear.

It seemed like everyone saw that Clay was deaf before I did. He was so active all the time. He could climb on anything. He played. He laughed. He cried. He made sounds. Clay learned to walk by the time he was eleven months old. I had no reason to believe that something was wrong with him.

The boys kept me very busy, and all I could think of was meeting Bruce. I didn't care about the lack of housing or the inconvenience, I just wanted to go meet Bruce and have my family together again. I applied for a passport right away, even before Bruce's transfer to Germany came through. I hoped maybe we would find a doctor in Germany who could help Clay. I heard they had good doctors there and I was hopeful. Preparing for a trip overseas was a lot of work. After I got things all taken care of, I kissed my mom good-bye. I knew that it would be two years before I would see her again. My brother Slim tried to talk me out of going, but I told him, "I already made up my mind and I am going." I even sold my car to Mr. Lenord, the sheriff.

Early one October morning, Mr. Lenord drove me and Monty and Darrell and Clay to Many. The boys were now two, three, and four years old. I couldn't wait for my port call to come in. Bruce's mom and dad didn't have a telephone, so I arranged to have the call made to his Uncle Lee and Aunt Zula, who lived nearby. Every morning Uncle Lee would come by, and as soon as I heard his old '47 Chevrolet pick-up, I'd run out to meet him on the front porch. I would eagerly ask, "Did my port call come in?"

His reply was always the same. "No, sister, I'll let you know when it does!" This went on for two months.

Chapter 4. Frankfurt, Germany, 1957

Finally, one day in December, 1957, my port call came in. I was so excited. Our plane was going to leave from Shreveport, Louisiana. Aunt Zula said, "If you insist on that trip to Germany with these three little boys, you should buy a harness for Monty and Darrell, or you will end up losing one of them at the New York airport." So I took her advice and bought a harness for the two older boys. I also bought them each a long coat and each a pair of boots. I'll never forget the morning of December 12, 1957. Try to imagine, if you can, a small-town girl, someone who had never even been out of her home state before she married, in a big-city airport such as Idlewild, now called Kennedy Airport, in New York. I was trying to keep up with a four-year-old, a three-year-old, and a two-year-old. Aunt Zula had been right about the harness. The airport was crowded and the boys stumbled and fell a lot. I was going around in circles trying to locate my luggage. My inexperience must have been quite obvious—I could see that we were attracting attention! I don't know if I was leading the three boys or they were leading me.

After going out and back through the swinging doors several times, it seemed like we were right back where we just got off the plane. Someone yelled very loud, "Hey lady, get away from there." Good Lord! We were back on the runway, and the wind from the planes almost scooped us up! Scared to death, I managed to get back inside the terminal. I finally located my luggage and heard someone say, "May I help you?" That was like sweet music to my ears.

He was an army sergeant. I said, "Please, would you call me a cab so I can get out of here." We got the cab and went to the Army Terminal, which was about an hour away from Idlewild, to wait for our plane to Germany. I have never seen so many wives with crying babies as I saw gathered at that terminal, all of us waiting to join our husbands.

We stayed at the terminal three or four days, waiting for the weather to clear. Snow was falling and the boys were having fun playing in it. It was the first snow they'd ever seen. It rarely snows in Louisiana. Finally we were to leave for Idlewild Airport on an army bus which managed to break down on route to the airport. We had to double up on another army bus. We were packed like sardines in a can. A young GI was kind enough to give me his seat and help me with the boys. I don't know how I would have managed without his help. I wish I could thank him, but I didn't even know his name.

Close to midnight, we boarded a four-engine Seaborn Western passenger plane. We settled down and soon took off. Flying at night is a very beautiful experience. I leaned back and gazed at the stars. I was on my way at last to meet Bruce! Around seven or eight that night we landed at Rhein Main Airport in Frankfurt, Germany. I was going through customs, having my passport checked, when I looked up to see Bruce walking in. Was I ever glad to see him! I flew into his arms. We were both so happy to see each other again. The boys hadn't seen their father in eleven months and they walked up to him and said, "Hi Daddy," as casually as if they had said good-bye the

Left to right, Monty (three), Darrell (two), and Clay (one).

day before. I had thought they would be jumping with joy, but children are unpredictable. From Rhein Main Airport we drove to the new apartment Bruce had found for us. It was nicely furnished. I thought the apartment looked beautiful. Some of Bruce's friends had hung a big "Welcome Home" banner on the wall above the sofa. Our family was together again at last.

There was only one problem with our apartment: it was on the third floor. But it was roomy and comfortable, with a big picture window in the living room. The boys used to press their noses against that window looking out. The back of the house faced an apple orchard. The weather, however, was gloomy and hazy and very cold, quite a contrast to the weather we'd just left behind in Louisiana. It was three months before we saw the sun again.

I was always worrying about the boys when they played outside. The apartment was on a very busy corner. I was always afraid that Clay might take a notion to cross the street. Being deaf, he wouldn't be bothered by noises—not even oncoming cars or trucks. I was always on the balcony checking on them as they played in the playground below. Monty and Darrell were not much older than Clay, and I was not sure at that point if they really understood that their little brother could not hear. I told them to watch their little brother and not let him go in the road, because he couldn't hear. I think they sensed that something was not right and that he needed to be protected.

Once we were settled in our apartment, we started to get very anxious to take Clay to the United States Armed Forces Hospital in Wiesbaden. We had high hopes that one of the doctors there could help Clay. Finally the day arrived for our appointment. I explained to Clay, by gesturing to him, that we were going to see a doctor who would look in his ears and do some tests with him. Of course, Clay was only two years old. To him it was just an adventure.

Doctor Visit

The U. S. A. F. Hospital in Wiesbaden was located at the Lindsey Air Station. Bruce and I both hoped that the doctor, a middle-aged and soft-spoken man, would have encouraging news for us. The doctor made us feel at ease. He and his staff spent most of the morning running different tests on Clay. One test involved putting ice-water in both of his ears. The doctor explained that Clay would lean to the side if he could hear at all. I watched the process very slowly, each second a tick of hope, hope, hope. I felt sure the doctor would hear my heart pounding. After what seemed like an eternity, I saw Clay lean a very little to the left side. The doctor also tested him with a tuning-fork and an audiometer.

After all the tests were run, the doctor called us into his office. The diagnosis was the same: Clay had probably been deaf since birth. He went on to explain the complicated and delicate workings of the outer, middle, and inner ear. The outer ear is the part we can see. The middle ear contains the eardrum and a set of three tiny bones that transmit sound impulses to the inner ear. In the inner ear, a small organ shaped like a snail-shell, called the cochlea, relays those sound impulses to the auditory nerve, which channels them to the brain. Damage to the bones or eardrum (considered middle-ear hearing loss) can often be fixed, but damage to the vital center of hearing, the cochlea, cannot in most cases be repaired. Nerve tissue cannot repair itself once it has been injured or destroyed. Inner-ear damage is also known as sensorineural loss, or nerve deafness, and that was what he said Clay had. The doctor explained that Clay could hear a very little bit at a low frequencies, but that he could hear nothing at high frequencies. The doctor compared this to trying to hear a ship's whistle, the sound coming far away across the water.

Deafness can be genetically transmitted (inherited), or it can result from other factors, such as sickness before or after birth, lack of oxygen during delivery, injury, reaction to drug or alcohol, Rh factor, infection, or any number of other things. While the doctor was explaining all of this to me, I was wondering in which one of these factors explained Clay's deafness. I haven't been able to trace any deafness in the family, so it probably wasn't hereditary. As far as I knew, I hadn't had measles or any other illness during my pregnancy. My doctor had given me something for morning sickness, but I hadn't taken it for very long. I don't drink, and I have never smoked. I have Rh-negative blood and Bruce has O-positive, but when I asked the doctor if that might have caused Clay's deafness, he said no. I couldn't help remembering how fast Clay was born—in the time it took Bruce to fetch my suitcase from the parking lot. The doctor did say that lack of oxygen during delivery could sometimes be a cause of deafness. I wondered, would things have been different if the nurses had checked me in faster when I was in labor? Of course, I will never really know what caused the deafness, but I am not convinced that Clay was born deaf.

I think God gave me a very special kind of patience with Clay. I always tried very hard to understand what he wanted or needed, or what he was trying to say to me. Sometimes he would point to the cabinet, and if I didn't get what he wanted, he got very frustrated. It was like playing charades. As Clay got older, if I didn't understand him right away, he would get very angry and bang his head on the floor, sometimes so hard that I was afraid he would hurt his head. I guess that was his way of venting frustration.

I began to observe him more closely, to better understand what he wanted. This was all new to me, and I knew that I had a lot to learn by observing his every movement. I soon learned that it was a waste of my time and effort to try and communicate with Clay unless he was looking right at me. Sometimes it was hard to get his attention. I had to wave my arms in every direction until he took notice. Another method I used, whenever we lived in a house with wooden floors, was to stomp hard on the floor. Clay could feel the vibration and he would know that I wanted him to look at me. Once I got his attention, he'd turn to face me and study my lips, expressions, and gestures and try to make sense of what I was saying to him. I played a lot of charades with him when he was a small child. Each member of the family developed his own technique to communicate with Clay. Darrell and Monty were only three and four years old when we learned that Clay was deaf. Among the boys, Monty was always the leader, and Darrell and Clay just went along with whatever Monty wanted to do. They all learned, as I did, that Clay had to be facing them in order to understand what they were saying. If they wanted Clay to come, they would signal, "come on." They played charades with him also.

I realize now that it must have been just as frustrating for Clay to make us understand him, maybe even more so because we could hear. He finally outgrew the temper tantrums, and sometimes he used his deafness to his advantage. If Clay thought that I would scold him for something, he would deliberately not look at me.

From the time he learned to walk, it seemed there was nothing I could put out of his reach. He would climb like a little monkey. One day, I left him upstairs taking a nap while I went down to the basement to do some laundry. While I was busy in the laundry room, and Monty and Darrell were playing in their room, Clay woke up and pulled a chair to the kitchen cabinet where I kept the baby aspirin. He climbed the chair to the top of the cabinet and ate every aspirin in the almost-full bottle. They were orange flavored, and I guess he liked them. When I came back upstairs and saw the empty bottle I called the hospital in panic. The nurse I talked to said not to let him sleep too long. He was fine, but he sure did give me a good scare.

Chapter 5. The Delights of Paris: Summer of 1959

By the time we had been in Germany for two years, we had saved enough money for a trip to Paris to visit Charlotte and Bill, old friends from the States. I was very excited about the trip. I'd never dreamed that a poor little Cajun girl like me would ever have the opportunity to go to Paris! Clay was almost four now, and Darrell and Monty were five and six years old. We loaded the boys in a '54 Ford that Bruce had bought from his friend Sergeant Simmons and headed out for Paris.

We drove through the countryside, passing fields of colorful tulips and other flowers, haystacks, chickens running across the roads, and farmers working in the fields. I could see huge piles of hay, and sometimes a large barn in the distance. It was so relaxing to see the countryside this way. The boys were taking in the scenery as well, and they mostly behaved themselves while we drove. When we crossed the French border, a gendarme (policeman) checked our passports. He didn't stamp my passport and I was disappointed. I wanted that French seal on my passport—I was afraid that my friends in the States might not believe that I'd been to Paris, and if my passport wasn't stamped with the French seal, how could I prove that I had been there? We drove a mile further and I finally asked Bruce to turn around. "Why?" he asked. "I want the gendarme to stamp my passport." He laughed but turned the car around. Bruce told the gendarme I would like my passport stamped with the French seal. I got that stamp! Now I could prove to my friends beyond a doubt that I had really been to Paris. As a Cajun, this was very important to me.

The next day I was anxious to do some sightseeing. On the way to Paris I had come across only two French words that I didn't understand. We had stopped at a roadside café and I asked for an aspirin. The waitress didn't understand me. I patted my head and told her in French that I had a headache. Finally, she said "Aspro." I was afraid the French language would be really different from the Cajun French that I knew, but the only other word I found different on our trip was automobile. In Louisiana we say, "an shaww," but in Paris they say "vatour." Since I was born of Cajun parents and had known French even before I learned English, I had no trouble with the language in Paris. I understood what people were saying and they understood me. We walked on the streets of Paris and saw a lot of different little shops. We went inside a garden supply store, where I wanted to buy seeds to mail to my mother in Louisiana. I wanted to see if they would grow in Louisiana. The clerk said to me in French, "You will have a pretty garden."

I explained to her, also in French, "The seeds are not for me. I am going to mail them to my mother in Louisiana."

She was very surprised. "You not from Paris, no?"

"No, I am from Mamou, Louisiana."

"I thought you were from Paris," she said with a smile.

Naturally, we toured the Eiffel Tower. I still have a bracelet I bought at a souvenir stand at the base of the tower. Bill took lots of pictures and even a video of us about midway up the Tower. Bruce went all the way to the top, but the boys and I stopped about half-way.

We visited the Arc de Triomphe and France's Tomb of the Unknown Soldier of World War I. We went to the Louvre, where we saw the *Mona Lisa* and the *Venus de Milo*. We visited the Cathedral of Notre Dame, the most famous of Paris's many beautiful churches. It was breath-taking. We went to Versailles, where the peace conference meetings were held after World War I. The gates at Versailles have pure gold on them.

We took the children to the Paris Zoo, one of the largest zoos in Europe. The boys liked the animals, especially the monkeys, giraffes, elephants, lions, and the peacocks and other beautiful birds. The peacocks spread their large colorful tails just like a huge fan. We had one eventful day of sight-seeing, and by the end of it, the children were tired. In the late afternoon, we headed back to the apartment, where we fed and bathed the children. They were talking about all they had seen at the zoo. I included Clay in the conversation by making gestures about the animals. I imitated the monkeys scratching their backs and pointed to my own back, acting like I had a monkey's long tail. Clay laughed and thought his mother was very funny.

Folies-Bergére

That night, we had a sitter to come stay with the children while we all went to the Folies-Bergére, which was the most beautiful performance I had ever seen. The girls were stunning, and the costumes were out of this world! The show was so colorful—the scenes would change before you realized what was happening, and the girls could really dance. I enjoyed the chorus line and the single dance by a boy and girl. They danced so gracefully. When the single dance was over, a chandelier came down very slowly from the ceiling. There were girls between the lights on the chandelier, but every other girl was actually a mannequin. The girls stood so still it was hard to tell which was a girl and which was a mannequin! When the chandelier reached the stage, the live girls stood up and performed one last dance, a farewell dance, and then the show was over. That evening in Paris is one I will always remember.

After one glorious week in "Gay Paree," we headed back to Wiesbaden. We thanked Bill and Charlotte for a great time and invited them to visit us in Germany. That fall, Monty was old enough to start school. Bruce offered to take him to school the first day. Monty was a very handsome little boy with his freshly cut dark hair and brown eyes. I dressed him in a red sweater and the new jeans I had bought for him. He was really looking forward to going to school. Bruce took Monty to school in Wiesbaden, and when Bruce got back, he said, "Would you believe that his teacher is from Lafayette, Louisiana?"

"You're kidding me!" Lafayette is not far from Mamou, where I was raised. *What a small world we live in*, I thought.

Monty was very proud to be going to school. We made arrangements for him to ride the bus to school, so that I would I have more time to spend with Darrell and Clay. Darrell wanted to go to school too, so I enrolled him in a little day-care center where they read to the children, let them color and put puzzles together, and sometimes took them on field trips. Clay would walk with me to the bus stop. He started crying because he wanted to go to school with Darrell. One day I brought Clay to the day-care center. I explained to the lady in charge, Miss Deal, that Clay was deaf but that he really wanted to go to school with his brother. "Is he potty trained?" she asked. When I said that he was, she said, "Let him come." So in the fall of 1959, all three of my boys were going to school. Clay enjoyed riding the bus to school with Darrell. He played with the other children and brought back pretty pictures that he had colored. The boys only went to school for a half day. It was working out just fine.

One night while we were still in Wiesbaden, the weather was bad and we heard a very loud thunder. Clay ran into our bedroom. I thought, *he must have heard that*. I cuddled him in the bed with us.

I kept telling Bruce, "He must have heard that." If only he could hear. I thought to myself, *when we get back to the States, I will take him to another doctor.* I think Bruce was afraid to build up my hopes and he didn't say anything to encourage me.

Chapter 6. Return to the States, 1960

I was just as excited about going home as I had been to go to Germany two years before, probably even more so. I hoped to find the right school for Clay and to learn more about deafness. I had to learn how to communicate with him; we all did. We got up early on the day of our flight, and I dressed the boys in their new coats and boots. They were so cute all dressed up, and they were excited about riding in a big plane. We had a good flight and a safe landing at Idlewild Airport in New York, and I was grateful to have Bruce with me to help with the boys in the airport. This time I didn't need a harness for Monty and Darrell.

It felt good to see the Statue of Liberty and to know we were back in the States. We had shipped our car ahead, so Bruce took a cab to

Refueling in Shannon, Ireland, on our way back to the States.

Brooklyn Army Terminal to pick it up while I stayed with the boys in an airport hotel. As soon as Bruce returned with the car, we headed for Mobile, Alabama, where he would be stationed next. We drove through the beautiful Smoky Mountains of Tennessee. There was snow on the mountains. In some places where the snow was melting, little streams of water ran down from the peaks. I thought the mountains were pretty and I hoped to go back one day. We drove straight to Redstone Arsenal in Alabama.

We didn't have any trouble finding a house. Bruce had met a sergeant in Germany who owned a house that we could rent. It was a brick home with three bedrooms and a fenced-in back yard, and it was only about seven miles from the base. It seemed to take forever to get our furniture out of storage. In the meantime, Bruce checked out five Army cots from the base. I bought cheap dishes, one electric skillet, and a couple of cheap pots to get by until we could get our furniture. For about three months we ate our meals off of orange crates.

After about three months of living like this, our furniture finally arrived. It was good to have all the comforts of home again, including my comfortable bed. Bruce went to work and I got the house looking like home again with our old familiar furnishings.

Adventures in School

Once back in the States, Monty quickly settled back into the first grade. Because of the recent Christmas holidays, he hadn't missed that much school. My next priority was to find the right school for Clay and enroll him as soon as possible. We looked all over Mobile and inquired everywhere, but we couldn't find a school with a program for deaf children. There was nothing. My heart sank. He would soon be five years old, and we just had to find a school for him.

After much searching and inquiring, we heard of a school called the Line Avenue School in Shreveport, Louisiana. Barksdale Air Force Base is nearby in Bossier, with the Red River separating Shreveport and Bossier City. We wrote to the Line Avenue School for information about their program for deaf children. They wrote back that all the students, both hearing and deaf, ate in the same cafeteria and played on the same playground. The deaf students had special classes, in separate rooms, with certified teachers who had been trained to teach deaf children. They told us that if Clay was accepted, we'd be responsible for his transportation, as there was no bus service.

We had no choice but to put in for a transfer to Shreveport. It would mean taking Monty out of school again, but there was nothing else we could do. Clay had to be in school. Bruce's transfer request was turned down because he'd been in Mobile less than six months, but I was desperate. We had to find a school for Clay, and soon. Bruce had an idea. His father was pretty good friends with U.S. Senator Allen J. Ellender. Mr. Rivers had already spoken to Senator Ellender about the problems we were having finding a school for Clay. The senator had told Mr. Rivers, "If ever I can help you, let me know." So Bruce reapplied for a transfer to Barksdale on humanitarian grounds, arguing that our need to educate our deaf son counted as benefiting society.

Bruce mailed a copy of his transfer application to Senator Ellender. Less than two weeks later, we received a telegram approving of the transfer.

We bought a three-bedroom brick house in a subdivision named Shady Grove, about one mile from the base. The subdivision was about seven miles from the Line Avenue School, and there was an elementary school nearby for Monty and Darrell. The houses all had big pecan trees on the lots, so there was a lot of shade for the boys to play under. I was glad the kitchen faced the front so I could keep an eye on the boys while I fixed our evening meals.

Shortly after we got settled in, Bruce and I took Clay to the Line Avenue School. The school was in older red brick building. We went to the principal's office. He introduced himself as Mr. Clark. He was middle aged and soft spoken. He was very pleasant to us and showed us the room where the deaf children were taught. I met Clay's new teachers, Mrs. Bloomer and Mrs. Gibbs. They were pleased to meet us and took a liking to Clay right away. I would have to take Clay to school by eight-thirty in the morning and pick him up by three o'clock in the afternoon. We were so happy that we finally found a school for Clay.

Line Avenue School wanted us to take Clay to Tulane Medical Center in New Orleans, four hundred miles away, for a full evaluation. We made an appointment for the evaluation. I asked someone to come to stay with Monty and Darrell, since we had to leave so early in the morning for the drive to New Orleans. I was happy to have found a school for Clay, but I was afraid to build my hopes again that maybe something could be done for Clay. Still, I was hoping something could be done to help Clay hear.

We arrived at the Tulane Medical Center around ten o'clock in the morning. We met first with a woman doctor who asked me a lot of questions about my pregnancy. After I answered as many questions as I could, she started Clay's evaluation. She arranged blocks on a table and stacked three of them, one on top of the other. Then she scattered the blocks and gestured to Clay to stack them. Clay thought that she was playing a game with him, and he enjoyed games. She had him play a few different games and work with some large puzzle pieces to see if he could understand what to do with them. Sometimes he did what was expected of him, but other times, if the test was a little more complicated, he would just scatter the pieces around, not knowing what to do with them. This went on for about one hour.

Next, we were told to bring Clay to a different room for a hearing test. The doctor placed earphones on Clay and told him to raise his right hand if he heard something. My heart was pounding so fast I just knew the doctor would hear it. While he was being tested, I thought I saw his green eyes light up, and I wondered if maybe he could hear the tones. He raised his hand, but I think he was just enjoying the attention. It seemed like we waited for hours before the doctor could talk to us, but last he came into the room where we were waiting. He explained the results, much like the doctors at Fort Polk and Wiesbaden had. He said that Clay was deaf, and probably had been since birth. He could hear very little in his left ear, and only on a low frequency.

Clay was tired and fell asleep on the ride back to Shreveport. I was quiet while Bruce drove back. I had so many thoughts and questions going through my head. Clay's deafness seemed so final, so permanent. I looked at my sleeping baby in my arms. He was the picture of health. His face was round and he had a pretty curl on top of his head. He had a big chest and was sort of husky looking. Just to look at him, no one would guess that he was deaf. Deafness is an invisible handicap. While Bruce was driving, I made myself a promise. I would do everything in my power to help educate my son. He would not beg on the streets. He would not sell pencils on the street corner and have people feeling sorry for him. I was going to help educate him, so help me God.

Clay turned five in the fall of 1960 and started school. I fell into a very busy routine of getting up early, helping Monty and Darrell get ready for school, helping Clay get dressed, and fixing breakfast for all of them. Monty and Darrell rode a bus to school, which helped make the mornings easier. Around eight o'clock I drove the seven miles to Line Avenue School, dropped Clay off, and drove the seven miles back home. I got back home around 9:00 A.M. I would straighten up the house, do the laundry, and cook lunch, since Bruce came home for lunch every day. At exactly 2:00 P.M. I'd set out for school again to pick up Clay.

Line Avenue School had three rooms set aside for deaf children. I felt very fortunate that Clay had an excellent teacher. Her name was Helen Bloomer and she soon earned my respect and admiration.

Helen Bloomer and the boys in her first-grade class. Clay is in the middle of the bottom row.

She was like a miracle worker. I visited the school often, at least once or twice a week. I wanted to learn all I could about Clay's silent world, so I could be even more of a help to him. I observed everything Mrs. Bloomer did in the classroom. Mrs. Bloomer wanted to meet the rest of the family, so she visited us at home.

Mrs. Bloomer had a class of about eight children, five boys and three girls. She believed that every deaf child deserved an opportunity to communicate orally, so she worked very hard to teach them to talk. She'd sit Clay on her lap so that he was facing her—the deaf child always has to face whoever is talking, so that he or she can pick up lipreading and facial expressions. Facial expressions play a big part in helping the deaf child understand what is being said. Mrs. Bloomer placed Clay's small hand on the side of her throat so he could he feel the vibration of her vocal cords. Then she made sounds for him to feel: *ba, ba, ba, ba* to teach him the sound of B. She made Clay repeat and repeat and repeat. She held up a feather and blew on it. That was to get the P sound, *paw, paw, paw.* Clay would blow on the feather and feel his breath on his hand. I sat quietly in the room and took in her every movement.

One thing I learned over the years was the importance of teaching the deaf child the same as what you'd teach the hearing child, or as close to the same as possible. Hearing and deaf children alike need to learn to behave themselves, and also to work toward independence. We mothers were told never to feel sorry for our deaf children or to give in to them; that would defeat the whole purpose of their training. We were told to let our children dress themselves every day. I would set his jeans and shirt and sweater out every day, and Clay learned to dress himself at the age of five. Sometimes he skipped a button hole and he would have to start buttoning his shirt all over again, but he always wanted to do it himself.

Chapter 7. A Wake-Up Call

I thought that I had accepted the fact that Clay was deaf, but it turned out that acceptance was easier said than done. Deep down there was still room for a tiny and stubborn hope that something could be done to cure my child's deafness, or that a miracle would happen. I guess I never did bury that tiny hope; I still carry it deep inside.

The base in Shreveport had a big hospital, and it wouldn't even cost anything to bring Clay in for a check-up and consultation with a doctor. No one needed to know that I brought Clay. I felt that I had to try, just one more time. I made an appointment for Clay, but I didn't tell Bruce. He would discourage another doctor visit and didn't want to give me false hope.

After the doctor examined Clay, she looked at me, hard. Surely she recognized that I was clinging to that tiny bit of hope. She said in a very stern, cold, and harsh tone, "Your little boy is deaf. The best thing you can do for him is to educate him." I don't know what I was expecting, but not this cold, cruel voice. Her attitude hit a nerve, and I felt weak. How can she do this to me? How can she destroy that last tiny bit of hope? She made it so final, so permanent. It was like she had thrown a pitcher of ice-cold water right in my face. I wanted to attack her, to claw her face bloody. I wanted to hurt her as she was hurting me. What right did she have to do this to me, to interfere with my happiness, with Bruce and my three handsome little boys?

Clay's silent world frightened me. I lived in a different world, a very noisy hearing world, a noisy hearing world that Clay knew nothing about. I knew that I had to learn to understand his world. How could I do that, when it was so different from my world? How could I reach him? How could I educate my deaf little boy when I was not educated myself? I knew that I would have to conquer these challenges with much strength and courage.

I know now that the doctor at the base was not trying to be cruel. She was trying to wake me up, make me face reality, and accept Clay as he is: deaf. The only way she could do this was by killing off that last tiny hope. The doctor suggested a hearing aid for Clay. It was supposed to help him learn to control his voice, not so much to hear, but to be aware of the pitch of his voice. If I remember correctly, the hearing aid was very expensive. I think it cost $400. But even in the sixties, that was quite a bit of money. The hearing aid was pretty large—about two inches by two inches, including the batteries. A cord ran behind Clay's neck to connect the hearing aid to earphones

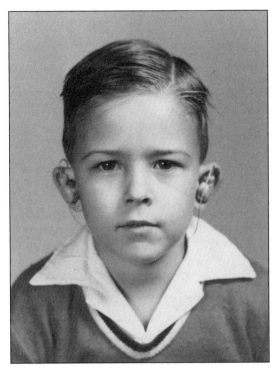

Clay with his hearing aid.

in both his ears. I sewed a little strap to hold the cord against his chest under his clothes. He could keep spare batteries in a little cloth sack that I made for him. Clay never did like to wear it. I got in the habit of checking, when I picked him up from school, to see if he was wearing the hearing aid. He would take it off as soon as we got back home. After about two years he refused to wear it at all.

Clay had a very deep voice, and it was generally a pleasant voice, unless he really wanted something. Then he made all kinds of loud, unpleasant noises like *Aw, Ba, Ba, Ba*. I can truthfully say there was only one time I was embarrassed by his noises. There was a little store on the corner by Barksdale A.F.B. where they sold a variety of things. After I picked up Clay from school one day, I stopped at that store to buy something. Clay picked up a big toy truck, but I told him "No" and put it back on the shelf. I didn't have enough money with me to buy the truck, but I didn't know how to get Clay to understand that.

Every time I put the truck back on the shelf, he grabbed it again, and he started making an awful very loud noise, *Aw, Ba, Ba, Ba.* The other customers in the store all stopped what they were doing and looked at us. Well, what was I to do but hurry out of there? That was the only time that I can remember being embarrassed by his deafness.

Darrell was now in the first grade and Monty was in the second grade. They rode the bus every day to Curtis School, a few miles from the subdivision where we lived. I continued to drive Clay to Line Avenue School every day and visited his classroom as often as I could. We drove over the Red River and past Centenary College. The ride was pleasant, and Clay knew our routine. All the while, I was learning more and more about the deaf world. Children who have been born deaf have to learn the names of all the objects in their lives, what the things and people around them are called. They can learn to identify the names of the objects through pictures. These pictures, Mrs. Bloomer explained to the mothers, should be appealing: bright, colorful, and clear.

I went around the neighborhood and asked for my neighbors' old magazines. I explained to them what I needed them for, and they would save their magazines for me. We searched for pictures that were just right—a table, a chair, an airplane, a car, a house—anything that was clear and colorful. I bought poster paper at the corner store. I cut cards from the poster paper and pasted the cutout pictures onto the cards. We did the same thing with colors—I colored large circles of different colors and pasted them on cards. I set aside a regular time every day of the week, usually after supper, to work with Clay. I was very serious about our tutoring sessions, and tried to stick to the schedule so that Clay would take the lessons seriously.

During the lessons, I would make Clay sit in a chair facing me. I would hold up one of the flash cards, name the object or color on the card, and try to make Clay repeat after me, the same way I'd observed Mrs. Bloomer doing it. She had warned me not to get discouraged, that it would take a lot of hard work and a lot of repetition. And repeat, repeat, repeat we did.

Unlike most five-year-old children, Clay never actually said anything very plainly. He made grunt-like noises and pointed to things that he wanted. He tried to say words, but he wasn't clear enough to be understood. If he wanted something—a drink of water, or a cookie, whatever—I tried to make him say the name before I'd give it to him. Mrs. Bloomer suggested that we do this, to encourage him to talk. The hope was that Clay would associate the name with the item that he wanted, so whenever he wanted something badly, I would do my best to try and make him say it. He would try and repeat it after me but he still couldn't say anything plainly.

I made a point to tell all of our neighbors that Clay was deaf, in case they saw him playing in the road or doing something that he shouldn't be doing. We lived in a nice neighborhood with a lot of military families. There were a lot of kids in the neighborhood, and they all played together after school. The other children knew Clay was deaf, but they tried to include him in their games. There were a lot of big trees in the empty lot close by. The boys formed a club and built a tree house, with its own ladder for climbing up and down. Clay liked to climb up to into the tree house. The kids in the neighborhood developed their own methods of communicating with Clay, mostly by motioning him to "Come on." Clay seemed to know what they wanted, and he played right along with them. They rode their bikes in the neighborhood and played marbles after school. Sometimes they just ran among the trees pretending they were cowboys and Indians. The kids liked to play with Clay, and it didn't seem to matter to them that he was deaf.

When Darrell was about six years old, he developed a persistent cough; he would cough all night! The doctor said that Darrell needed his tonsils removed, so we made arrangements for the operation at Schumpert Hospital in Shreveport. Darrell was in the hospital for about three days recovering from the surgery. At the hospital he shared a room with another little boy. I went to see him one day after I'd picked up Clay at school, and the other little boy's mother was reading him a book. While I was there, she said to Darrell, "I bet your mom reads to you."

"No, she doesn't have time." Darrell replied.

My heart sank. Did Darrell feel neglected? I was so busy trying to help Clay learn to talk, was I neglecting Monty and Darrell? They were not much older than Clay. While I drove back home I pondered that question. Was I neglecting my other children by trying to help Clay? I think all parents of a handicapped child ask themselves the same question—we want so much to help the handicapped child that we probably all feel at times that we are neglecting the rest of the family.

Once in a while, Mrs. Bloomer invited all the mothers to come in for a discussion about how our deaf children were affecting our families. We had the discussions early in the morning, before class started. Sometimes we even wrote papers about our deaf children. One day, another mother in the group was reading out loud what she had written, and I was surprised to learn that her husband was having a hard time accepting their deaf son. She said that her husband didn't know how to handle and discipline their little boy at home. The discussion made me realize that other people had problems with their deaf children—it made me realize that I wasn't alone with my problems. Each one of us had a deaf child, and it was good for us to share the experiences that we encountered in our daily lives.

I met a lady in our subdivision, Arlene Yakub, whose son Johnny was deaf as well. Arlene and I became friends. I noticed that Arlene was very good with Johnny, that she really knew how to handle him. One day Arlene said, "Mary, you are not talking enough to Clay. You have to talk all the time." She added, "Would you like me to help you work with Clay?"

"Sure," I answered. I was happy to have someone volunteer, someone with a bit more experience. Arlene agreed to come as often as she could. She came by sometimes on Saturday mornings. She did lessons with Clay just as Mrs. Bloomer did—she held Clay on her lap, with his hand on her throat, and made him repeat after her. She started with B: *ba, ba, bow*. Three or four times they repeated this. Clay hadn't said anything very clearly yet, but this particular morning he was trying hard. Arlene said, "*ba, ba, bow*." I heard Clay say, "*ba, ba, bow*." He said "*bow*" very clearly, too. Such a small word, but he said it. If he could say "bow," I thought, he could say anything. I felt a swelling in my throat and tears in my eyes. I wanted to run in the street and shout. "Hey everyone, Clay said "*bow*."

From that day on, Clay called Arlene "Bow" whenever he saw her. He thought that her name was Bow. Arlene really tried to help me, and she encouraged me to keep working with Clay. She told me to look at him and let him see my lips, eyes, and facial expressions. It was very important for Clay to see my face while I talked to him, and he learned to tell a lot about what I was saying by my facial expressions and body language. After I heard Clay say "bow," I was so encouraged that I worked harder than ever. I made signs and taped them all over the house. On every light switch, I posted a card that said "light." On the bathroom door, I posted a card that said "bathroom." Where the phone hung on the kitchen wall, I put a card right below it that said "telephone." Our house was practically wallpapered with Clay's cards.

Mr. and Mrs. Rivers came to visit one weekend. Many was about one hundred miles away from where we lived, and they were getting up in age, so they didn't get to come over that often.

Mrs. Rivers asked me, "What are all these signs for?" I explained how I was using the signs to help Clay learn to talk. Mrs. Rivers was not someone to give out compliments very easily, but I learned through other family members that she was very proud of me for trying so hard to help Clay. She was crazy about all of her grandchildren, and she didn't treat Clay any differently than the others. She just didn't know any way to communicate with him other than through gestures.

Clay was always very happy to see his grandparents. They kept a cow at home, fenced in behind their house. We were at their house one day and we heard Clay making a very loud noise. We ran to the back of the house to see what was wrong. Someone had left the gate open, but Clay knew that his grandma kept that gate closed so that the cow wouldn't get out. Clay let his grandma know that the gate was open, and Grandma gave him a big hug and thanked him helping to keep the cow from getting out.

I kept on visiting Clay's school as often as I could. I sat in the back of the room and observed Mrs. Bloomer's work with the children. I learned a lot by observing her. She explained the purpose of everything she did. I learned that feeling the objects was very important to deaf children. They make the most of their active senses—sight, touch, and smell—to compensate for their loss of hearing. By smelling and touching, they can better understand what's going on. As a result, deaf children are very sensitive to vibrations, and they can feel some sounds, including music playing. When someone enters a room and a deaf person turns around to see who walked in, it's because he or she felt the change in the air. This is why so many young mothers, like myself, believe our deaf children can hear, when in reality the children are simply being alert.

Mrs. Bloomer understood the importance of hard work and repetition. She told me not to get discouraged, and to keep on working with Clay at home as often as possible. I stuck firmly to my schedule; Saturday and Sundays were no exception. Every day at 4 o'clock, I went out and looked for Clay so we could do our lesson. He would often be riding his bike or playing outside with the other boys in the neighborhood. Clay knew what I wanted, and he would deliberately not look my way. Sometimes I asked one of the boys to touch his shoulder and point to me. When I finally did get his attention, I would motion to him, "Come on." If he was having a good time he would be reluctant to follow me back into the house, but I stuck firmly to my schedule. Every day we worked for about one hour. It was our routine, and Clay knew better than to try to argue himself out of it.

I was pleased that Clay was able to enjoy music and rhythm. He took up tap dancing at school, and he looked forward to his weekly lessons. He looked so adorable in his black trousers, white shirt, black bow-tie and shiny black tap shoes. Mrs. Bloomer would hold each child's hand on top of the piano and encourage them to feel the vibrations of the notes as they were struck. They could feel the music through the piano or through the wood floor. Once a year the children put on a dance recital. They enjoyed performing as much as we parents enjoyed watching them perform. I was surprised how in step they were to the music, and they looked so pleased that we were enjoying the performance so much.

Clay was a handsome little boy. It seemed there was so much that he wanted to say to me. There was a real closeness between us. He could always sense if there was something bothering me. He'd look at me with a questioning expression and hold out his little hands, palms up, as if to ask me, "What's wrong, Mommy?" Clay thought that unless I was smiling there was something wrong. If I looked happy and cheerful, so did he. Clay seems to sense my moods even today. It is hard for me to hide my true feelings from him.

There is great pleasure in bringing up a deaf child, in watching him learn and grow up. I had a feeling of real accomplishment. I knew that he was a very special child who saw the world in a special way. I needed a lot of patience and a lot of love for my deaf child.

Chapter 8. Bicycle Days

When Clay was five years old, we bought each of the boys a shiny red bicycle for Christmas. It was Clay's first two-wheeler and he learned to ride his bike along with the other boys. But I wondered how I could teach Clay not to go in the road. I had an idea that I thought might work. I took Clay by the hand, and we walked to the end of the sidewalk. I took a piece of white chalk and chalked a line across the sidewalk. I talked and gestured to him, telling him not to go in the street. I made the motion of driving a car, and then I made a fist with my right hand and hit the palm of my left hand, trying to explain that a car might hit him if he went into the street. I explained to him that when he reached this white line, he had to turn around and come back home. He nodded as though he understood what I had said, but I still worried about his safety, so I kept an eye on him. I also depended on Monty and Darrell to help keep an eye on Clay.

I made a point of reminding all of my neighbors that Clay was deaf, and that if they found Clay playing in the street while they were driving, there was no point in honking the horn at him. I thought it best to forewarn them, and save them frustration and anger. It was a nice neighborhood and everyone knew each other, but I do remember one incident very well. I had picked up Clay at school, and the boys were all playing together in front of the house while I went inside to start our evening meal. I was peeling potatoes when all of a sudden the kitchen door was jerked open. A woman poked her head inside the kitchen and said, "Clay was in the road; I nearly ran over him." It was Sue, the English girl who lived across the street. I was flabbergasted. The nerve of her, jerking my door open and telling me that she almost ran over Clay! I swung around to face her, and in the same tone of voice that she had just used, I said, "Well, watch where you're going. I can't tie him to a tree." I was angry and also hurt. I wished that people would be a bit more understanding. After all, deaf kids are still just kids. They want to play and have fun, just as hearing children do. Clay didn't realize the dangers of the road. I went outside and gestured at Clay, telling him again not to ride his bike in the street. He saw that I was very angry. I wanted Clay to live as normal a life as possible. I wanted him to be able to do things as well as the hearing children. I wanted Clay to have a happy childhood and I tried to treat him the same as I treated Monty and Darrell.

We didn't give Clay any special privileges just because he was deaf, but I also didn't let anyone mistreat him if I could help it. I recall one incident where someone tried. The window above my kitchen sink let me keep an eye on the boys while they played. I looked out of the window one Saturday afternoon and I saw a little girl riding her bike around the block. Clay was in front of the house, where I could see him, playing with a hula hoop. Each time the little girl passed Clay, she stuck her tongue out at him and said "Dummy." I saw her do this several times. A while later, the doorbell rang, and there stood that little girl. She was about ten or twelve years old.

"Clay slapped me," she said.

I replied, "That's good for you. I saw you stick your tongue out at him, and call him names."

"But he can't hear."

"That's right, he can't hear, but he can see, and he saw you calling him names and sticking your tongue out at him." She gave me a stunned look and left. She didn't bother Clay any more after that incident.

Meanwhile, Clay was making good progress at school. He said "Mother" and "Father" very well, he could say "water" and "cookie," and he had learned to say, "May I go to the bathroom?" I continued to visit the school and do whatever I could to help Clay. My whole family tried to help out. As Monty and Darrell grew older, they started to ask us questions. What was wrong with Clay's ears? Why didn't he hear? I tried to explain to my six- and seven-year-old sons that the nerve in Clay's ear was dead, and that his ears couldn't pick up sounds like theirs could. They just said, "Oh," and start playing again.

Although I tried hard, sometimes I didn't understand Clay, and when that happened he looked very disgusted with me. The older he got, the easier it became to understand him, and things started to ease up a bit as the whole family became better at understanding him. Clay learned to try using his voice to ask for things, rather than just pointing to the things that he wanted. I didn't understand everything that he was saying, but because he started to say some of the words more clearly, I could usually make out what he wanted.

Patricia Sue Rivers

Clay had been in Line Ave. School for two years when I woke up one morning with morning sickness. I knew that I was pregnant when my coffee came up as fast as I drank it—I could never hold my coffee down early in a pregnancy. I went to see a doctor at Barksdale Air Force Base, and he confirmed that I was pregnant and the baby was due in December. Since I had three boys already, I naturally hoped the new baby was a girl. I had not planned on getting pregnant again, but now that I was, I made up my mind to not spend the whole nine months worrying about whether my baby could hear. I decided that I would accept whatever the Lord gave me. While I was in Germany, a friend of mine had said something that was a lot of comfort to me: "Did you ever stop and think maybe God gave you a deaf child because He knew you would take good care of him?" I had never actually thought of it that way before he said it, but I never forgot his words.

Soon school was out for the summer and I got some rest from my daily drives and school visits. The base had a nice swimming pool, so I took the boys there to swim. Clay had learned to swim well. They also had a nice bowling alley, and sometimes we took the boys bowling, or went to see a Saturday matinee. The boys were big enough now that I could drop them off to see a movie and pick them up afterwards. I was also getting pretty big. I was very big by the time school started again in the fall, but Christmas came and went with no baby.

I finally had my baby on a rainy Friday afternoon late in December, while Bruce, Monty, Darrell, and Clay sat in the car outside the base hospital. It was an easy delivery. Afterwards, I told the nurse to hand me the telephone, so that I could call my mother.

When my mother answered the phone, I said in French, "Mama, I have my baby."

She said—more like a question—"Not a girl?"

"Yes, mama, a girl, and a beautiful one at that."

She had a head full of black hair that went down to her neck. I called her "Papoose" the minute I saw her, because she looked like an American Indian baby with all that black hair. She was rosy and beautiful, and I was thrilled to have a daughter. Bruce took a leave and took care of the boys while I was in the hospital. After three days, I was ready to go home with our new baby girl. The boys were waiting for us in the hospital lobby. While the nurse was wheeling me out with the baby in my arms, the boys ran to meet us and pulled the blanket back to see their baby sister. They couldn't wait any longer to see the baby. The other people in the lobby got a chuckle out of that.

There was a lady with pretty red hair who lived next door to us, and her name was Patricia. Clay called her "Pa-Ti-Ta," for Patricia. I thought Patricia was a pretty name, so I named my baby Patricia Sue, with "Sue" coming from the English girl who lived across the street. (After the bicycle incident, we became pretty good friends.) The mother of one of Clay's classmates offered to pick Clay up for two weeks, until I was able to drive to school again. Her son, Jerald, was a cute little boy in Mrs. Bloomer's class, and they lived near us. Jerald had a sister about twelve years old. Her name was Janice, and she was also deaf. She had beautiful red hair. Sometimes Bruce drove the children to school after Patricia was born, and he said, "Janice looks so proud when I pick them up."

Clay was very proud of his new baby sister. As soon as he came in from school, he went straight to my bedroom and make sure she was okay before he went out to play. He never went out to play without checking on the baby first. His pride and concern for the baby fascinated me. One day when Patricia was only about two or three weeks old, I had her bassinet in the kitchen, below the wall phone. Suddenly the telephone rang, and she let out a loud cry. It was a friend of mine calling, and when I told her the phone had woken up the baby, she apologized. But I just laughed, relieved, because now I knew that this baby could hear. The more my friend apologized, the more I laughed. *Thank God*, I thought, *my new baby girl can hear.*

Before long, I was able to resume the drives to and from Line Ave. School. It was a very cold January. I'd feed Patricia early and let her take her nap. At exactly 2:15, I would start the car and let it warm up. I put the bassinet next to me in the front seat. At 2:30, I would get Patricia, lay her down in the bassinet, and drive to Clay's school. It wasn't easy to make two trips to school, driving a total of twenty-eight miles, every weekday with a new baby. If I hadn't stuck to my busy schedule, I would never have made it. One of my neighbors said, "I don't see how you do it, with a new baby and all." I didn't want sympathy. Missing out on neighborly chit-chat and coffee breaks didn't bother me. I had a job to do. I had good neighbors and they seem to understand my priorities.

When Patricia was three months old, we had her christened. Soon afterwards, she came down with a steady cough. My mother had come in for the christening, and before she left, she told me, "You better take that baby to the doctor." I called the Barksdale base hospital and made an appointment for her. At the hospital, I had to hold her tiny little body while they X-rayed her small chest. The doctor said she had a touch of pneumonia. I thought this might be my fault, for taking her out in all kinds of weather. She was admitted to the hospital, and I adjusted my schedule. As soon as I dropped Clay off at Line Avenue School, I went directly to the hospital nursery. I held my baby, and if the nurses were very busy, I fed her too. Then I drove back to get Clay, brought him home, fixed supper for the family, and then returned to the hospital. After about a week, Patricia was well enough to come home.

I managed to get through another school term. Pretty soon it was spring, and then summer and school was out. I still encouraged Clay to talk, although his speech was very hard to understand. He could say quite a few things now, and he could put a few sentences together: "May I have some water?" "Where is Monty?" "Where is Darrell?" He could say "baby" clearly. I drilled him on the colors. Clay had a deep voice, and I loved the way he said "purple." It sounded like "Puu-ple." I continued to work with Clay in the summer, and I had more time now at home. I felt more relaxed and I was enjoying my family.

When Patricia was almost two years old, I bought her a plastic pool. I filled it half-full of water and let her splash in it. One day Clay

Everyone is all dressed up for Patricia's first Easter service.

and I were sitting on the front lawn and watching her play. Clay started acting up about something that he wanted. He kept on until he made me very angry. Leaving Patricia in the pool, I grabbed Clay's arm and made him go inside, where I spanked his bottom. The whole time I was spanking him, he cried, "Baby, baby, baby." He disregarded his own plight, because he was worried about his baby sister alone in the yard, even though I could see her from where we were inside the house.

I continued to start our tutoring lessons around 2:00 P.M. every-day of the week. I sat Patricia in her high chair, and she watched us work together. I held up a picture-card and made Clay repeat, re-peat, and repeat. I was so busy trying to teach Clay that I didn't re-alize Patricia was picking up what I was trying to teach her brother, and she learned to talk at a very early age. By the time Patricia turned two, it seemed like she never stopped talking. She chattered nonstop. One day we were at my mother's and she remarked, "Boy, she can talk."

I said, "You told me that you prayed she could talk, so let her talk."

Luckily, Bruce and I had a good marriage. We both love children, and in spite of our difficulties, we both had enough love to give all our children. I honestly think that Clay's deafness helped us to be a more close-knit family. I learned that you just have to love your children and do your best with them. Love them, set a good example for them, take them to church on Sundays, strive to educate them, and hope for the best. That is about all any parent can do. The rest is up to the child.

Chapter 9. Back to Texas

When Patricia was about two years old, Bruce got orders for a transfer to Bergstrom Air Force Base in Austin, Texas. He had only two more years before retirement from twenty years' active duty, and I had hoped we could have stayed at Bossier City until Bruce retired. I hated the thought of selling our home, and I wondered what to do about Clay's education. He was making such good progress at Line Avenue School. So many thoughts ran through my mind. How would he adjust to change? What about his friends? Clay had his own friends at Line Avenue School. He had become very close to Micah Roberts. Micah, a handsome little boy with dark curly hair and big brown eyes, was about the same age as Clay. They had been going to school together for the past four years, and they got along well together. There were also Ronnie, Claude, and a cute little girl named Bobby Sue. Clay had the same classmates for almost four years! How would he feel leaving them and how would he adjust to a new environment? What kind of school would he go to in Texas? Would it be the right school for Clay? How would I know if the school was right for him? What about teachers— would they have teachers certified to teach deaf children? I asked myself all these questions.

I talked to Mrs. Bloomer about the transfer to Austin, and she told me there was a good school in Austin—the Texas School for the Deaf, or TSD. It had both a residential and a day program. I wrote to the school and received a letter back saying that Clay would be accepted as a day student. That was our one consolation about the move, but time was getting close for our transfer and we still had not found a buyer for our home. We had to let it revert to the man who had sold it to us, and we took a loss on the sale.

After Clay finished his fourth term at Line Avenue School, we moved to Austin, where we first lived as newlyweds. This time, though, we lived in a duplex apartment on the base. Luckily for us, there was a public school right behind our home where we enrolled Monty and Darrell. Monty was in the sixth grade and Darrell was in the fifth grade; both boys made friends easily, and they looked forward to attending a new school. I went to the school to meet with their teachers and get them settled in their new classrooms.

The Texas School for the Deaf was on South Congress Avenue in Austin, about seven miles from the base. We took a drive over to the school and enrolled Clay without any trouble. It was a nice school, sitting on several acres of land. Some of the residential students lived in cottages, with about eight students to a cottage, during the school term. These cottages looked like comfortable homes. The students were served home-cooked meals and ate together at a table. They had a very comfortable environment. The TSD staff was really nice to us. We met Clay's new teacher, Mrs. Mary Snell. She was his first black teacher, and she earned my highest respect. She was good with the children and they liked her.

I fixed one bedroom for Clay. Monty and Darrell shared one bedroom, and Patricia slept in the third bedroom with me and Bruce. One day, Clay fell asleep upstairs after school. A little while later, while the rest of the family was sitting in the living room, Clay came down the stairs fully dressed in a clean shirt and jeans. We asked where he was going, and he answered, "School." After Clay's nap, he thought it was the next day! We all laughed, and Clay got angry at us for laughing at him.

After about a week, I told Bruce that I was ready to drive Clay to school again. The drive to TSD went smoothly. I observed a very old boat in a pasture while I was driving, and I thought to myself, *this is a good landmark for me to remember, when I drive back home.* The boat made me think of Noah's Ark, because it had very high sides.

I dropped Clay off at school, and on the drive back to the base, I was looking for that old boat when I glanced in the rearview mirror and saw two men driving behind me. My first thought was, "They sure do wear big hats in Texas." Their car stayed behind me, but I didn't pay too much attention to it, because I was still looking for that old boat. When I reached the main highway, west toward Bergstrom Air Force Base, the two men who'd been tailing me pulled me over. Those big hats were state troopers! They told me that I had been wavering across the yellow line. I explained to the state troopers that we had just moved to Austin, that I had a deaf child to take to school, and that I had been trying to memorize the way to get home. I must have sounded convincing because they only gave me a warning ticket. When I got back home I said to Bruce, "Would you believe I got a ticket?"

All he said was "Yep." I have reached the conclusion that nothing I do surprises Bruce.

Learning to Sign

Since I started my education in deafness, I've learned that there is a controversy about methods of teaching deaf children. Some schools prefer the "oral" method, which is what Clay had been learning at Line Avenue School, while others teach signing and fingerspelling. It's very difficult for a parent to know which method is best for their child—most parents tend to go along with the method their child's school uses, and hope that method works for him or her. I was so happy just to have Clay in school that I didn't question the teaching method. I also did not realize that the method could make a big difference in Clay's life after he was out of school and adjusting to the hearing world.

In fingerspelling, special positions of the fingers and hands each represent different letters of the alphabet. Anyone, deaf or hearing, can use the fingerspelling to spell out words, and the system is easy to learn. At the Texas School for the Deaf, the children were taught to fingerspell, but it was all new to me. I explained to Miss Snell that at Line Avenue School they taught the children to lipread and not fingerspell; in fact, they discouraged fingerspelling. I will never forget Miss Snell's reply: "The most important thing is talk to your deaf child. Talk with your mouth, talk with your hands—I don't care how you talk, but talk, talk, talk."

So I decided to learn the manual alphabet. Miss Snell gave me a little reference card for the alphabet, and it seemed truly to be a miraculous thing. I studied the little card, and I practiced, and it seemed

Clay at the Texas School for the Deaf.

that I learned the alphabet overnight. I continued to talk to Clay as before, but now I fingerspelled while I was talking. Clay would fingerspell back to me. We were actually communicating! Finally, Clay and I were able to get to know each other. I felt like a whole new door had been opened to both of us. He could learn more about my "hearing world" and I could learn more about his "silent world." So we talked, we practiced, and we laughed at our mistakes—but we were communicating.

Monty and Darrell learned to fingerspell, too. Even Patricia, as young as she was, started to pick it up. She watched and studied while Clay and I signed, and she tried to imitate us. Bruce, on the other hand, chose not to fingerspell with Clay. He said that he preferred talking to his son. Bruce said that Clay understood him and he understood Clay. Was this the best method for Clay? Would Clay have developed better speech if he'd continued in the oral method like he was learning at Line Avenue School with Mrs. Bloomer?

What would happen when Clay had to compete with the hearing world? I had so many questions, and I still do.

We started a new daily routine. Monty and Darrell walked to school on the base, although sometimes I dropped them off on my way to TSD. When I returned home, I straightened up the house, cooked lunch for Bruce, and did the laundry. Bruce could walk to the house for dinner, and he often did so, which let me keep the car. After lunch, I put Patricia down for her nap so we could leave at 2:30 to make the seven-mile drive to school to pick up Clay.

I visited Miss Snell's class just as I had visited Mrs. Bloomer's class. She had a slightly larger class, and they had a lot of discussion in that classroom. If one of the students had a birthday, the students would discuss the details of the birthday. Did he have a cake? What color was the cake? How many candles were on the cake? How old was the birthday boy or girl? Miss Snell also talked to the class about the days of the week and the dates. "Today is Monday, January 5. What do we do on Mondays? We go to the library." She used every opportunity to start a discussion. She told me to do the same, to use every opportunity to talk to Clay. I learned many things by observing teachers working with deaf children.

Soon it was the end of the school year, and summer again. The boys played Little League baseball. Their team was called the Braves, and Bruce volunteered to be their coach. Clay was on the same team as his brothers. Darrell was pitcher, while Monty and Clay played outfield. Clay kept his eyes on the ball, and he was good at catching it. Monty was too. At the end of the summer season, the Braves were county champs, and all our boys got trophies. They were proud of their trophies and displayed them in their bedrooms. We had a watermelon party for a celebration. I always enjoyed the games and watching the boys play ball—I used to sneak them bubble-gum in the dug out. We were a team.

The boys also enjoyed bowling. There was a nice bowling alley on the base, and sometimes I bowled with them. I won a small trophy that summer for being the most consistent bowler. It was the first time in my life that I won a trophy for anything, and I was very proud of that small trophy. To hear me talk about it, you would think the trophy was three feet tall instead of just three inches! The base had a nice nursery where I sometimes left Patricia while I went bowling. With her dark hair and brown eyes and long lashes, she was a beautiful baby girl, and the women in the nursery enjoyed keeping her. Sometimes the boys went to see a Saturday movie, and other times they went swimming. There was a really nice pool on the base and they were all good swimmers. We all had a good time that summer, but it went by very fast, and soon it was time to shop for new clothes and get ready to go back to school.

Bruce

In 1966, Bruce retired with an honorable discharge at the age of thirty-seven, at the rank of Technical Sergeant. He was also awarded an Air Force Commendation medal. I cleaned the apartment, and we passed our final Air Force inspection before checking out of base housing. After checking out of the apartment, we got a motel room and got ready for the retirement ceremony. I had bought each of the boys a red pullover shirt to wear to the ceremony, and I asked Bruce to go to the base exchange and buy Patricia a new dress. He came back with a little white dress with bright purple circles on a fine overlay. I didn't like it at first, but it looked so cute on her that I decided it was the most adorable little girl's dress that I had ever seen. Bruce took his shower after he got back from shopping for me, and while he was in there, I heard him yell. A scorpion had bitten him on the ankle, and his ankle swelled from the bite, but by the time of the retirement ceremony the next morning, the swelling had gone down. We drove to base headquarters at Bergstrom. When Bruce's name was called, the whole family stood with him while the colonel handed him his discharge. The colonel said to Bruce, "You have a nice family, Sergeant."

Now that Bruce was discharged from active duty, our plan was to head to Baton Rouge and enroll Clay at the Louisiana State School for the Deaf (LSSD). Bruce had always had a love for learning, and in his life he had educated himself by reading. I had always said that if he had the right opportunity, he would have made a fine history teacher. After the retirement ceremony, we headed toward Baton Rouge with four kids, no house, and no job. We had shipped our furniture ahead, so we piled the kids in the car and took off. We thought that we would find a house quickly and get settled in, and that Bruce would have no problem finding a job. After all, he was only thirty-seven, and he had his military experience behind him.

One of my sisters, Gert, lived in Donaldsonville, only a few miles from Baton Rouge. She took care of Patricia while the rest of us went house-hunting. It was a very hot July that year, and the kids got hot and tired and fussy from being in the car for so long. After driving and looking all day for a house, we didn't find anything, and that night we checked into a motel. Gert called to see if we had found anything. I felt so down and discouraged that I was afraid if I got on the phone I would break down and cry, so I didn't even talk to her. Bruce told her that we still hadn't found anything. The next morning we got up early and spent the day house-hunting again, but still no luck.

The Mississippi River separates East and West Baton Rouge. The Louisiana State School for the Deaf is on the east side of the river. After we spent another day looking and still not finding a house to rent, Gert suggested that we look on the west side of the river, in a community called Port Allen. We decided to give it a try, and Gert came along with us while we looked. Driving around Port Allen, we saw an empty house on the corner of Eucalyptus Street, in the West Side Village neighborhood. The screen door was about to fall off, and the grass in the front yard was waist-high. Gert said, "Here is a house." We all laughed. But after looking elsewhere all day and not finding anything, it wasn't funny anymore. That house was all we could find. It was a very small three bedroom house, and the previous occupants hadn't even bothered to sweep the floors! My disappointment must have been obvious, because Darrell said, "We'll help you clean it up, Mom."

So we rented that small house, and everyone pitched in to make it a home. Bruce cut the grass and fixed the screen door. That was a big improvement. I swept and mopped the floors thoroughly. Darrell volunteered to wax them. Soon our furniture arrived from Bergstrom, and I was able to unpack the boxes and start trying to make it look like home. With a little work, the house turned out to be not so bad, even if it was still small for a family the size of ours.

There was only one problem left. The Louisiana School for the Deaf was in East Baton Rouge, and we were living in West Baton

Rouge. In 1966, to cross the Mississippi River you either had to ride a ferry boat or you had to drive all the way around on the old Huey P. Long Bridge. The drive took anywhere from forty-five minutes to an hour, depending on the traffic. A new bridge was under construction but far from being finished.

Gert must have read my thoughts, because she said, "You managed to take Clay to school every day and pick him up for the past seven years. Why don't you let him stay at school through the week?" Leave Clay at school? Could I do that? He was my little boy. We were finally learning about our different worlds. I never dreamed that I would ever have to make such a decision, but I thought about her suggestion. Clay was almost twelve years old. If I wanted him to be a day student, I'd have to ride the ferryboat with him every morning, or drive with him and Patricia in a lot of traffic. I didn't like those options, but I also wasn't crazy about the idea of leaving Clay at school for a week at a time. Bruce and I talked about it, and we considered the needs of our three other children as well. We decided to try residential life for Clay and see how it worked out. We'd leave him at school through the week, and take him home on the weekends. It seemed like a good compromise.

Every day, Bruce left early in the morning to look for a job. He applied at all the nearby chemical plants. We felt sure that he would get a call before much longer, but we kept waiting. We were living on the little bit of savings that we had, and that was going fast. The School for the Deaf told me that I would have to label all of Clay's clothes, for laundry identification. I ordered name labels and sewed them in all his new school clothes. I sewed his name inside his shirt collars, and in his pants, pajamas, and shorts. I had a lump in my throat as I sewed these labels. I hated the thought of leaving him for a whole week at a time, but it just seemed that I didn't have a choice. I wanted Clay to go to school and get an education. He didn't have enough hearing to go to a public school. He would never understand what the teachers said, and the kids would probably laugh and make fun of him. I enrolled Monty and Darrell into a school in Port Allen. They had already made friends in the neighborhood and were looking forward to the new school. A bus was going to pick them up right by the house so that was no problem.

Chapter 10. Louisiana State School for the Deaf

School always started around Clay's birthday, September 6. He turned twelve that year. I packed up his clothes, and Bruce and I accompanied him to his first day at the new school. We rode the ferryboat across the Mississippi River. Clay thought that was fun! I had a lump in my throat at the thought of leaving him at school for a week. We got to school around one o'clock in the afternoon. The school was an old red brick building with a black wrought-iron fence around it. We went directly to the principal's office. The principal, a middle-aged man, sat behind a wooden desk and motioned for us to sit in desk chairs in front of him.

The principal did a lot of talking, and he was hesitating about something. When he said, "The school is real crowded," I began to get a strange feeling. Suddenly he said outright, "We can't take your son." I felt like the room was spinning around me. I thought that surely I hadn't understood him correctly, but I heard him say again, "There is no room for Clay." That was the last straw. The hot, sweaty summer, the kids, moving, Bruce not having a job—I just couldn't take any more disappointment. Why else had we moved here, but to get Clay in this school? My anger boiled over and I broke down and cried. I wanted to scream, "It's not fair. I can't take it anymore." At that moment, I didn't care who saw me or heard me crying, or how loud I was hollering. All I cared about was my son going to school.

Mr. Phillips, the assistant principal, was looking at me, and I saw sympathy in his face. Somehow I got my strength back, and the anger I had been feeling hardened into determination. I stood up and looked at the principal and I said between sobs, "We wrote you a letter and you said Clay could come to school here. I still have the letter. If it is a chest of drawers you need, I'll bring it! If it is a bed you need, I'll bring it." I looked at him good and hard and I said, "I'll bring anything you need, but my son is coming to school here. I still have the letter you wrote." I made up my mind right then that I would go to any length necessary to get Clay in this school. Clay watched me, upset and crying, and I don't know what he must have thought.

Mr. Phillips was looking at me with such a kind face it made me even more upset! I'm not sure what the principal's reason was for not wanting to register Clay, or what changed his mind. All I know is that after the principal got me upset like that, he said, "Let's walk around and see what we can do." So he took us on a tour of the grounds and dormitories. The school was old, but it was nice. They had one academic building for younger children and another for older ones. They had a nice cafeteria and an infirmary, with a nurse on duty at all times and a doctor on call. That was reassuring. The dormitories were nice, too. We found one room where Clay could stay. The principal explained, "I thought that the dormitories were full, but I see I have room for Clay." After all of that, he decided that Clay could attend their school after all. The principal agreed that Clay could stay in the dormitory from Monday through Friday, and then come spend the weekend at home with his family.

There were about six boys to a dormitory room. Each boy had his own bed and a closet. Each shelf was labeled, one for shirts, one for socks, and so forth. They were taught to keep their clothes very neat, and both the closets and the rooms were orderly. The students made their beds every morning and then went to the cafeteria, where a hot breakfast was served.

Classes were from 8:00 A.M. to 3:00 P.M. Clay was reading and learning how to put sentences together. He was also taught mathematics, English, and history. As he got older, he also studied woodworking, and he made some neat things like wooden bowls, birdhouses, and fruit bowls. Clay came home one weekend and surprised me with a large fruit bowl that he had made at school. I still have the bowl today, and Clay still loves woodworking.

After classes were done for the day, the students could play ball or relax in a large room where there was a television. There was also a game room with a pool table. Clay enjoyed playing pool with his friends. They even had a large indoor heated pool, which was very nice. LSSD had their own football team, and Clay's friend, Micah Roberts, from Line Avenue School, was at LSSD and on the football team. Gerald Bamburg, another old classmate from Line Avenue School, was also at LSSD, and I felt better knowing that Clay had his old friends around. They were happy to see him, too, after two years. I felt much better on my way back home to the west side of Baton Rouge.

Clay adjusted well, and he didn't seem to mind staying at school through the week. In addition to having his old friends from Line Avenue School, he made new friends, and he felt right at home at LSSD. Every Friday at 3 o'clock sharp I was there to pick up Clay. He looked forward to riding the ferry. The Mississippi was a beautiful sight, and Patricia and I looked forward to the trip, too. We took Clay back to school on Sunday night or sometimes early Monday morning. If I was planning something special, like a special dinner at home, I would go and get him during the week. The best thing about leaving Clay at school during the week was that I could now spend more time with Patricia, Monty, Darrell, and Bruce. After all, I'd managed to keep Clay at home for twelve years, in spite of Bruce's tours of duty. Some of the kids at LSSD had been enrolled at a very early age and got to go home only on holidays and summer vacation because their parents lived far away. I felt lucky that I could pick Clay up every weekend.

In 1967, the fourteenth annual LSSD Gym Circus was presented on a Friday night. The purpose of the annual gym circus is to provide the students with a bigger incentive in their daily physical education classes, as well as to provide parents and friends with an opportunity to see what the students were learning in those classes. Clay was in the advanced tumbling demonstration. The boys ran out into the gym wearing their physical education uniforms and did tumbles, one after another. It was a perfect formation. The program was a big success and a very enjoyable evening. I was beginning to feel better now about the school, and I was glad that Clay was getting a good education. The school mailed out a progress report to the parents about every six weeks. LSSD also printed a magazine called *The Pelican*, where we read about the children's activities and what they were doing in school. The students wrote about trips that they went on. *The Pelican* was very informative, and I enjoyed reading it. Since Clay graduated from LSSD, *The Pelican* published a poem that I wrote, titled "No Time For Me."

Clay had adjusted to school very well, so all that was left was for Bruce to find a job. Every morning he got up and shaved and show-

No Time For Me

I can look. I can see. I can smell and feel and touch.
    In this old busy world that has no time for me.
For I can not "hear" you see. In my "silent world" I beg for work.
    In this old, busy, hearing world, that has no time for me.
        They are afraid if they hire me
I'll slow them down you see and have no time for me.
    So with my God beside me, I walk along,
Always looking, you see, for I know the day will come
        When He will slow them down.
The ones who have no time for me, will be glad to notice me.

ered and went out job hunting. He put in his application at all the plants in the area. One day he was called for an interview at one of the plants. We were both excited, and I felt sure they would hire him. He was still young and healthy, and he had an excellent service record. He was gone most of the morning. Around noon he came back home, looking very disgusted. "Would you believe they said that I was too old for the job?" I couldn't believe it. He was only thirty-seven; he couldn't be too old.

Our savings was getting lower every day. Bruce kept on looking and finally got a job with Swift Meat Packing Company on North Boulevard. They hired him as a shipping clerk. We also found a little larger house to buy in Port Allen on Rosedale Road. The house was on a corner right by the levee on the Mississippi River. Patricia started at a school only one block away from the new house, and Monty and Darrell were now in high school. Clay was doing well in school, and we still picked him up every Friday. He didn't like it if we were late to pick him up, and he would tell us so.

Monty and Darrell needed a new winter coat, so we went to this nice big store called Goudchaux's in Baton Rouge. The saleslady was very nice. I asked her if it was hard to get a job there and the saleslady said that if I was interested in a job, she would take me upstairs and introduce me to the manager. He was an older man. He said, "So, you want a job?"

"Yes, I would like to work here, and I can use the money," I said.

He pointed to Patricia and said, "What you gonna do with her?"

"I'll take care of her," I said.

Monty and Darrell were laughing at me for trying to get a job. They said, "We came to buy a coat and now mama is looking for a job!" When I came back downstairs, I told them that I got the job. With four kids in school, we could certainly use the extra money.

I hired the sweetest black woman, Mrs. Kelly, to come stay with Patricia while I worked. I picked her up every day before I went to work. The children loved Mrs. Kelly. She called Darrell "Dale." One day, when Mrs. Kelly went in the backyard to hang clothes, she started hollering, "Dale! Dale! Dale! Get that snake out of here!" Darrell went out to see what she wanted, and he saw that there really was a snake in the yard. Mrs. Kelly was afraid to hang the clothes with the snake there, so Darrell killed the snake with a shovel. Mrs. Kelly was also afraid of our pet rooster, which we had raised from a small chick we bought one Easter. After it was grown, the rooster got a little feisty. It would jump up and peck at our legs. Every day, when Mrs. Kelly went out to hang clothes, she would ask Dale to get the rooster out of her way. Mrs. Kelly took excellent care of my children while I worked, and I will always be grateful to her for that.

At Goudchaux's, they started me in the nurses' uniform section. The company provided me with white uniforms to wear while I sold them. I learned a lot about the different brands and styles of uniforms. For instance, I learned that nurses like to have front pockets in their uniforms. One day I surprised Mrs. Kelly with a white uniform. She was so proud of that uniform.

"I'll wear it to church," she said.

"You'll be the best dressed gal in church," I replied.

While I was at Goudchaux's, I worked on commission, and I also got a discount on clothes. I bought all the boys' school clothes with that discount. Patricia and the boys were all doing well in school, and Patricia liked Mrs. Kelly. It seemed like all was going well. I even remodeled the kitchen in the house we bought. I had the cabinets made over and a dishwasher put in.

Clay is Missing

Early one afternoon, while I was working, I got a call from LSSD. It was the physical education teacher. "Mrs. Rivers, we cannot find Clay anywhere! We looked all over the campus!"

My heart sank! "How long has he been missing?"

"We've been looking for him for at least two hours!"

I called Bruce at Swift and Company, "Honey, the school called and they can't find Clay." I was on the verge of crying.

"What do you mean they can't find Clay?"

"The school just called me and said they haven't been able to find Clay for the past two hours. Go home and get a picture of Clay and take it to the police station. Go now!"

Bruce said, "Settle down, I will get a picture and take it to the police station." But I couldn't settle down. I couldn't imagine where Clay might be. Why couldn't the school find him? Maybe he fell asleep somewhere? I imagined all sorts of things.

Before long, Bruce called. "Clay is home!" Oh my God, I wondered, how did he get home from East Baton Rouge, all the way across the Mississippi River? Bruce said that he didn't know, but he was pretty sure Clay wouldn't run away again. Bruce had scolded Clay for running away and given him a good spanking. Then he put Clay in the car and took him back to school. The teacher said that they would keep an eye on him, but Bruce just said, "He won't run away again."

Later I tried to find out how Clay had gotten home, across that busy bridge. I asked him if someone had picked him up, and he nodded his head. I asked Clay why he had run away, and Clay said, "I don't like the teacher." It looked like the teacher had scolded him for some reason, and he just decided to come home. I was still curious as to how Clay got home, so I kept asking him. Eventually he told me that he had walked to the Frosty Top root beer stand on the corner by the school. When he saw a bus with a sign in front that read "Port Allen," he got on the bus and came back home. I talked to him and explained, "Mother and Daddy were very worried about you. I didn't know where you were or what happened to you. Clay, you must never run away again." Clay never did run away from LSSD again.

One Friday when I picked Clay up at school, he said that he wanted to get a hamburger at the Frosty Top. He loved hamburgers and French fries. I pulled up at the drive-in, but he wanted me to get out and order for him. I said, "No, you will have to go in and order your hamburger."

Clay signed to me, "The girl will not understand me."

I signed back to Clay, "If the girl cannot understand what you want, write down what you want."

He was reluctant at first, but he realized that I wasn't going to go in and order for him, so he finally got out of the car. A few minutes later Clay came out with a big smile on his face and a hamburger in his hand. One step closer to independence! I was trying to teach Clay to be independent, not to depend on me for everything that he wanted.

While Clay was a residential student at LSSD, I did not visit the classroom as often as I had visited in TSD and Line Avenue School. The teachers had their own ways of doing things. On special occasions, I would bake cupcakes and take them to the whole class. The teacher encouraged this, and it gave her something to write in the newsletter—"Clay's mother brought cupcakes to school. They were good." The teacher would ask Clay, "What did you do at home over the weekend?" This was a good opening for a discussion. Clay would tell them, "I rode the horse, I went bowling, I went skating," or "I went to the movies." Since most of the students were residential, the teachers welcomed any outside news to use for a discussion.

After we had been living in West Baton Rouge for three or four years, we decided to apply for a GI loan to build a larger house in East Baton Rouge. Patricia was in elementary school now, and Monty and Darrell were in junior high. The loan was approved, and we built a nice, roomy four-bedroom brick house right off of Florida Boulevard. We had enjoyed our home on Rosedale, but I welcomed the extra bedroom. It meant that when Clay came home on weekends, he had his own room. Clay was almost grown now, and he was getting particular about his appearance. I washed and pressed all his clothes, enough for a school week. When we took him back to school on Sunday nights, I would walk to the dorm with him and help him place his clothes in the closet.

Mother

My dear mother had once remarked, "I will probably not live to see Bruce retire." She had lived to see that, although by now her health was very poor. A little over a year after Bruce retired, my mother died a horrible death. Her bathroom was just off the bedroom, and since it was so cold in the house, she kept a small gas heater in the bathroom wall, burning low. She was under medication at the time. She must have gotten up during the night to use the bathroom, and the long flannel nightgown she always wore brushed against that small heater. Not realizing that her gown had caught fire, she got back into bed. When she woke up again, her bed was on fire. The neighbors thought they heard her screaming, and they called my niece Jody, who lived in Mamou.

By the time Jody got there, my mother was standing in the kitchen, dazed and shocked, in a puddle of ashes, with only a piece of elastic left as visible evidence of clothing. Her nightgown had burned completely off. Her bed was one big blaze of fire and the house was filled with smoke. Jody called the fire department and an ambulance, and my mother was rushed to the hospital in Mamou. Jody called me at home to tell me, and we went to see her in the hospital.

The first thing she asked me was, "Where are the boys?"

"They are all in the hall, Mom."

"I want to see them." Monty and Darrell and Clay came in and stood at her bed. They had a sad look on their faces. She had always been crazy about my boys. Here in the hospital, her body was swollen beyond recognition. Her breast was charcoal black. Mercifully, her beautiful face was untouched.

She looked at me and said, "My house burned to the ground."

Her little house, the one she'd worked so hard for and was so proud of, the house we'd bought by picking cotton and saving money.

"No, Mama, I swear the house is still there!"

"You must not swear, baby."

I promised her that the house was still standing, and that we would clean it up for her. She died three days later, from second and third degree burns. She was seventy-two years old. Her face, her beautiful face, looked at peace lying in her coffin.

I still miss calling her on the phone and talking in French with her. Bruce is from north Louisiana and he doesn't speak French, so the only time I have an opportunity to have a real French conversation is when I get together with my sisters and brothers. I miss the sound of my mother's voice, her laughter. No matter how hard life was for her, she could always laugh back at it.

I am happy to say that I kept my promise to my mother about having my marriage to Bruce blessed in a church. One year after he retired, we had our marriage blessed by Father Donahue at Holy Family Church in Port Allen. The next day Monty and Darrell told their teachers at school, "Mom and Daddy got married last night." I wondered what the teacher thought. I wanted to give the priest something for blessing our marriage, so I went by his house one day and gave him a bottle of good bourbon.

I said, "Father, I sort of hesitated about giving you this."

He smiled and said, "Don't hesitate again."

Chapter 11. Life Changes

In almost no time it seemed Monty and Darrell were in high school and dating. They always had a crowd of young people visiting our comfortable home. I enjoyed their friends, and they took a liking to me right away. I always did like to spend time with the younger generation. Sometimes on Friday nights I took Clay to the roller-skating rink. He enjoyed skating and was very good on the skates. He had his own group of friends, and sometimes we all went to see a movie together. Monty fell in love with Brenda La Blanc, a Cajun girl who was brought up in West Baton Rouge. Monty was only eighteen years old, but he told me that he and Brenda wanted to get married. Monty was pretty headstrong, so I didn't even try and talk him out of marrying his high-school sweetheart. He and Brenda had a beautiful church wedding.

Less than a month later, Darrell also married his high school sweetheart, Pauline Sheldon. He was only seventeen. Things were happening very fast all around me at the age of thirty-nine! The house was suddenly much quieter with only Bruce, Patricia, and myself left at home while Clay was at school. Patricia was in the fifth grade. She and Clay have always been close, and she had been able to communicate with him in American Sign Language since she was four years old. She looked forward to coming with me to pick him up at school on Fridays.

Soon after Monty and Darrell got married, I woke up feeling sick to my stomach. I couldn't make it to the bathroom. I had to throw up in the kitchen sink! Darrell, who was living with us for a couple of months, had just come out of the shower and was walking down the hall drying his hair, slinging a towel back and forth across his head. When he saw me, he said hoarsely, "What are you throwing up for?"

I started crying and said, "What does anyone throw up for?" I knew without a doubt I was pregnant again, at thirty-nine years old. I didn't want to wait to find out for sure, so I went to see a doctor in Baton Rouge for a urine test. The test was positive. The doctor gave me a big lecture about being pregnant and I was a high-risk patient, but I was happy. I drove down Florida Boulevard with tears rolling down my cheeks. I couldn't get used to raising Patricia with no other children at home. Most women my age would probably be ready to jump into the river at the thought of having another baby, but I was truly and honestly very happy. My three boys had been born so close together; now I would have time to really enjoy this baby.

Darrell's wife, Pauline, was expecting a baby in March, my first grandchild. My fifth baby was due in June. So my daughter-in-law and I were both pregnant at the same time! I called Monty's house early one morning to share the good news. Brenda was in another room when I called. When she walked in, Monty was sitting on the edge of the bed, white as a sheet. She asked, "Monty, what's wrong?"

He said, "Mama is pregnant." Brenda was the new bride and I was the pregnant one! They couldn't get over it. Once Bruce got over the shock, he was happy, too. Patricia was also very excited, and she told every one at school that her mommy was going to have a baby. When Clay came home the following weekend, I told him about the baby. He laughed and motioned to me, "Too old!" He thought that I was kidding him. Clay didn't believe me until I actually started showing, and even then, he looked awfully surprised.

Clay was seventeen years old now, and a junior in high school. One Friday afternoon, when I picked him up at school, he pointed to a girl. He said, "I like her. She's from Sulphur, Louisiana, which is close to DeQuincy. Her name is Karen Mae Stevenson. She has been going to LSSD since she was three years old. She rides the bus home to visit her parents." I was a little surprised that Clay said that he liked her. He hadn't showed any particular interest in any girl before this. He had a group of friends that would meet him at the skating rink on Saturday night, but no special girlfriend.

I told Clay, "She's a pretty girl."

"I would like for you to meet her sometime."

"Yes, that would be nice," I signed to Clay. After that, we didn't see Karen for a while, and I thought maybe Clay had forgotten all about her. I was having a good pregnancy, and I kept getting bigger. I quit my job at Goudchaux's after working there for over three years because I thought that I should take care of myself. Every Friday, Patricia and I went to pick up Clay at school. I tried to be on time because he didn't like it if I was running late. He would look at me and sign, "You're late."

Another Move

Bruce came in from work one day and said, "I was offered a job as a security officer in DeQuincy at Louisiana Correctional Institutional School for first offenders." It would mean a better salary and retirement program, but it also meant moving again. We talked it over with Monty and Darrell. Darrell said, "If Dad wants to take the job, I can pick up Clay on Fridays and bring him to my house." We visited DeQuincy, an old railroad town with a population a little more than five thousand. There were a lot of tall pine trees in this part of the state. The small town was friendly and it felt homey—like the whole town was one big family. We decided that this small town, with its tall pines and friendly people, would be a good place to settle down and raise our last baby. After looking all day, we found a three-bedroom brick house for sale, close to DeQuincy High School. We bought the house and Bruce accepted the job.

Soon after we made the decision, my first grandson, Jeremy Bruce, was born. He had the prettiest golden curls I'd ever seen. Shortly after he was born, we made the move to DeQuincy and settled in. Clay didn't seem to mind us moving. He just said, "Darrell better not be late picking me up."

One night in June, a sharp pain woke me up, and I knew that it was time. Clay was home for the summer. He and Patricia were asleep in their rooms, and Bruce was on the night shift. At 2:00 A.M., I called Bruce.

"It's time for me to go to the hospital."

"Are you having contractions?"

"Yes, hurry."

"I'll be right over." He came home right away and drove me seventeen miles to the hospital. Although Patricia had asked me to wake her up, I left without disturbing either her or Clay. Around 4:30 A.M., our fourth son was born. He looked just like his daddy, so we named him Bruce Jr. I felt wonderful after Bruce Jr. was born—I felt like I was twenty-five instead of forty. Patricia was in junior high now, and I had no schedule to keep. I had time to relax and enjoy my baby.

That summer, Clay visited Karen Stevenson, the girl that he had pointed out to me at LSSD. Her parents lived only seventeen miles from DeQuincy. Clay was handsome, and he kept himself very neat. He had blond hair, green eyes and a fair complexion. He liked to dress in western-cut jeans and western shirts. He was tall and carried himself well. In the fall we took him back to LSSD to begin his senior year. In May 1974, we celebrated Clay's graduation. We went to Darrell's house. Darrell had bought Clay a white shirt and a pair of black pants for his commencement ceremony. Clay looked happy. All of us went to the commencement ceremony, including Bruce Jr., who was now learning to walk and talk.

We sat in the school auditorium. The graduation march began to play, and I saw Clay standing tall and proud in his green cap and gown, walking slowly toward the stage. I got all choked up, a lump in my throat and tears in my eyes. *Dear God*, I thought, *it was a long hard journey, but we made it.*

With the help of God and the love of a close-knit family, we had all come a long way from the early days at Line Avenue School. We'd made it this far by loving, caring, and working together. There were no miracles, just hard work.

Clay's graduation picture at LSSD, May 1974.

Chapter 12. The Hearing World

After graduation, Clay moved in with us in DeQuincy. We were happy to have him at home again, but Clay was not a little boy anymore. He was a man with needs of his own. Being out of school meant a very big adjustment for him. He didn't know anyone down here, and he missed his friends at LSSD. I heard that the city was hiring young men and boys to pick up fallen tree limbs, and I thought that Clay had to start somewhere.

I called the mayor. I said, "Clay is deaf. He just graduated from LSSD. He is looking for a job. Can you use him picking up the limbs?"

"Can he talk?"

"No, not very much but I am sure he will understand what to do."

The mayor agreed that they could try it out, and the city gave Clay a job. Now that he finally had a chance to meet other boys his age, he made friends easily.

I told Clay to carry a pen and notepad with him in case he didn't understand what was said. Clay rode in a city truck all day and drove around the city picking up limbs. When he came back home at the end of the day, I asked him if he liked the job, and he signed to me, "It's okay." He didn't make much money working for the city, so I asked one of my neighbors to let Clay cut his grass, to give him something to do while earning spending money. For a while, Clay looked lost and miserable. He reminded me of the captured lions on *Wild Kingdom*. He missed his friends in Baton Rouge, and he couldn't communicate very well with anyone outside the family. He looked so unhappy, my heart went out to him.

Clay found out that there was a skating rink in DeQuincy. He came home from work one day and said, "I am going skating Saturday." On Saturday night he came back from the rink around 11:30 P.M., looking happy and excited. "I met some girls," he signed to me. "I had a good time." I told him that I was glad for him, and he signed that he planned to go again the next week. I was so pleased that Clay had finally met some young people and enjoyed himself.

Once I asked him directly, "Clay, why don't you ask a hearing girl to go out with you?" Clay only shrugged his shoulders. I didn't bring it up again. I figured that it was Clay's choice to make, not mine. However, he continued to drive to Sulphur to see Karen Stevenson. Karen was a pretty, petite girl, with long medium-brown hair and green eyes and a very bright, keen, alert look. She was always quick to catch on to things. I think she had more hearing then Clay did. I had a feeling that Clay was very interested in Karen, and I was glad that he had at least one deaf friend close by that he could visit.

Clay Goes to College

One day I was listening to the radio while dusting the furniture. When the music stopped playing, they made an announcement that there was a program for deaf students at Lamar University in Beaumont, Texas, about fifty miles away. My mind started racing. I thought how wonderful it would be if Clay could further his education; if he went to college, he could get a better job. I could hardly wait for Clay to come back from his tree-gathering job. He deserved something better than picking up limbs for minimum wages. I was grateful the city had given him a job, but I knew that Clay could do better for himself.

When Clay got home, I told him what I had heard on the radio. I was excited and signing very quickly. I asked him, "Would you like to go to college?"

Clay's face lit up and, without hesitation, he said a simple "Yes." Going to college had been his dream and mine, but until that day I hadn't realized that there was a college close by that taught the deaf. I had just considered myself lucky that Clay finished school.

We wrote to Lamar University and made arrangements for an interview. After the interview, they suggested that Clay might do better at Lee Junior College, which also had a program for deaf students. Lee was in Baytown, just outside of Houston, and about 100 miles from DeQuincy. Clay said that he was interested in studying graphic arts, and in the fall of that year, we drove to Lee Junior College and enrolled Clay as a graphic arts student. We found him a nice apartment close to campus. He shared the apartment with three or four other boys; one or two of the boys could hear, and the rest were deaf. Clay looked happy again—he made new friends, and he had plenty of people to communicate with.

At college, Clay did well with his studies in graphic arts. When he came home on weekends, he brought some books to show us what he was learning. Clay showed me how they applied color to a picture. I found that very interesting. When he visited on weekends and holidays, he went to see Karen Stevenson in Sulphur, and I started to feel that it was getting serious between the two of them.

A Fair Chance

Time went by quickly while Clay was attending Lee Junior College. I was enjoying Bruce Jr., who we called B.J. He was a good baby and it was a pleasure to be with him. Patricia also enjoyed her baby brother. After two years, Clay completed his course at Lee Junior College and came home again. Once again, we were happy to have Clay back home with us. The next step was to find him a job.

The city of Lake Charles, Louisiana, about twenty-five miles from DeQuincy, was the home of Lake Charles American Press, as well as several other print shops. Clay and I went out there one day to look for a job. I thought that with his degree in graphic arts, he would have no problem finding a job, but I was wrong. Lake Charles American Press had no openings, but Clay filled out applications in the event that something came up. From the Lake Charles American Press, we went to several other print shops, one after another. Each print shop we visited would refer Clay to a different print shop. After the third or fourth "referral," I realized what was going on. They were afraid to hire a deaf person!

It was a hot afternoon, and Clay hit a chain-link fence as we walked from one shop to another. "They don't want to hire me because I am deaf." That came out pretty plain! I told Clay that we would keep looking until we found something, but he insisted that no one would hire him because he was deaf. He was very upset, and I was totally disgusted. This situation was completely unfair. Deaf people should be given a chance on the basis of their ability, and not rejected simply because they are deaf. Deaf people want a chance to become useful citizens in their communities, just like everyone else. Clay was educated, and he would have been able to do these jobs, if someone had given him a fair chance.

The telephone, which plays such an important role in the hearing world, has been a real barrier to the deaf. Ironically, Alexander Graham Bell, the inventor of the telephone, was originally an instructor of deaf children. His wife was deaf, and his mother was hard of hearing. But the hearing world's dependence on the telephone has prevented deaf people from getting both jobs and fair treatment. *"Sorry, we need someone who can use the phone."* That's a favorite line. Another favorite threat against deaf people is the word "dangerous." *"Sorry, the job is too dangerous."* That one really gets to me. Crossing the street is dangerous for deaf and hearing alike. Unfortunately, in a small town like DeQuincy, a deaf person's opportunities are very limited.

After we got the runaround from the print shops, we both felt pretty discouraged. In desperation, I called the plant manager at the Boise Southern plywood company. I introduced myself and said, "I am calling for my son Clay. He is deaf, but all he needs is a chance to prove his ability. He is young, healthy, and educated. He graduated from the School for the Deaf in Baton Rouge and completed a two-year course in graphic arts at Lee Junior College in Baytown.

I feel sure that he would learn quickly if given the opportunity." I paused, hoping that he would be willing to give Clay a chance.

The line got quiet and I heard him say, "I'm sorry the job is too dangerous"! I was beginning to hate that word! Then he said, "You have my sympathy."

That was like a slap in the face. "Hell, I don't want sympathy!" Instead of screaming in the phone, I said, "Thank you, I don't want your sympathy. I want a job for my son!" I didn't want sympathy, and I didn't need it. I just wanted a fair break for my son.

From the time Bruce and I first found out that our child was deaf, we worked hard to educate him. Our son went to school for fifteen, twenty years, believing he was going to make something of himself so he wouldn't have to depend on a hand-out or charity. He worked hard to get that education. He made sacrifices, living away from family so that he could go to school. At the end of all that, his reward was to be told that the job is too dangerous? Dangerous? If the job was that dangerous, they could install flashing warning lights. A warning light works just as well as a loud bell.

Dear God, I asked myself, *when will hearing people realize that deaf people are still people?* They are people with real feelings, the same as you and me. Not being able to hear doesn't make them any less human. Deaf people have intelligence, talents, and abilities. It's about time deaf people become part of the community, welcomed as a valuable resource. No more excuses, and no more sympathy! Deaf people want a chance and a job to prove their ability.

A Job for Clay

I had called the manager at Boise Southern because Bruce had started working there on weekends, to make some extra money while Clay was attending Lee Junior College. Some time after my "phone interview," the plant got a new manager. Bruce had a chance to talk to him one evening, and Bruce said, "My son is deaf and he is having a hard time finding a job. It seems like people are afraid to hire a deaf person. He has two years college and is living with us now."

"How old is your son, Mr. Rivers?"

"He will be twenty-one in September."

"Send Clay over here I'll give him a job!"

Bruce came back home and told Clay about it. We were all so happy! Clay Rivers was the first deaf person hired by the Boise Southern plant in DeQuincy. They trained Clay to operate a forklift loader, and he set out to prove that he could do the job.

Clay became one of the best forklift operators out there. This was a whole new world for him. I suggested that Clay take a tablet and pencil in case the men at work didn't understand him. One advantage that Clay had at the plant was the noise didn't bother him. Clay taught fingerspelling and some basic signs to some of the other employees, which enabled everybody in his department to communicate above the noise of the machinery. Soon after they hired Clay, Boise Southern hired another deaf man, Richard Clement. They both worked in the shipping department, and their department won the plant's safety award that year. The *DeQuincy News*, our weekly newspaper, wrote an article about Clay and Richard and what a valuable resource they were for Boise Southern.

In July of 1977, the newsletter at Boise Southern had a picture of the shipping crew along with this caption:

SHIPPING RECORD SET. The shipping department at the DeQuincy plywood mill shipped a record 10,122,000 board feet of plywood during June, completing the month with an inventory of under 100,000 board feet. This surpasses the previous record of 10,060,000 board feet shipped in December 1976.

Clay got along well with the other employees. After working with Clay and getting to know him, they pretty much forgot about Clay's handicap. He was a person, another employee. They all treated Clay as an individual and did not look down on him because he was deaf. Both Richard and Clay were cited as having "excellent" attendance records and no job injuries while on the job. In fact, both of them were awarded three safety awards for their "outstanding" safety achievements. The plant manager said that they were, "without a doubt, valuable employees."

Chapter 13. Clay Gets Married

One afternoon late that summer, after Clay came home from work, I walked into his bedroom to talk with him. I still have a vivid memory of Clay lying on one of the twin beds, all stretched out with his arms folded in back of his head. Clay stared up at the ceiling like he was deep in thought. He looked at me and said, as clearly as he could: "I want to get married."

I replied, "I love having you home, Clay, and taking care of you—why do you want to get married?"

He looked at me and simply said, "I am lonely. You have father and I have no one. I went to school longer than Monty and Darrell did."

Well, I couldn't argue there. He would soon be twenty-one. Clay said, "I have nothing to do but watch television when I get off work. I am lonely and I need someone. I want to marry Karen." I could certainly understand that. Karen was a very pretty, sweet, intelligent girl. If this was his decision, it was his choice. I gave him a big hug and offered my congratulations.

Clay and Karen were married on August 6, 1977. They had a beautiful church wedding. Karen wore a simple, long, white dress with long sleeves and a V-neck. She wore a wide-brimmed hat, and her brown hair hung softly to her shoulders. She was a lovely bride, and Clay was a handsome groom. He wore a black tuxedo and bow-tie, and a white ruffled shirt. They made a handsome couple. Clay and Karen drove to Galveston, Texas, for their honeymoon. They enjoyed the sun and the beach in Galveston. They shopped and brought back souvenirs for the family. They came back to DeQuincy looking tanned, fit, and healthy.

Trailers and Telephones

After their honeymoon, Clay and Karen bought a trailer and rented a tree-shaded lot for it. They looked happy and very much in love, like they were crazy about each other. One day, shortly after they were married, I was looking over our weekly newspaper and I saw an ad for three acres of land with trailer hookup and deep well, just outside the city limits. It was for sale at a very good price, and sounded like a good deal. I went by their trailer and showed them the ad in the paper. They said they would go take a look at it.

Clay and Karen drove by my house the next day. Clay said, "We drove out there, but we can't find the land for sale." I offered to go help them find it. We headed out south of the city limits to find the land, and after driving around for a while, we saw a "For Sale" sign on a beautiful corner lot with tall pine trees. Clay and Karen loved it! We went back home and I called the owner. I told him, "Consider the land sold, if my son can get a bank loan."

They bought the land and moved their trailer over. It was a beautiful piece of land, and only about five miles from my house. Clay was so proud of his land. He had a small garden, where he raised peas, cucumbers, and tomatoes for me. He also raised big beautiful pigeons on his land. He built some really nice cages for the pigeons, and he enjoyed feeding and taking care of them.

Clay also planted fruit trees. I went over there one day and walked around with him, looking at the trees. Clay broke a leaf from a lemon tree and held the leaf up to my nose. He said, "Smell, Mother."

I smelled the leaf and thought, *Oh God, if he could only hear.* In that moment, I was deeply touched by Clay's gesture, that he wanted me to smell the lemon leaf, and it just got to me. Of course I never let him know that; I smelled the leaf and told Clay, "It smells good."

A Baby Born to Clay and Karen

Clay and Karen were so happy together. Karen was a good homemaker and enjoyed cooking and reading in her spare time. I would have them over for dinner often. One evening when they were at our house, during the summer after they were married, Karen asked for our attention. She signed and said, "I am going to have a baby."

I hugged her and said, "That's great!" I was very happy for them! "Let me know if I can help you in any way."

"I will be fine," she answered. Karen liked being independent. She liked doing things herself. That night, I wondered how they would manage without being able to hear the baby crying. What if the baby was choking? I imagined the worst possible things that could happen to a newborn baby, and I was very concerned. Of course, I didn't let on that I was concerned.

Karen's pregnancy went well, and in February 1979 she gave birth to a beautiful and healthy baby girl. While Karen was in the hospital, Patricia went to see her. Patricia said that Clay and Karen hit the metal bed with a teaspoon to see if the baby could hear the noise.

Clay's daughter Katrina Lois at the age of two.

She was really touched by that. The noise made the baby cry, and Clay and Karen looked at each other and smiled. Their baby girl could hear!

Clay and Karen named their beautiful daughter Katrina Lois. She brought so much joy to them. When Clay and Karen brought Katrina home from the hospital, they installed a special system of microphones and lights that was called a "baby cry." A microphone hung over Katrina's baby bed, and every time she cried, a light flickered. That was how they knew their baby was crying. They also had an alarm clock with a flashing light buzzer, and that is how Clay woke up in the morning. Their doorbell was even wired to a light, so instead of a buzzing noise, a light would flash if someone was at the door. When I saw how well they were both managing the new baby, my anxiety was relieved. They took excellent care of Katrina.

By the time Katrina was two years old, she had picked up signing and fingerspelling, and she could communicate anything to Clay and Karen. It amazed and fascinated me to see how fast she could move her tiny hands to talk with them. Since Karen had fairly clear speech, she also talked to Katrina, who understood her perfectly, and Katrina learned to talk very well. She amused herself by playing in her bedroom with her dolls and her Easy-Bake oven.

One day, when Katrina was about four years old, Karen was out hanging clothes and Katrina started screaming. Karen did not hear her crying, of course, and kept on hanging clothes, but Katrina was standing in a huge pile of ants. Finally, Karen saw Katrina crying, and walked over to her. That's when Karen saw the ants all over Katrina's little legs. She grabbed her and went in the house and ran cold water on her legs.

Chapter 14. Back to Work

When Bruce Jr. was in the first grade and Patricia was a senior in high school, I accidentally found a job. I went to see my family doctor in Sulphur for a check-up, and at one point I had to take something to a lab at the hospital across the street. At the lab, I started talking with a nice girl who worked in public relations for the hospital. I said, "I would like a job like this, but I don't have a high school education."

"I don't either," she said. I was surprised to hear that she didn't have a high school education. "Why don't you put in your application?"

"Well, I can speak French and I know how to communicate in American Sign Language."

"That would be helpful here at the hospital," she said.

I went to the personnel office across the street and asked for an application. I walked back to my car, filled out the application, and turned it back in to the personnel office. I went back home and told Bruce that I had applied for a job. "I don't want to intrude on Clay and Karen's life," I told him. "I think it would be good for me if I went to work."

Bruce said, "If that is what you want to do." Bruce always left working up to me. If I chose to stay home or if I wanted to work, it was fine with him either way. He wanted me to do whatever made me happy. Before long, the hospital called and offered me a job as an operator on the night and evening shifts. They trained me to operate the switchboard and to admit patients. I was also responsible for handling ambulance calls and for calling the fire department in case of fire. I caught on quickly, and I really did enjoy working the switchboard. Sometimes I had to work the three-to-eleven shift. When I was on that shift, I asked Bruce's mother or grandma, who was now living near us in DeQuincy, to come stay with Bruce Jr.

For a year, I worked nights, but then an operator on a different shift quit, and the supervisor called me at home and offered me her job. It meant working Thursday and Friday evenings, and all night Saturday and Sunday.

"I'll take the job if I can have an occasional weekend off to spend with my family and go to church on Sundays," I said.

"I can work something out," she replied.

I accepted the new position. I loved working the switchboard. But more than anything else, I loved being able to help my children. The extra money I made working at the hospital really came in handy for the whole family. I thought about helping Clay and Karen out, and helping Darrell with his tuition. He was at Louisiana State University now, studying chemical engineering.

The first thing I bought was a chain link fence for the land behind Clay and Karen's trailer, so that Katrina could have a safe place to play. I worried about what would happen to Clay, Karen, and Katrina in case of a real emergency, so I decided to have a telephone put in. I was excited about the telephone. I wanted to be able to talk to my granddaughter. She learned to dial my number if she wanted to talk to me, and she often did that. One day I cooked a good dinner and wanted to invite them all over. I wondered if Katrina could give Karen the message, but I figured I'd try. I dialed their number.

Katrina picked up the phone and said, "Hello."

"Katrina, this is Maw-Maw. Tell mama and daddy to come eat dinner with Maw-Maw."

"Okay, Maw-Maw, I will tell them." I wasn't sure that she could make them understand her—after all, she was only two. But after a while, Clay and Karen drove up, just in time for dinner. She had given them the message. After that, Katrina relayed many messages to her parents.

The telephone gave me peace of mind. One night, when Bruce was working and B.J. had already gone to bed, the telephone rang. It was Karen. She was trying to tell me something, but she sounded like she was in pain, and I could hear her crying. It sounded like she said, "Mary, come quick."

I called Patricia, who was studying at a friend's house, because she was a little closer to where Clay and Karen lived. "Tricia, Karen called and she sounds like she is in pain."

"I'll go see, Mama," she said. She was there in five minutes. When she saw Karen doubled over in pain, she rushed her to the hospital, the same one where I worked, and Karen was admitted for emergency surgery. The doctor said that there was something wrong with her small intestine, causing a blockage in her digestive system, and he would have to operate right away. The surgery went well and she was out of the hospital by the end of the week. Patricia's best friend, Stephanie Hyatt, had brought Katrina to our house. Karen's mother, Mae, told me that God must have directed me to put a telephone in their trailer. I think the Lord has directed me in every decision concerning my children.

Addition to the Trailer

One day after work I stopped to visit my niece in Sulphur. She and her husband also lived in a trailer. They recently added a new room, about twelve feet by thirty-six feet, to their trailer. It contained one large open space and a bedroom, with nice paneling, a ceiling fan, and sliding glass doors at one end. My niece said, "We are building a new house and will sell the trailer and room." I immediately thought of Clay and Karen. They could use all that extra space!

"How much do you want for the room?"

"Why, do you want to buy it? I will sell it to you for a thousand dollars," she said.

I thought for a minute. It would cost a lot to move that room to DeQuincy. "Let me check into it, I'll let you know." I found someone who'd move it for $700. That made a total of $1,700, but that was still a bargain. I was so excited that I stopped by Clay's trailer on my way home to tell him.

He was washing his truck in the front yard when I got there. Their dog, Shep, came to greet me, as always. I kept saying, "Clay, I want to talk to you," and he kept washing his truck. Finally he rinsed off the soap-suds and came over to sit by me on the glider in the yard.

I told him about the room. I was happy and excited, and I said "Clay, I want to buy that room for you." He looked surprised and his eyes lit up. "You and Karen go look at it and let me know what you think." While they went to look, I made the moving arrangements. Clay and Karen loved the trailer, and they were just as excited about it as I had been.

I needed to borrow money to get the trailer for them, but I'd never borrowed money in my name before. I wanted to do this on my own—my gift to Clay and Karen. I went to the bank where Bruce and I had an account. I told the manager, "I need to borrow $1,700." He didn't even ask me what for, and approved of the loan instantly. I was proud that I was able to borrow the money to improve Clay and Karen's home.

The moving went off without too many complications. Clay and Karen placed the room right in the front of their trailer. The wood-working skills that Clay had learned at LSSD now came in handy. He removed the window, where the room joined, and converted the window space to attractive book-shelves. He did a skillful job, and it looked very nice when he was done.

You're Fired

Two weeks after taking out the loan, on a beautiful, sunny Thursday, I drove my usual seventeen miles to work. I had been working for two years now, and I was really enjoying my job. Darrell and Pauline were going through a divorce, so I was helping him pay his tuition at Louisiana State University. I drove along, thinking as usual about my family, how all was well with them. Bruce Jr. had gotten over his cold, and today was even my payday. When I got to the hospital, I had some time before I had to clock in for work, so I went to the personnel office to pick up my check.

The personnel manager, the same one who had hired me two years ago, handed me my check and said, "You're fired." I thought he was joking. I had been working for two years and hardly missed a day's work. I was a good, dependable employee. Why would he fire me? I thought about the $1,700 I had just borrowed from the bank; I thought about Darrell's tuition.

He said, "You made unauthorized calls to your home."

Weak, shocked, with tears in my eyes, I replied, "Yes, sir, I did. I called my home. My little boy was sick. I called him to remind him to take his medicine." I stood there, holding my check, and added, "I need my job; I'll pay for the calls."

The personnel manager just looked at me and said, "We have to let you go, Mary."

I went to see the administrator of the hospital. I told him, "I just got fired for making calls to my home to check on my son. I didn't neglect my calls to the hospital. I put my son on hold while I answered the incoming calls. Other women call their homes, and they haven't been fired. I need this job."

"I am sorry, Mary," he said. "We have to let you go."

Ten minutes later, still holding the check, I walked back to the car.

I knew my supervisor didn't like me—she made no bones about it, but I could take it, I needed the job. But to fire me over some calls to my house to check on my son who was sick? I could understand being put on probation or making me pay for the calls, but fired? Driving back home, I thought about how fast our lives can change. Less than one hour ago, I was on top of the world, and now I had tears rolling down my face.

I was still very upset when I got home. Bruce put his arms around me and told me, "Don't worry about it. I will enjoy having you home."

"But what about the money I owe the bank?"

"I told you not to worry about it." Thank God that Bruce was such an understanding husband and father.

I wrote to the unemployment office in Baton Rouge and argued my case. My argument was, if I was a marginal employee, why would they keep me on the switchboard for two years answering ambulance calls and fire alerts? Other women made calls to their homes and were not fired. I just happened to live a few miles further. After arguing by mail for a few months, one day I went to the post office and found my mailbox stuffed with $1,700 in back pay. I took that money straight to the bank. After paying off my loan, I had ten cents left, but that was okay. I had won my case, and the bank loan was now paid in full.

Chapter 15. Beginning Again

Clay had been employed with Boise Southern for several years when the plant had to close because of a cutback in wood sales. That put Clay out of work again, just as Karen was expecting their second child. Armed with enthusiastic letters of recommendation from his supervisors, he started looking for a job.

On September 17, 1984, Clay and Karen's son was born. They named him Clayton Lee Rivers. We called him Lee, and like his older sister Katrina, he could hear and talk, and was very alert. Karen took good care of her children. She was a good mother, and she and Clay seemed very happy. Clay finally found a job in a print shop in DeRidder, Louisiana, about twenty-five miles away. A year later the shop went out of business, putting Clay out of work again.

There was a small church in their neighborhood. One day Karen told me, "We have an interpreter for the deaf at church, a man named John." She looked happy as she was telling me this, and I said that I was happy for her. Clay offered to watch the children while Karen went to church. After that, I started to notice a change in Karen. She started dressing up more and wearing jewelry. John visited them at home, and I could see more changes coming over Karen. At first it was just little things—how Karen wouldn't help Clay put the kids' coats on when they were done visiting, she would only stand around and watch Clay get the kids ready.

One day, Tricia and I were sitting on our lawn. I said, "Karen sure did get religious all of a sudden. I just hope it is for the right reason."

"Mama, you ought to be ashamed of yourself."

"I hope so," I muttered.

Around Christmas time, when Lee was two years old and Katrina seven, Karen went to church and didn't come back home. Clay was worried about her. He loved Karen and trusted her, and he had no clue that she had run off with John. After a week went by with no word from Karen, I called her mother.

"Mae," I said, "if she was my daughter, I would report her missing. I am worried about her."

"Maybe I will," she said.

Katrina had said to Mae, "John is taking my mommy away from my daddy. My daddy doesn't know it." I had thought Clay and Karen had the perfect marriage, and that they got along great. They had been sweethearts since they were both students at the Louisiana State School for the Deaf. I was totally taken by surprise that Karen left Clay and the children. Clay was hurt beyond description. He was crazy about his wife, and he hadn't seen this coming. He thought Karen had just enjoyed going to church. I would see him driving Lee around town to amuse him. I am sure Lee missed his mommy, and Clay was trying to keep him happy.

Looking back now, I can only speculate as to why Karen left. She was sent to LSSD at the age of three. She only visited her parents in Sulphur on holidays and every other weekend. She married at seventeen. Clay had a hard time keeping a job—through no fault of his own, the economy being what it was. Karen couldn't find a job at all. There were very few people that she could communicate with besides her family and Clay's. She was lonely and bored, and she spent a great deal of time reading romance novels at home. To her, John must have seemed like a romantic foreigner from a wide-open, exciting, and very new world.

Karen never came back, and she and Clay have been separated since 1986. Clay was devastated, and it was hard for him to raise two children while holding down a job. Eventually Clay closed the trailer and took Katrina and Lee to Baton Rouge, where he found employment in a print shop. He found an apartment—I made many trips over there to help him out with the children. Lee was only two, and the lady next door offered to keep him while Clay worked.

Lee used to ride his little tricycle on the sidewalk in front of the apartment building. One day Lee signed to his dad, "I don't know which apartment is ours. They all look alike." Clay had a ceramic Indian, about three feet tall, and he signed to Lee, "I will put the Indian in the window, and then you can tell which apartment is ours." So Lee looked for the Indian in the window when he wanted to go back inside.

There was a fenced-in swimming pool. I used to sit by the pool and watch the children swim. Katrina learned to swim like a fish. I used to hold my breath while waiting for her head to pop out of the water. Clay played with them in the pool when he came in from work.

A few years after Clay and the kids moved, Patricia heard that Blue Cross and Blue Shield of Louisiana had a job opening in Baton Rouge, in their printing department. She knew that Blue Cross had a reputation for hiring deaf individuals, so she told Clay about the job opening. She also helped him draft and submit his resume. Blue Cross called and asked Clay to come in for an interview. Patricia can interpret very well, and she does it faster than I do, so she interpreted for Clay at his interview. After the interview, Clay kept working at the print shop, hoping that he would be offered a job at Blue Cross and Blue Shield. Patricia called them periodically, to remind them that Clay was very interested in working for them. After about a year of waiting, they did call Clay, and now he works in the mailroom. He has been with the company for ten years now, and he loves his job.

Clay did a splendid job raising his children. He went to work every weekday and devoted all his spare time to Lee and Katrina. He kept his apartment nice, became a good cook, and did the laundry. Katrina told me her dad made "a great Mr. Mom." I looked after Clay's land and trailer back in DeQuincy. Later, I sold them for him, so that he could build or buy a house in Baton Rouge. In the early years after Karen left, Katrina mothered Lee and read to him in the evenings. Things got a little easier for Clay after both children were in school. Katrina was an "A" student. She adjusted to the abrupt changes very well. She had many friends, and she taught them sign language so they could communicate with her dad. Clay did everything he could to make his children happy. He played with them. He acted silly with them. I am very proud of Clay and his little family.

Chapter 16. Telling My Story

Now that my children were grown and out on their own, I wanted to do something. I had learned so much while raising a deaf child: The shock of realizing my child was deaf; the glass bubble I imagined him living in; his struggles to cope with the hearing world, and mine to get him an education. I wanted to share my experiences with others. After I got fired from my job at the hospital in Sulphur, I had a lot of time on my hands. The following summer, in 1981, I suddenly wanted to share my story with everyone. I sat at my dining-room table with a pencil and loose-leaf paper. I didn't know how to type and I knew nothing about computers. I realized that in order to write my story I would have to improve my English.

First I took a correspondence course in writing from the Newspaper Institute of America. The lessons were short stories that I had to rewrite. That was good practice for me, and the course was very helpful. Every month I mailed in my lessons, and each lesson was corrected and graded and returned to me. I was embarrassed about how bad my spelling was when I first started the lessons, so I bought a dictionary and improved my spelling while I completed my lessons. I did one lesson a month for two years, at which time I completed the course and passed with a "B" average. By the time I received my certificate of membership from the Newspaper Institute of America, I was really interested in writing my story.

The first article I wrote was called "Count Your Blessings," which was published in the *Lake Charles American Press*. I was so thrilled to see my article in print. Next, remembering the times that Clay could not find work, I wrote a poem, "No Time For Me." My poem was published in the *American Poetry Anthology* and also in *The Pelican*, the news magazine published monthly by LSSD. Darrell said, "Mother, you like to write so much—why don't you go back to school and learn how to write?"

I was forty-nine years old, but I liked his suggestion. I said, "I think I will." So back to school I went.

We lived near DeQuincy High School, so I inquired there about adult education classes. I found out the school had classes for adults on Tuesdays and Thursday nights, so I enrolled. It had been thirty-five years since I'd dropped out of high school in Mamou, Louisiana. After six months of night classes, I took the GED test. I was surprised to find that I scored very high in math, which I had always thought was my weakest subject. I scored pretty high in the other subjects, too.

I was fifty years old when I received my high school equivalency diploma. I was as excited as a teenager going to her first prom. Needless to say, I framed my diploma, and I have it hanging on the wall in my office. I wasn't satisfied with an equivalency diploma, though. I had already started drafting my story, which I called "Silent World."

I love writing, and I wanted to keep improving my English so that some day I could get my book published.

After finishing the rough draft of "Silent World," I enrolled at McNeese State University in Lake Charles, Louisiana, about a twenty-five-mile drive from DeQuincy. First I took remedial classes in English, history, speech, and typing. A few years earlier, I had borrowed a typewriter and taught myself to type, but decided to take typing at McNeese anyway. Since I'd been out of school for thirty-five years, there was a lot I wanted to learn. There were a few other people my age on campus, and I loved going to college and learning again. I went to McNeese for a year, and would have continued going, but the tuition was sharply increased after that first year. Bruce Jr. was a junior in high school when I started going to McNeese, and I thought that I'd better save my money to pay for his college tuition.

Katrina, Lee, and Kassidi

Katrina got married at the age of seventeen to a man named Geram Baldman from Sulphur. The following year, she gave birth to a beautiful baby girl. She named her daughter Kassidi Page. As I write this story, Kassidi is five years old. She is sweet and lovable, and she can hear and talk very well. After about one year of marriage, Katrina and Geram separated, and she moved back with her father in Baton Rouge. She called me one day, very excited, and said "Maw-Maw, I passed the test."

"What test?" I asked.

"To do interpreting for the deaf. I scored a level five, as high as you can score." She had always been interested in doing interpretation for the deaf.

"That is wonderful, Katrina!"

Katrina is now a certified interpreter for the deaf, and she did interpretation at LSU for a while. She has her own apartment and she is raising Kassidi on her own. She likes her independence.

Chapter 17. A Few Thoughts

I was in the grocery store one day when a deaf boy came up to me and handed me a manual-alphabet card. He was trying to get customers to give him "donations" in exchange for these cards. I was furious! I gave him a good scolding, and he was surprised that I knew how to sign. I told him that I had a deaf son, and that my son was working just as hard as he was able to work, and that he could go to work too. I resented that this deaf boy was acting like a beggar. Not only was begging against the law, but it was a bad reflection on intelligent and hard-working deaf people.

I still get a chill up my spine when I hear someone described as "deaf and dumb." Maybe "dumb" originally meant "not able to speak," but who wants to be called dumb? If deaf people don't speak, it is not because they can't speak, but because they can't control the intonation of their voice. If they don't speak, it's because they prefer not to speak. Nowadays we use the word "dumb" to mean "stupid" or "ignorant," and deafness has nothing to do with lack of intelligence.

Sometimes, when I look at Clay and see those expressive blue-green eyes, it hurts to think that he will have to go through life not only not hearing, but being treated differently. It hurts me to see people stare at him when he tries to communicate, even though I know they only stare out of curiosity.

I don't know why the Lord chose to give me a deaf child. I do not question it. I learned to accept it, and I gave up wishing for a miracle long ago. God has his reasons. I do not have that much education, but I write as honestly as I can, in the hope that my story may reassure someone else, maybe a young parent who just found out their child is deaf. To that parent, I would say, "It is not the end of the world. Your deaf child will bring you much happiness and pleasure. Just please educate your deaf child. Learn all that you can about how to help your child get a good education. Find out about the school near you and their methods of teaching, and decide which method is best for your child. Be proud of your deaf child as I am of Clay." All parents of deaf children should remember, first and foremost, the deaf child is still a child, a child with real feelings, the same as you and me. Once you understand that, you're halfway there.

If hearing people knew how to communicate with deaf people, it would save a lot of the frustration, wasted time, and misunderstandings that currently cause bad feelings between those in the deaf world and those in the hearing world. I would especially like to see doctors, teachers, nurses, and police officers know how to communicate with deaf people in case of a real emergency. If a doctor knew sign and could communicate with a deaf person, just think how much time that would save. The doctor wouldn't have to find an interpreter, and the time saved could very well save the deaf person's life. If a deaf person gets in an automobile accident, he's like a caged animal, at the mercy of a doctor or nurse who can't even communicate with him. If a deaf person breaks the law, he's thrown into a jail cell and deprived of the right to make a phone call, just because no one can communicate with that deaf person. So America, I say to you, learn to communicate with the deaf.

Changes

Technology has come a long way since 1981, when I wrote the first draft of this book, sitting at my dining-room table and using only a pencil and loose-leaf paper. The world of the deaf has been greatly improved. Scientists have invented the cochlear implant, a device that can help some deaf people to hear. From what I understand, though, the implant is not right for every deaf person. If you are deaf and thinking about an implant, you should ask your physician many questions, and also do your own research on it.

When Clay was growing up, the telephone was a barrier to him, but technology has changed that as well. Today deaf people have access to the TTY telephone, which is a telephone with a small type-writer-like keyboard. The deaf person can type a message, and the person receiving the message can read it on an LCD display or print it out. Today deaf people also have access to videophones that allow them to see each other and have a conversation. Pagers have also become very popular with deaf people. The deaf person hooks the pager, which is about the size of a cell phone, to his belt or clothing, and then he can feel it vibrate when he receives a call. The computer is also an important mode of access for the deaf world, and deaf people can now enjoy communicating with friends through e-mail.

All of these technologies are a big improvement for deaf people. We had none of those things while Clay was growing up. I felt fortunate just that he could go to a school that had certified teachers of the deaf. The computer has opened new lines of communication for our family.

Not too long ago, I knew nothing about computers. I walked into our local library and saw five or six computers lined up against the wall. I asked one of the ladies working there if anyone could use the computers, and she said that they were for public use. I told her that I wanted to learn how to use them, and she gave me a password and helped me get started. I learned to e-mail my children.

I went to the library every day for a whole year to use the computers. Bruce decided if I was that interested in computers, he might as well buy one for me. Monty came over and hooked it up for me. I thoroughly enjoy learning more about it every day, but the best thing about it is that I can communicate with Clay. I have learned so much since I first started writing my story. In spite of all the changes that have been happening, some things haven't changed at all. Clay and I still have the closeness that we shared in his childhood. He is still very intuitive, and he can look at me and immediately sense my mood, if I'm keeping good news from him or if something is bothering me. Clay and I are like old friends.

Chapter 18. A Word from Clay

As you know by now, I feel closer to my mother and sister than anyone else, probably because they learned to communicate with me better than anyone else in the family. I remember when Patricia was born. She was pink like a rose bursting to bloom. She would wrap her tiny finger tightly around my finger. I would check on her after school to be sure she was all right. Usually she was sound asleep. She smelled of baby powder and baby lotion. I was too young to remember our trip to Germany, but I do remember Line Avenue School in Shreveport, Louisiana. I remember my teacher, Mrs. Bloomer, and my classmates, including my best friend Micah Roberts. Mrs. Bloomer was a good teacher. She didn't want us to sign, and she was firm about it. While in her class, I learned to say some words, and even put them into sentences. My first sentences were, "May I have some water?" and "May I go to the bathroom?"

Eventually I learned sentences that were a little more complicated. I can remember my mother bringing me to school in the morning and picking me up in the afternoon. My mother is a happy, jolly person who always tries to see the bright side of things, so whenever she wasn't smiling I would worry. I wanted to know why she wasn't smiling. I would raise my hands to her and gesture, why wasn't she smiling? She would break out in a big smile, pat my shoulder, and assure me everything was fine. My mother was also very firm when it came to my study time. She had a certain time set aside for our studies, and there was no getting out of it. We would usually study sometime after supper, around seven or eight o'clock. On weekends we studied around two or three in the afternoon.

My mother used flash cards with pictures on them, and she used a large board with circles with all the colors. We would sit at the dining table. She would hold my hand to her throat, so that I could feel the vibration, and she would say, purple, p-u-r-p-l-e, purple. She would say purple over and over and make me repeat after her until she was satisfied I did my best. Between my mother's help and Mrs. Bloomer's class, I learned many words. We fell into a routine—my mother took me to school in the morning and picked me up after school, then supper at 6:00 P.M. and study period at 7:00 P.M. On weekends, we spent an extra hour studying. Sometimes I would see my mother looking for me and I would pretend not to see her, so that I could continue playing outside. She soon caught on to my trick and made me look at her. She was very determined about our study time and always insisted I come into the house.

By now I could make myself understood instead of just gesturing to things I wanted. When I was around seven years old, I noticed how easy it was for my mother to talk to Monty and Darrell. I pointed to my mouth and said, "me nothing." My mother knelt down besides me and took my hand in hers. Her face was very serious, and slowly she said, "Clay, you cannot hear, and that is why you cannot talk, but I will teach you to talk. You will have to go to a special school. I will help you, Clay." At the age of seven I realized, in my small child's mind, that I was different.

My family didn't treat me as though I were different. If I needed a spanking, I got one, just like Monty and Darrell. There were times when we had to be corrected. I played with all the neighborhood kids after school. They knew that I was deaf, but it didn't seem to bother them. We played ball and made tree houses in the backyard. We played tag, marbles, and other games that seven and eight year olds play. When I was about ten years old, my father transferred to Bergstrom Air Force Base in Austin, Texas. My mother and father enrolled me at the Texas School for the Deaf. The kids there talked in sign language, and that was where I learned to sign. My mother learned the manual alphabet, and it opened a whole new world for us. My mother and I could actually communicate. My father chose to talk to me rather than sign. Most of the time, I could read his lips and understand him. If I didn't understand my father or mother, she would spell out the words using the manual alphabet.

Life was so much easier for me, now that my mother could sign to me. We learned together. She learned more about the world I lived in, and I learned more about her hearing world. I had many questions to ask her. I remember asking my mother if water made noise, and I was surprised when she said that it did. She held my hand under the bathtub faucet and let me feel the water. She said that while the water was running, it made a noise. There were so many things to learn about this hearing world. I made new friends at the Texas School for the Deaf and I liked it.

When I was twelve years old, my dad retired from the U.S. Air Force and we moved to Baton Rouge, Louisiana. I remember going to school with my mother and father. We rode the ferry across the Mississippi River. We sat in a small office where the principal was sitting behind a desk. He said there wasn't any room for me at the school. My mother broke down and cried. She was very angry, and she kept saying, "I wrote you a letter, you said my son could come to school here." She told other people in the office, "He said my son could come to school here and now he won't take him." My dad tried to calm her down, and that upset her even more. Mother shouted, "No! I will not be quiet! Clay will go to school here even if I have to go see the governor!" The principal invited my parents to walk around on the school ground. Later, he decided that there was room for me at the Louisiana State School for the Deaf. My mother smiled again. She placed all my clothes in the closet. She said that either she or my father would come get me on Fridays.

I enjoyed going to the Louisiana State School for the Deaf. There were many activities to keep us busy. We had a heated swimming pool I enjoyed very much. There was a center where students could enjoy hamburgers and a Coke after school. My mother and father kept their promise to pick me up after school every Friday. Mother did my laundry when I was home, and I went skating on Saturday nights with Monty and Darrell. I learned to roller skate very well, and I enjoyed my weekends at home.

On Monday mornings, my father would bring me back to school on his way to work, or sometimes my mother would bring me back. I always looked forward to the next Friday, when I could go home again. We kept this routine until the year before I graduated, when my father got a job at a correctional school in DeQuincy, Louisiana, and my parents moved there. After they moved, Darrell picked me up on weekends until I graduated in May of 1984. My mother bought me a pair of black slacks and a white shirt to wear for my graduation, under the green cap and gown.

By this time I had a new baby brother. We called him B.J., short for Bruce Jr. B.J. was learning to walk around the time of my graduation. I had been surprised to have a new baby brother. After graduation, I moved in with my parents in DeQuincy. It was nice for a while, but I soon became very bored. I couldn't communicate with anyone other than my parents. I missed my friends in school. I got a job picking up tree limbs for the city of DeQuincy, and it was better than sitting at home being bored. My mother begged me to ask a girl out to a movie or something, but I didn't want to, because I felt that I couldn't communicate well enough to ask a hearing girl on a date. So I watched television at home with my parents, and I was lonely and bored. I missed my deaf friends in Baton Rouge. I had a few temper tantrums at home because I was so miserable. I never did drink or smoke, though, and I still don't care for either one.

I came in from work one day and my mother looked excited. She said, "Clay, would you like to further your education and go to college?"

"Sure," I responded.

She told me that she heard about Lee Junior College on the radio, and that they could teach deaf students. The next thing I knew, I was studying graphic arts at Lee Junior College in Baytown, Texas. I came back home occasionally. My mother gave me the blue 1967 Mustang that she had bought while we lived in Baton Rouge. I enjoyed going to college and spending time with deaf friends again. After attending Lee Junior College for two years I received a bachelor's degree in graphic arts. I was looking forward to getting a job.

First my mother and I went to the American Press in Lake Charles, Louisiana, but they weren't hiring. My mother and I went to other print shops, but each printing shop would just refer me to another. It didn't take me long to realize what they were doing. They were not interested in hiring a deaf person, so they were getting rid of me. After all the schooling, the studying, working hard, only to be turned down. Why wouldn't the hearing people at least give me a chance? By now I was feeling very disgusted with this hearing world. My mother was trying to talk to me and cheer me up but I knew she was just as disgusted as I was. As we were walking back to the car I said, "They don't want to hire me because I am deaf. Leave me alone!" I shouted as loud as I could.

Eventually I got a job driving a forklift for Boise Southern, a wood processing plant located about five miles from our home. I had one advantage over the hearing people—the noise inside the plant didn't bother me. Some of the men showed an interest in learning sign language. I gave them some of my cards, and a few men learned a few signs. I learned what signals to use on the shipping floor, and I carried a pencil and a small tablet in my shirt pocket so that I could write when the other men didn't understand me.

Things were much better for me now. I was happy to have a job, and I was adjusting to the hearing world. I met an old friend, Karen, who used to go to school with me at LSSD. We started dating, and soon a romance developed. Karen and I had a beautiful church wedding and eight wonderful years followed. I thought Karen and I had the perfect marriage. However, Karen met a hearing man at church and just walked out, leaving my two kids and me behind.

My world was falling apart. I didn't understand why Karen just walked out on us. I guess I would have lost my mind if it had not been for the children. After several months, when I realized that Karen wasn't coming back, I decided to try and go on with my life. My daughter, Katrina, was eight years old, and my son, Lee, was two. I gathered my family and our belongings and moved to Baton Rouge, Louisiana, to make a new life for us. I found a job in a print shop and I found an apartment in a nice neighborhood. I enrolled Katrina and Lee in the best schools. It has been fourteen years now since Karen left, and it has not been easy being both a father and a mother to Katrina and Lee. I felt the pain of Karen leaving us for a long time, but each day it hurts a little less. Today I live for my children. Katrina and Lee are both exceptionally good students. While Katrina was in the fifth grade she was voted class president. Lee received certificates for honor roll and perfect attendance.

The children and I are members of a local Catholic church, where the children attend regular religious instruction. We attend Mass at the Catholic Deaf Center on the campus of the Louisiana State School for the Deaf. My daughter, Katrina, is grown now, and I enjoy spending time with her daughter, my little granddaughter, Kassidi. She will be six this year and she can sign very well. Katrina works as an interpreter for the deaf, and she enjoys her job. My son, Lee, graduated from Redemptorist Catholic School this year, and plans to attend Louisiana State University. I am enjoying my job at Blue Cross and Blue Shield of Louisiana. I work in the mail room. I am still a single parent. I am active in church and I drive the church van on Saturdays, picking up deaf people who don't have a way to go to church. Maybe I will do little odd jobs for them.

The woodworking skills I learned at LSSD come in handy. I love working with wood in my spare time. I am very fortunate to have such a wonderful family. My mother and father, my brothers, and my sister Patricia have always been very supportive of me through the years. My grandmother Devillier was a very strong person who was full of determination, and she instilled that same determination in me over the years. I thank God for my two beautiful children and my darling little Kassidi. All I really want out of life is a good job for my family and to give them a good education. I am very thankful for the study time my mother insisted upon, and I am thankful that she encouraged education, family, and spiritual life for all of us. Without my mother's help, I may never have learned to say "purple." Thank you, Mother, for sharing our story. My mother and I are like old friends.

Deaf People Have Rights

To all my deaf friends, deaf people have a right to prove themselves as first-class citizens. They have a right to vote and be represented. As tax-paying citizens they have a right to access to news media. All television stations should have an interpreter (I wrote to our local station to express the need for an interpreter, and we now have one). To all my deaf friends I say: Be a proud citizen. Set an example for others who are deaf. Vote and fight for your rights. Demand interpreters or captioning on your local television station. You have just as much right as hearing people. Never settle for less.

Between Two Worlds

Dvora Shurman

Preface

I was part of my deaf parents, their ears, their voice to the hearing world, Mother and me sharing the task of being the mother.

This book is a double helix, around the core of deafness and society, and my own duality in the deaf and hearing worlds. Elements wind together:

- within the community of my deaf parents,
- in the society of people who can hear,
- and my split life inside and outside those worlds.

Daughter of Deaf Parents without Signing?

Language is not only spoken or written words, but incorporates the entire body, through the mind, beyond the limits of words.

More important than any physical handicap was societal perception of deaf people. Mother forbade me to use sign language, since her teachers at the school for the deaf told her that signing was only for people who were born deaf. But sign language, expressed with intelligence, wit, and thematic and cultural integrity, has the power to do what any art aspires to do: affect people's attitudes. Sign language is deep, and it's natural; it involves not only the left brain's logical mind but also the spatial perceptions of the intuitive right brain.

But Mother did not use sign language with me. Since she had no language before the age of five, her brain was not configured for "grammar," but it was open to signing, and to spatial perceptions.

My hands were locked. Yet, watching my parents, body language and deep connections developed.

In these stories I journey back into memories. Like the infant in King Solomon's dream, the struggle between Mother and her sister Ella pulled me in two parallel lives, with two mothers. I perceived my dichotomy, not being a self but rather a messenger. I found healing for myself, as someone with Memory.

Deafness as Social Handicap, and Shame

In journaling, using both storytelling and movement, stories came alive and revised themselves! I reentered memories, resolved conflicts, by giving voices—and "listening"—to other people. I pried stories out of memories, then reconsidered them with amazement and new understanding. I also recognized shame—I had been taught to be ashamed of my deaf parents.

Using dreamlike journaling, I unfolded the layers of myself. Unhappy episodes became more-than-personal facets of a broad human drama. I reconsidered Mother, her disappointments, frustrations, anger, and anxieties. In imagined dialogue my father "told me" he loved me. Out of depths of understanding my father's spirit informs my life, enthusiasm, and ability to rise as a phoenix from my mother's misery.

Then I discovered Father Antonio Provolo, the Italian priest responsible for taking away sign language from deaf children—from my parents and from me.

Telling these stories I drew understanding from them, coming to celebrate that I am my deaf parents' daughter. May this book inspire my readers toward a similar understanding.

Acknowledgments

I thank and bless my mentors,

- Neighbor and dean of children's literature in Israel, Yehuda Atlas;
- My father who is with me in spirit, inspiring my laughter;
- Professor Joseph Lukinsky, who introduced me to storytelling;
- Professor David Kraemer, who brought me research on deafness in Judaism;

- Johanna Reiss, teacher of writing workshops. With her I opened my Pandora's box of SHAME through stories; and
- Dear friend Roberta Barr, who encourages me from Florida by e-mail and phone, and believes in me.

Chapter 1. Sam and Anna: History and Childhood

My mother told me stories. Stories of her life that I heard over and over.

I sit beside Mother and listen as she retells this story. "I love to dance. Yes, Deaf, but feel music in my body, natural. I always dance, dance in street when hearing children play games I don't understand. I am seven when dancing teacher walk by, see me. He stop, watch, and smile, and ask childrens where I live. They point, my house, and we go to Ma. He tell her it's wonderful, the little girl dance beautiful, want to give me lessons, free! I go three years, know to dance!"

She stops her story to stand and sway, dancing, kicking back her slender legs in the Charleston, laughing and bouncing. Then she sits down, sad.

"Nineteen-eighteen, for two years I had bad sickness, flu from Europe. My hair fell out, weak, tired. Nineteen-twenty at last okay, go out, but late for me to find a husband. Twenty-three years old, in Milwaukee the Jewish Deaf men are few, all born deaf. I do not want deaf children. In Chicago many Jewish deaf, make parties and dances! I go to Chicago."

She smiles dreamily. "There I meet Emmanuel. Tall, handsome, dark hair smooth back. The best dancer, like me, graceful, perfect time. We move together. Two-step, waltz, Charleston. Wonderful time. I am in love! Emmanuel come to Milwaukee to my family. Sister Ella flirt with him, not nice!

"Three years I go to Chicago. Men flock around when I enter. I stand up tall, head back, ropes of crystal beads, grey satin chemise. Fingers flash: 'Anna from Milwaukee! Now watch her dance.'"

Mother remembers, the memory spinning again and again, Emmanuel quickly moving toward her, signing, "At last. You came! You look so fine! Come, we dance."

Anna dressed up for partying.

"I step into his arms. Others move back to watch. The band plays a waltz, we spin about the room. Everyone raises arms, applause. Like Dolores del Rio in the movies. I wave, smiles."

She stops in a quiet remembering pause, then,

"One day I am hot, in August. Take paper fan from beaded bag. Emmanuel bring me to table for lemonade and cookies. Many pretty ladies rush up, sign: 'Oh Emmanuel, you dance nice. Give me one dance.'

"I watch, angry, counting. Four years I come to Chicago. I dance with Emmanuel. He come to Milwaukee, we go out to movies. He say I am pretty, good for nice times. I say what about marry, and he shake his finger: Not yet. I am twenty-six, almost twenty-seven, my friends all marry. Only me not.

"I'm mad, arms across chest, foot tapping. I don't see Sam from Milwaukee, next to me. Short, not tall, not like Emmanuel, only eighteen. Young kid, full of good spirits, laughs and sings. Clumsy dancer, no balance, from getting deaf."

Father tells the story this way,

"I watch Anna, thinking: 'I have a good job. Time to settle down. Not a born-deaf girl, only a Jewish girl for me. Anna is the best. So pretty, good dancer, bright eyes, full of life. I must act now.'"

He goes straight to the point, doesn't waste time or words. He touches Anna's arm to get her attention. "Anna," he begins, "You're so lovely. I love you."

Back to Mother.

"I stare at him. This young kid, this clumsy dancer. Loves me? Foolish! He is nothing like Emmanuel. Emmanuel! Where? In the middle of pretty girls, flirting.

"I signs to Sam: Later. Then quick clicking steps across the room, to Emmanuel. I sign: 'You forget me?'"

Signing is visible, so everyone can see what's going on. Her face talks even more than her hands, with her teeth and chin set, lips tight. She brushes back her fine, wavy hair, loosened by the dancing, that flies about her face.

Emmanuel takes Anna by the arm: "Anna, I tell you again. I like you. Of course. Very much. You're pretty. A fine dancer. But I'm not looking to marry. Not yet. Just good times, no more."

Anna stamps her foot. "Three years? Not love?" Emmanuel looks at her coldly. It's clear he does not love her. Anna reacts sharply.

"You make me a fool. I finish with you. I marry someone else. You see!" She turns away, thinking: "I fix him! I swear. Marry the next man who ask me. Doesn't matter who. Swear to God." She returns to her lemonade, and Sam.

Sam signs: "You mad? I make you smile. Come, dance." She accepts, pirouetting around him, keeping her eye on Emmanuel. As the party ends the Milwaukee group head home by train. Sam walks beside Anna, asks permission to take her arm, to keep his balance in the dark. She thinks, "Right, he makes me feel better."

Sam tells the story.

"I am romantic, love flourishing phrases, the flowery language of the titles in Rudolf Valentino's flicks. I can remember tunes the band played, still dancing in my head. I learned songs in English and Yiddish, before I lost my hearing. I still can hear the tunes. As the train pulls in, I ask gallantly, 'May I have the pleasure of escorting you home?'"

Anna:

"I nods my head, quick. On the streetcar he tell about his job, sings and makes me laugh. I feel good. He say he can come next Saturday.

"I tells Sam: 'I finish all eight grades of Binner School. I work, seamstress, piece work, hard work. I am very good, very fast. In the shop we all are deaf girls. I have many friends among the girls. We get little money but we have good times together.'"

Sam:

"A month of Saturdays is all it took. I took her to films starring Dolores del Rio, the Latin dancer, to German band concerts in the park with the strong oompah beat we both loved. Then I proposed. 'It's true, I'm only eighteen, but I am smart, have a good job, a blueprint draftsman. I went to high school. I want to settle down with a wife. You are so graceful, pretty, smiling, and not born deaf. You are the girl for me. Will you marry me?'" Anna accepts, smiling sweetly.

Anna:

"I swore, didn't I! Swore to marry the first man who asks. Good, Sam was born hearing. He's good nature, has a good job. He loves me. He laughs a lot, but I don't understand what is funny. No matter. There's no one else, Jewish, not born deaf. I want to be a housewife, a mother. That's enough."

Sam:

"I am gallant, romantic, know I must ask Anna's father for his consent. The next day, dressed in my holiday suit, I knocked on the door. Her father came out. I took off my fedora, bowed, and said, 'Sir, I've come to ask for Anna's hand in marriage. I love her and can provide for her.'

"Her father, taken aback, was thinking: 'Sam's family is low class and poor. But Anna is twenty-seven and deaf. She needs a husband.' He smiled at Sam, and said, 'Of course, Son.'"

Like in fairy tales, they were married, and I was born. To tell their stories?

Anna

Mildred, Anna's youngest sister, wrote, "I sat down to imagine Anna's journey to America."

At the end of the nineteenth century, in a *shtetl* (village) in Russia, lived Masha Saffro, with chestnut-brown hair, soft gray-brown eyes, sweet and petite. Times were hard for East European Jews, especially for a girl who had no dowry. Auburn-haired Jacob Schefrin, nearly six feet tall, lean and handsome, shunned the idea of arranged marriages and married her. Lacking a dowry, Masha's parents undertook to house their daughter and her family. In time Masha and Jacob had five children, which meant that there were twelve people living in that crowded house.

When Anna and her twin sister were twenty months old, they caught scarlet fever. Her sister died, and Anna lost her hearing. She

Anna and her siblings.

soon forgot the words she had once known, since no one in the village knew anything about teaching deaf children. She had no way to understand or be understood.

Masha's older brothers had settled in America. They wrote to Jacob: "It's good here in Milwaukee. There's work for everyone. Joe's got a pushcart, and we take in tailoring. Come. Stay with us until you find work and save money for boat tickets for the family."

Jacob set off, with kisses and tears, leaving the family behind. He did manage only a year later to send steerage tickets, but to Canada, not to Ellis Island. He knew immigration authorities did not allow deaf and handicapped people to enter. The Canadian border was easier to cross.

Ella already was taking care of her deaf sister. She would stamp her foot, shake her fist, pull and slap Anna to make her behave. With five children, Rose still a baby, Sam, just two, Anna four, Ella eight, and Bertha the eldest, ten, Masha organized the voyage. She assigned each daughter a task, "Bertha, you take Sam. You're strong, so you can carry him part of the way. Ella, you're my right-hand daughter, so you'll take care of Anna. Watch her all the time, and hold her hand tight. Don't let her wander away."

Without proper papers, they set out to cross the Russian border. As they walked in the deep woods, their "underground" guide heard a border patrol approaching. He told Masha to hurry, picked Anna up, dashed ahead, and disappeared into the woods. Masha and the other children didn't have time to cross before the soldiers arrived. Anna was alone in Poland. She ran about, looking for Ella, making frightened whimpering sounds, and wandered out of sight.

Masha was distraught: "My poor little deaf baby. If the border patrol finds her, we'll be arrested, sent back, or worse. If they don't find her, wild animals might hurt her. I have to give myself up to the soldiers. Children, come!"

Masha reached the nearby outpost, and opened the door. There was Anna, her face streaked with dirt and tears, sitting on a blonde soldier's lap. When Anna saw Masha, she jumped off the soldier's lap and ran to her mother.

The soldier smiled reassuringly. "This must be your little girl. I heard her crying, and found her. She's deaf, yes? Hard for you." He looked at Masha, at the children trailing her, and said, "You can go on. There won't be any trouble."

Masha and the children finally boarded a boat to Canada. Packed in with other families, they slept on their packets in steerage for nearly three weeks. Poor Anna didn't understand what was happening. The waves, the winds, the movement of the ship in the water frightened her. The odors of the unwashed steerage passengers nauseated her. She clung tightly to Ella; remembering their experience at the border, Ella clung to Anna, too. But by the end of that voyage Ella was never able to forgive her sister for being such a burden.

From the port, Masha crossed the border to reach Milwaukee, where they walked to the address on Walnut Street that Jacob had sent to her. They were "home."

Milwaukee 1900

In 1994, I visited an exhibition at the Milwaukee Municipal Museum, "150 years of the Jewish Community of Milwaukee." A reporter for a Catholic newspaper forwarded photos of me with his article about Milwaukee's Jews. From that article I understood more about my own parents and their immigrant families.

Immigrants

Women like Masha were the heroines of the new American frontier at the beginning of the twentieth century, even if many of them struggled with English. They bore the heavy burdens of raising families in unfamiliar surroundings, yet they rose to the challenge with the help of young social workers and teachers. The Settlement House community center served the needs of immigrants on Walnut Street and was the center of the Jewish community.

Milwaukee was an ideal city for new immigrants. In the 1840s, German socialists fled their homeland for Wisconsin's green pastures, which were so much like Germany. These liberal thinkers were active in politics. They introduced kindergartens to America, became local and national leaders, writers and teachers, and brilliant international politicians, like Golda Meir.[1]

Large numbers of immigrants fleeing eastern Europe's mayhem against Jews expanded the Jewish population in Milwaukee to 20,000 between 1875 and 1895, and the community took over the abandoned London Factory to serve as a shelter over their heads. Educated young women formed social service organizations and community centers to help the newcomers adjust. The Settlement House raised money selling the *Settlement House Cook Book*, which became a classic of Jewish cookery. Mount Sinai Hospital, established in 1913 to offer medical service to the needy, was considered an exemplary facility for the entire city. (I was born there, as was my second son.)

Both my grandfathers, like many European immigrants, began life in America as peddlers. Such peddlers soon opened small groceries and shops, or worked as tailors and shoemakers.[2] At first my grandfather Jacob Schefrin supported his family with his pushcart, buying and selling scrap metal. After the five-year required waiting period, he passed the citizenship test easily, and told Masha, "I'm going to take good care of you here, in the melting pot, America. I am an American now."

One evening he rushed in to report: "I'm in a real business! Mr. Locher, the German who buys my scrap, asked me to work with him. He has a foundry melting scrap metal on the south side, near the factories."

Masha smiled, pleased for him, and quietly served Jacob a cup of tea, with two sugar lumps to hold between his teeth as he drank. He thought, with no care for his wife and family, "What do I need with Jewish neighbors? I'm associating with Americans."

Little Anna

He moved his family away from Walnut Street, from the Jewish neighborhood, but his partner never invited Jacob to his home. Masha was uprooted, with no compatible Yiddish-speaking neighbors. She had to do her kosher food shopping in her old neighborhood, riding two trolley cars to get there. She was very much alone, with little English, trying to manage a houseful of children. Especially Anna.

Anna was five years old when the family came to Milwaukee. Left without language in her early years, she had missed the developmental window for forming grammar rules in her brain. She was frustrated, made almost crazy by the language wall, not understanding and not being understood. She threw food, broke dishes, or ran about the room screaming, making wailing noises, pulling at her mother's apron.

The social worker at Settlement House heard about Anna from Masha's former neighbors. She came to visit, and explained, "You're lucky, living in Milwaukee. There's a fine school here, Paul Binner School for the Deaf. I'll take you to register her."

It wasn't so fine. Binner School taught only lipreading and forbade the use of sign language. Deaf children need more. They need signing to comprehend ideas, to organize their thinking. Anna did learn sewing and crafts, and excelled in these skills, which were visual and therefore understandable to her. But she did not discover how words make sense until she was ten years old, when she learned sign language from two girls who transferred from the Wisconsin School for the Deaf.

She had spent the first ten years of her life without communication or any understanding of the people and world around her. She had no sense of humor, for humor requires the ability to perceive meanings. Even when she finally learned to talk she could not communicate with her parents. Masha shook her head and shrugged her shoulders, hands held upward to say, "I don't understand." Anna and her parents would never understand one another.

Sam and His Family

Sam's parents, Harry and Ethel Becker, came from Slobodka, the Ukraine. Cousin Rebecca, the youngest daughter of Harry's older brother Abraham, kept a family chronicle. She recalled, "Harry married Ethel in Slobodka. The match was made through cousins who had moved to South Africa, and they sent the newlyweds money for boat tickets to join them. Harry and Ethel hurried to the seaport in Odessa, Russia, fleeing the czar's twenty-five-year draft of Jews,[3] but the ship to South Africa had already set sail."

Under the circumstances Harry couldn't wait, so they took the next ship out, to Canada. Maybe that was really his original plan! Sam's cousin Rebecca recalled, "Grandfather had previously brought his deaf cousin to relatives in Fond du Lac, where she could work and find a husband. He made that trip through Canada because the immigration authorities at Ellis Island would not have allowed her into the United States. He returned to Slobodka because he knew his wife, who had glaucoma, could not pass through immigration. After his wife died he came to Milwaukee alone. Seventy-five years old and strong, like his son Harry, he walked from the train station to his son Abraham's house, with his belongings in a basket on his back."

Rebecca continued, "Harry, however, was tiny and thin, from hunger and nature, but strong enough to carry heavy loads. Barely five feet tall, his body was taut, wiry, and powerful, his health excellent. Landing in Milwaukee with neither skills nor money, Harry began peddling coal. It brought him good money in the long winter but very little during the hot summers. He set up a small business from his backyard, selling coal by the bucket. He sold coal all his life. His skin was almost black from the coal dust that clung to his clothes and skin.

"Harry prayed every morning before starting his workday. Ethel, who was just as righteous, made him shake the coal dust from his trouser cuffs at night. She was making sure everyone got the full measure he paid for. To add to Harry's meager earnings she worked as an attendant at the *mikveh*, the ritual baths.

"In time they had seven children. First Al and Fanny, then Sam, followed by Morry, Sarah, and two others. Sam and Morry looked so much alike people took them for twins, but Morry was the bigger mischief maker. Their father Harry was given to practical jokes and shouting—he was wildly enthusiastic. Morry and your father picked up his wild humor and mischief, but Ethel, his wife, didn't understand his jokes, and pleaded with Harry to stop teasing."

My own connections with my father were deep. A look between us said more than words. We shared the slogan, "It's Not Fair," and we rebelled against the shaming, the demeaning our family suffered.

Sam's Story

Sarah, Sam's sister, told me, "Sam was born around 1903. We say around, because City Hall burned down with all the records. Sam was the jewel among the children, clever, affectionate, and brilliant. But he came down with a burning fever when he was seven years old. No doctor came to see him. We were so poor."

Sam recalled, "I was so cold Ma made me a bed in the kitchen near the stove. I was shaking and shivering. My brothers came to my bed dressed like devils, waving sharp claws, and scared me, so I fell out of bed and never heard again."

That sounds like hallucinations brought about by the fever. He lost both his hearing and his balance from the illness. There was no medical diagnosis, but mastoid infections and meningitis both show similar symptoms. Considering the headaches he had all his life, it was likely meningitis.

When Sam was born his parents named him Joshua, but they changed his name to Sam when he was ill, to outwit the Angel of Death. When Sam recovered, he slowly learned to walk again, carefully so as not to fall. Once he was stronger he entered the Paul Binner School for the Deaf. Because he could already read and write English and Yiddish, his language skills made the transition to lip-reading easy. He immediately associated lip shapes with words he already spoke and read.

Sam also experienced a phenomenon called "phantom voices," a lingering sensation, like that of an amputated limb. "I am not like the Deaf who never heard. I know what voices sound like, and music too. When people talk to me I don't just read their lips. I hear their voices. I studied with hearing people, too. After eighth grade I went on to high school."

His cousin Rebecca loved Sam so much that she became a teacher of deaf children, and worked some years later at the Binner School.

"Sam Becker, your cousin!" the principal exclaimed. "The best student we ever had. I didn't know deaf children could learn so much." Sam's niece Evelyn, who worshipped him, also became a teacher of deaf children.

Sadly, Sam was short-tempered and impulsive, a result of the damage to his brain. He recalled, "I went to high school to learn a trade, blueprinting. My friends in class loved my humor and helped me, explained when the teacher talked with his back to me. When the shop-work class made a strike against the teacher to protest an unfair grade to one boy, I left school with them because they were my friends."

Sam and Anna

Sam's lifelong "brain fever" affected his emotional stability, his education cut short because he could not let go of his anger. Yet, in the good times after World War I, he found a job. He told me: "I learned shop work, blueprinting and drafting, and worked as a draftsman for good money. So I was ready to settle down. I went after my heart's desire. I loved the most beautiful, most elegant Jewish deaf young woman in town, and she agreed to marry me! I was so lucky. Like me, she wasn't born deaf. We don't want deaf children. Deaf have so much trouble in the world."

I knew that story! They married, but neither Sam nor Anna knew much about sex. Anna acquired a husband, but never responded affectionately to him. She rejected Sam's family and his born-deaf friends, too, since her own father looked down on them. Her deafness bred isolation.

Sam soon lost the job as a draftsman. He claimed it was because his boss didn't understand his speech, but maybe he clowned around. His oldest brother would not give Sam a job in the stockroom of his grocery stores, not even when he was out of work. When his siblings mocked him, I was witness, "You! You are just a clown!"

Anna remembered, "Life was hard. After much time he got work, as a helper in bakery night shift. I wake him at 2:00 A.M. to leave the house. How to wake him? So hard life for us, we can't hear alarm clock. I sleep bad, wake up all the time, make sure he wake up. I lose thirty pounds one year. Then Father's friend Max, so clever, make a special clock. It flash a light and shake, so I wake up."

Chapter 2. My Childhood in Two Worlds

I remember my Father, singing! The songs he had heard before he became deaf remained in his memory, and he loves to sing them.

One day, when I am three years old and Father is working at night, Mother tells him to take me to the park after he wakes up in the afternoon. On the way Father says: "Remember, I can't talk to you while I walk. I can't look at your face. I have to look straight ahead to see where I am going. Otherwise I fall. So give me your hand, and I'll sing. A park song. My darling dotter," he jests, "I'm deaf, but I hear, inside my head, all the songs. I can sing them to you."

He sings "Walking through the Park" with a blissful smile and shining eyes. I know that song the way it's supposed to sound. I sing it with Aunt Mildred at Grandpa's house while she plays the piano. But Father's singing rises and falls, the notes stretched out. It's a haunting monotone that wavers up and down, varying intensity and tone with the words and mood, so that a stranger might wonder if he is in pain. It doesn't matter to me. I love the way his face shines as he sings. We walk happily toward the park down Tenth Street, past two-flat frame houses lining the street. I keep still so he won't fall, just listening, walking carefully, like him.

Singing and Signing

The park is just a playground, with a water fountain we call a "bubbler," swings, and slide. There Father pushes me on the swing awhile, and then we "talk."

Father says, "My darling dotter, to read your lips is hard and slow. Now we play. I teach you signs!" He takes me to the water fountain. "Water," he says, making the sign for water, three fingers extended in the shape of a W brought to his lips. I repeat it, delighted. More, I beg, and the lesson continues. "Milk?" His hands make motions like milking a cow. "Mother." Like an earring. "Father," like tipping the visor of a hat. "Eat," we act it out.

He gives me those signs in our playground, little gifts I take back home to Mother. When I use those few signs at home Mother is happy because she understands me. But it doesn't occur to her to teach me more, or encourage me to use signs. When I sign to ask Mother for milk, she can easily understand. Yet the "forbidden" remains, and we rarely sign. Instead I join the "battle of the lips," trying ever so hard to make the words shout on my lips!

Father and Little Me

Who cut off my hands?
Stole my childhood, my communication?

Father alone knows how to make me feel good. Like a puppy, he plays with me, hides under tables, and we laugh. He teases me, he teases Mother, but she runs from the room, shouting "not funny!" just like his mother.

Father's humor surfaces at supper time, our main meal, at five-thirty. I pass him a serving of mashed potatoes. He diligently masses the entire serving onto his fork, as Mother stares wide-eyed. I pass him a bowl of peas, ask him how many peas he wants. I carefully count them out, he returns a few, I exchange them, and so it goes. Mother turns her head away in disgust, but my little brother Marc digests fun with food. We are filled with good spirit, though we don't "talk."

Father often takes us out walking or visiting while Mother finds excuses to stay home, sewing. In summer he pulls me and my little brother down the street in the wooden wagon, a very expensive vehicle, but he has to have the best for his children. In winter he takes us to nearby Washington Park on the trolley car, with our sled. I hold my brother in front of me as we whiz down hills, screeching and laughing.

Deaf or Drunk!

Our play helps keep Father sane in his difficult world of deafness. His physical limitations pale against the effects of ignorance and prejudices, like being passed over for promotion, or seeing his siblings and coworkers laughing at him. He keeps the pain and anger inside, along with his frightful headaches.

Out for a walk, Father cautions me, "Never sign on the street. We don't want people to know we are deaf. They make bad signs, like putting fingers in their ears, like we have donkey ears. They call us dummies, think we're deaf and dumb, and they think dumb means stupid. They think being deaf means we also can't think, we're retarded."

Because he lost his balance along with his hearing, walking in the dark is a particularly serious problem. Often he comes home from work with a painful story to tell me. Only I receive and remember these stories full of rage. He can't tell Mother because she gets too upset and worried. More than once, he tells me, "There is a new policeman on the beat on the way to the bus. He stopped me, because he saw how I sway when I walk. He said, 'Come along now, I'll take you to jail, you drunk!'"

"I showed him the little card with the signs of the deaf alphabet, but the policeman only growled, 'Your speech is impossible to understand. You sure are drunk!' It took a lot of convincing for him to let me go on. Not everyone can understand the speech of the deaf."

That isn't the only problem he has. He lost his sense of time along with his hearing. Mother worries regularly, waiting for him to return home from work. He is often late, after stopping at the Deaf Club to play pinochle with deaf friends coming off night shifts at printing plants. They always play for money, and he always loses.

Physical Pain from Deafness

Our "talk" is beyond words. I notice the weariness in his face, the way he drags his body into the house, exhausted from working alongside great bakery ovens in the summer's heat. I hear Father in bed, tossing and turning with the excruciating headaches that remain from the illness that took away his hearing. "Daddy," I ask him, worried and wanting to help, "Why don't you take aspirin?"

He waves that question aside, drenched with perspiration that accompanied the pain, his eyes red from lack of sleep. "Aspirin, no. No help. Nothing helps." I want to be his angel, to rescue him from the curse of his pain, but of course I cannot.

One day when I am seven, he awakes after one of his headaches, dragging himself to a chair in the kitchen. Mother looks at him and quickly heats water to make him a cup of tea. I want to make him feel better, try to get his attention, but he turns his back to me. I stamp on the floor to get a response. No response. I tap his shoulder to get him to look at me. He turns away. I can't give up, and I try again, hitting his shoulder.

Then he blows up, gets out of his chair, grabs me, pulls me over his knees and spanks me, hard! I too lose control, fall on the floor, screaming in a temper tantrum because he won't talk to me! I kick and pound the floor, again and again. No one hears me! No one wants to hear me! No one can hear me! No one.

Mother and Me

Mother and I don't have to talk in words. Just being together and doing things together is a pleasure. I watch her embroider, or cook and bake, as she keeps up a running stream of commentary: "Scallop potatoes, delicious, you love. Watch, first I put butter, now potatoes slice. Next slice cheese, yellow color pretty, good taste. Paprika nice red, with salt and pepper."

She's thinking aloud. Otherwise she gets confused, loses track of what she is doing. She keeps up the patter until the casserole slides into the oven. She knows by the smell when to take it out, so we stay in the kitchen while it cooks.

Baking a cake is not a happy memory! Baking makes my mother confused and disorganized. "Dee, I make butter cake but not enough butter. Go to Mr. Goldstein, the grocery on the corner, ask for quarter pound butter, to charge to pay later."

This is an errand I hate to do because I know it's only the beginning. She doesn't have all the ingredients together yet. When I get home with the butter, she says, "Oh, not enough sugar," and sends me back to the grocer. I make one trip each for flour, sugar, and eggs. By the end, I can't face the grocer. I don't argue with Mother, because I know she can't help it, and when Mother asks for something I can't say no. The grocer is kind, smiles in welcome each and every time, and offers me a sweet from the candy counter to sweeten my sour face!

Doing the Laundry

In summer Mother and I do the laundry together, just the two of us. She calls to say: "Monday, laundry day. Come help. Busy all day so easy supper Heinz baked beans with wieners, you love. Also Jello."

The wicker laundry basket is loaded to overflowing. She carries it down the stairs as I follow with the cloth bag of clothespins, Fels

Naphtha soap in a box, and the soap bar, golden orange, for scrubbing stubborn spots. The glass blueing bottle nestles in the soft bed of clothes.

The laundry room is on the ground level of the apartment building. There's a cement floor, dim lightbulbs hang from the ceiling, and a vast drying space with parallel clotheslines enough for several families. No radiators, so it's cold in winter, and the clothes freeze on the lines.

Two washing machines stand beside deep cement tubs where the dirty water drains. The laundry room has a gas burner with an oval copper tub for heating water especially hot, hotter than the water that comes out of the faucets that fill the washing machine through a rubber hose.

Mother thinks aloud as she sorts, "Now make piles different kinds. For sheets, towels, make water hot." Mother heats water for the sheets and towels, as she washes our other clothing, the "color-fasts," as she explains. When I hear the machine stop, I pull her apron, and point, "Finish. All done."

She directs, "Now we squeeze. I put clothes in wringer, you turn the handle." Wringers are mounted on the machines, to squeeze the water out from the clothes. We lift the clean laundry out of the machine tub, one item at a time. She feeds each item between the two rolls, and I watch the water pour out of a shirt that turns into a flat pancake as it comes out the other side. I feed clothes too, knowing to keep my fingers far from the rollers.

In the belly of that basement we hang clothes together. I shake out a piece of laundry and pass it to Mama along with two clothespins. Those round wooden pegs don't have springs, just a slit cut between two legs that sit on the clothes draped over the clothesline. Mother holds clothespins in her mouth, straightening out a skirt or pair of trousers. "Good you come, help with sheets," she says. "I fold in half. You hold one side, pull so I hang sheet straight on clothesline."

Looking at Father's work clothes Mother sighs, "Hard work, your father's clothes from bakery, hard to clean. Have to shake first because full of flour. Then scrub with soap bar for sweat. To iron heavy canvas also much work." The apron, baker's hat, trousers, and shirt are a major part of wash day, especially in summer. Father showers and changes clothes at work, but the clothes he brings home are drenched with sweat and clotted with flour. He does his best to brush off the flour at work, but his sweat turns it into lumps that cling to the cloth.

We finally finish hanging the laundry to dry. Mother says, "We finish. Come now, upstairs home. I come back after supper to get dry clothes, tomorrow morning heavy clothes dry." Up the stairs we trudge, hungry for lunch, toasted cheese cut in neat strips. We have no need for words as we fill our hunger. Monday is under our control. We work together. I love doing the laundry.

Mother's Stories

Mother tells me stories, talks to me. She makes all my clothes, and talks to me endlessly as she sews. I listen with my eyes as Mother tries out recipes or sits sewing. She can't look at me while she works, so she talks. I listen and watch as she works. My hands lay still in my lap.

She isn't dumb, but I am. She does not let me use signs. "I am not born deaf. Teachers say signing only for born deaf."

I imagine her in school, deprived of sign language, knowing no language, trying to figure out what the teacher's lips are doing. Few words can be understood from lip shapes. Look at a mouth shaping *Pa* or *Ba*; there is no difference. She finds it hard to read my lips except for simple sentences, hard to pay attention to what I am saying for long. It is impossible for her to focus on more than a few short sentences. I try harder and harder to form words on my lips, but the more I strain the less she understands.

So instead of talking with me, she tells me stories of her childhood. They begin at the age of ten, when she first acquired language. Stories of her life that I've heard over and over, so often that I see them as pictures in my head. I know each one by heart. I relive them with her. These are not the traditional fairy stories of princesses and goblins. She had her own goblins and she was the princess.

The Dancing Master

Often she recalled, "I love so much to dance! I learn to dance, real dance. I am seven, play in the street, dancing, watch hearing children play games. Dancing teacher walks by, sees me. Asks children. They say I am deaf, show where family lives. He says to come, takes me home to my mother. Tells her he wants to give me lessons. Free! Because I am natural dancer! I know, really, to dance!"

Mother stands up and dances for me as she tells her story, kicks her feet, twirls and sways. Smiling, eyes shining, she tosses back her head, posing for me to admire her, her slender ankles and upright posture. She looks at me and sighs when she sits down. The meaning is clear: she is my beautiful mother, and I her clumsy daughter. "You know I want to call you Dolores, like Dolores del Rio, the dancer. Movies have words on the screen, so I go to movies, watch her dance. Grandma says no, not a good name. You are Dorothy, like her sister Dobbe in Russia."

Jello

The Jello story is always fun to hear. Mother recalls, as she prepares Jello for wash-day Mondays. "I go to friend for supper. Her mother make Jello. First time I see. Jello is from calf bones, not kosher. My mother doesn't make. The Jello quiver and shake. Like alive! I am scare, wonders, 'Will it jump off the dish?' My friend mother see my face so white. She touch my head to see if I have fever, but I just point my finger and shiver. She laugh, 'It's good, taste.' I love to eat Jello, ever since. You like too, good taste, pretty colors."

Signing Friends

Often she begins: "They don't teach sign at Binner School, but ten years old, at last I learn from Elizabeth. Elizabeth is my best friend. She come from the state school, live with her aunt to come to Paul Binner School, learn to read lips. Her family know that children who only sign, it's hard for them at work with hearing people, don't understand.

"When I learn signs I make friends, first Elizabeth, then Evelyn Plunkett. I have new baby sister Mildred, teach her signs. Ten years old, at last I talk to people and understand. Everyone see how happy I am. My friends and I sign with each other, have good times. We are friends now, always."

Why not sign with me too? I wonder.

Danger

This story teaches me that Mother's life was full of danger because she can't hear. I need to watch out for my parents, especially near trolley and train tracks.

Mother begins, "I never forget the train. I am eleven. Me and Elizabeth like to cross a little river, to woods the other side. We love to dance and run under the trees. We walk on the tracks. The bridge too far down. We aren't afraid on tracks. Deaf people feel vibrations, so we know when a train is coming, feel the heat of the train. One day a new fast train, rushing up, nearly crushing us. We don't feel the track in time, jump off the tracks. I fall far down. Where is Elizabeth? I am afraid. Is she dead? Then I see her, also fall down in bushes. We hug each other, cry. Bruises, scratches, but okay."

Marriage

She doesn't think how I might feel about what she is telling me. She confides in me about her love for Emmanuel. I don't like that story.

"I only marry Sam because I swore to marry the next man who ask me." Then she tells me again about her handsome beau, about being the belle of the ball. Mother's face speaks more than her words. The flush of excitement as she talks of dancing fades away as she thinks aloud. "Marriage! Only sewing, cooking, and taking care of children." Or the theme, "My sister Ella treat me bad." Always aloud, and she makes me her silent witness.

I watch her push Father away when he is affectionate, hugging and kissing her. She has no inhibitions about telling me of her sex life, such as it is. That was my early sex education! "When I marry your father he know nothing of sex. I know. Sex is for making babies. I want more, but my parents say two enough for a deaf couple."

She voices unhappiness and disappointment, not thinking of how I might feel. Mother's monotone, without the modulation, rhythms, and accents of hearing people, drones misery in my ears. She spreads a gray mist of frustration and loneliness through the stories she tells. Disappointment fills my ears and head, dancing round and round with her words.

Two Mothers

On heavy, muggy Midwestern summer days Mother gets up early to pull the window shades down tight. "Must to keep out heat, hot sun."

One such July day, the four-storied apartment building casts a protective shade, and the trees in the yard next door throw shadows over the yard. I sit on the gravel in the apartment courtyard, letting bits of crushed stone drop between my fingers, feeling the coolness of the gravel slipping and sliding along my sticky palm. Even in the shade rivulets of sweat run down my face and dampen my straggly hair.

The words I heard yesterday ricochet in my head. My tummy hurts, remembering. Ella took me for a drive yesterday. I didn't expect pleasant words from her. Usually her remarks begin or end with "I take you places but it's not because I love you. Just that your mother is deaf and she can't do these things."

This time was different. "Your mother is growing a baby in her tummy. He will be born soon. Your mother is deaf! She won't hear him cry. You have to take charge. You have to be the mother. Tell your mother when he cries. Otherwise she won't know. Now I'll buy you an ice cream cone."

I'm just four years old! The coldness of that ice cream sits in my aching stomach. As bits of stone slide between my fingers I remember: Mama can't hear. I must listen. When the baby cries, I will run to Mama and say, "Mama, baby cry."

"Dee, come! Supper!" Mother's high-pitched calling voice comes from the kitchen window. I brush the grit from my hands and knees, and climb up the dark, back stairway. Mother says, "Wash hands, then come sit. Surprise, something nice! Soon we have a new baby. He grow inside me, in my stomach. Come. Put your hand here. Feel the baby. He kicks!" She smiles, content.

I feel Mother's tummy swell up and down, jump at one side, then the other! Mother says, "The baby! Funny to see him move." She is happy, so I am, too. The next day I tell my playmates, "My mamma is growing a baby in her tummy!"

The neighbors are in an uproar. That afternoon one comes to the door, says to her: "You are deaf so you don't know anything. You should not talk about things like that to your daughter, about babies growing inside. Now all our children know! That's bad."

Mother and I don't know why it is bad. Our language is simple, direct, unadorned.

Mother goes to Mount Sinai Hospital in August for the baby to be born, so I stay with Grandpa Jacob and his family. When Mother brings the baby home, Grandpa brings me home, too. I run to Mama's room. She shows me the wicker bassinet touching her bed. "See! Your baby brother. Marc his name. Beautiful, yes? So big, strong. He weigh nine pounds, hard labor but I am natural mother, not too hard for me. I am good mother, can give him much milk. The same I did with you."

My very own brother! I adore our gorgeous baby with gold-brown ringlets, good-natured and gentle, bright, beautiful, and huge. I love to stroke his soft velvety skin, to hold him and kiss him. I am a good little mother. I don't have to come running to tell Mother he is crying. He seldom has a chance to cry, since both of us watch him closely for any sign of discomfort. Mother can sense every movement as she sleeps, for the bassinet touches her bed and shakes when "our" baby moves.

I remember Ella's orders. But I do not want to take care of my parents and I mustn't leave Mother alone with our baby. Sometimes Mother turns on me, "Go away. You want always to be with baby, push me. Not nice."

Six months later Mother tells me, "Marc wake up when I turn on light for your father to go to work. Marc sleep next to you now in your bedroom. If he cry, you come tell me."

He is really mine!

Up And Down the Dark Stairway

Ella orders, "You must tell us how Marc and your mother are. The Rosens, your upstairs neighbors, have a phone. You go upstairs, call us every day so we know if they are all right. Give them five cents."

Bother the neighbors? Every day? I don't want to ask Mrs. Rosen to go up and downstairs to tell me Ella is on the phone. Mrs. Rosen is old and fat. I talk back, amazing because I am usually so docile. "I can answer the phone. Get us a phone. You can call me."

I can still hear her words, her mocking voice. Ella jeers, "Foolish! What would your parents do with a phone?" As if it was for them, not me! I squeeze my eyes tight and ask again: "Please. A phone."

Ella laughs, harshly: "Coward, afraid to use the neighbor's phone. You're a baby, too! Your mother has two babies! Baby. Coward. Shame on you."

That word, "shame." I hear it so often I even know the hand sign: index finger of left hand extended as the index finger of the right hand slides down it, like scraping off something dirty. I feel it whenever Mrs. Rosen climbs down those steps from her apartment two floors up to ring the bell, "Come. Your aunt is on the phone."

Mother won't leave Marc to come with me, and he's too heavy to carry, so I go up alone, to hear what my aunt wants. Then I come back down, give Mother the message, tell her what Ella wants me to tell her, or ask her what Ella wants to know. Back I go with Mrs. Rosen, to report to Ella. No five-cent payment either, since I didn't make the call. Mrs. Rosen never complains. She takes it on herself to help "that poor deaf woman and her little child." The shame eats at me, deeper inside each time.

The Accident

I am six years old, Marc only twenty months. I am the Little Mother, always feeling responsible for my parents, for my brother. I have bad days, bad moods, having to give Ella reports, always doing things for other people. One day after school I walk home thinking, "I don't want to take care of my brother today. I'm good to him, never bother him, but Mother loves him, not me. If he cries when we play, she thinks I hurt him. She yells at me, and says I'm bad."

I don't usually think about such things. I try to turn the thoughts off, but they sour and fester inside. I am standing in the kitchen when Marc toddles in. He heads to the white enamel table, where the coffee percolator parts are drying. He reaches over, picks up the metal percolator stem, and heads out the kitchen door, into the dark stairway. I know he shouldn't have the percolator rod. It's sharp and hard. But if I try to take it away, he will scream. Mother can hear that noise, and I'll get blamed if he cries. I do not stop him.

Going down those dark steps with the metal rod in his mouth, he falls. The rod goes through his upper palate. A shriek, then gurgling sounds come through the half-open kitchen door. Doors open and slam; neighbors shout and scream. I can't move. The neighbor downstairs comes to get Mother. Who called a doctor, then an ambulance? I can't remember, though I keep seeing and hearing the sounds, and Mother sobbing, "My baby! He die?"

Neighbors crowd about Mother, too busy to notice me. I cringe into a corner, knowing, "It's my fault. I let him go out with the percolator stem. God will punish me."

Fortunately, the metal stem did not penetrate the bone of his palate, and Marc recovers quickly. Mother never asks me how he got hold of the percolator rod. Yet, from then on, Mother accompanies every request or remark with "Careful, he'll fall! Watch him. Watch out." Sometimes she suddenly cries out, "Poor Marc. Terrible!"

Every time, I remember that it's my fault. I know it, and I can't forget. I am bad. I saw him go out, and did nothing. I will keep that terrible secret all my life, waiting for God to punish me. Frightened at the top of stairwells, I don't dare to jump and run. I might fall. Life is like walking on eggs. I have a fear of going down steep hillsides, dark stairways. Guilt and shame are in the shadows that darken stairways.

With Father's Family

On Saturdays that I stay home, Father says happily, "Good. You can come to my family with me." Mother does not come along: "Marc naps now. You go, have good times. I stay home with the baby." A stickler for schedules, Father's day off or not, she feeds Marc exactly at noon, puts on his sleeping shirt, and sets him down for a nap.

Father and I walk the short block to North Avenue, where electric trolley cars run on the overhead wires. Less than a mile away, we enter Grandpa's ground-floor flat through the side yard, past a mound of coal. Picking our way down a gritty sidewalk, we leave footprints in a layer of coal dust. On Sabbath, Grandpa and Father's brothers go to synagogue, so Grandpa wears a white shirt. His skin is still stained dark by coal, but there is no dust clinging to his best clothes. He can hug the grandchildren, not keep them at arm's length.

The whole family comes for the Sabbath meal. From the yard we hear my aunts laughing and calling to one another. They arrive early to take care of Grandma's weekly chores, including dusting, vacuuming, and cleaning the floors. Grandma, short and round, in a shapeless housedress and a wraparound apron stained with grease, her hair under a head scarf, is at work preparing food for twenty people who come and leave at different times. She only dresses up at family celebrations.

The uncles eat early, so they can return to their stores. I sit quietly and listen to that noisy family. Grandpa's voice is loud, with harsh clipped tones, and everyone listens to him. He speaks quickly, to the point. "Sit. Eat. Go. Wait. Nu!" His voice rises to a high pitch when he gets excited, and his children join in, out-shouting one another.

Grandma never sits down except on holidays. Shuffling in loose slippers, she moves back and forth from the black coal stove in the kitchen to the dining table in the center of the flat. She greets everyone enthusiastically with big smacking kisses and smothering hugs. She folds me inside her fleshy arms, asking in Yiddish, how I am, how are Mama and Marc. I'm not used to such affection, and squirm inside.

My favorites are Aunt Sylvia and her little girls. Aunt Sylvia's hugs feel warm and comforting. Even Mother likes and trusts her. We visit her in her nearby apartment where I tickle her little girl under the chin.

My aunts all help their "Ma" cook and serve, chattering all the time, sitting down just long enough to make certain their own children are eating. Mickey, my age, vacuums under the table when dinner is over, but I just watch, knowing I'm an outsider. "She belongs to Schefrins," Father's sisters mutter. "Anna never comes, too good for us."

Big brother Al opens a grocery store, then expands to a chain, putting his brothers and brothers-in-law in charge of their own stores. Everyone but my deaf father, who begs, "Let me work for you. I can deliver groceries. I can keep the stockroom, clean, anything. Night work at the bakery is terrible."

All he gets are jeers and laughter from his family. I hear again in my head Al and his brothers and sisters, chanting, a Greek chorus,

"You can't hear. And you just make fun, foolish. We don't want you in the stores." I sit beside my Father, watching and listening, my head filled with his misery. It hurts me to see how they treat Father.

The best part of the Saturday visits comes after dinner. I climb upstairs with my three girl cousins, who live with their widowed mother Fanny in a tiny garret apartment. We huddle together on the window seat, the roof almost touching our heads, as we talk and laugh. I wish I could be with them, with my father, every Saturday, instead of going to the Schefrins. But I won't say it, can't say it, to anyone.

After the dishes are washed and house is in order, my aunts go shopping, their accommodation to life in America. They send my cousins to the movies, but I don't ask to go along. Knowing we are poor, I never ask my parents for money. But we really aren't poor compared to my widowed aunt with three children. I just think so, listening to Mother's family. I return home, exiled with Father, as my cousins go to the movies, spending the day together, twenty cousins, mine and yet not mine.

Father Rents a Car

My father is impulsive; he makes sudden decisions. One sunny Saturday when I am seven Father walks out the door with a big grin on his face, saying, "I'll be right back!" He returns an hour later, excited. "Max got a car, and he showed me how to drive. Now I'm going to take you for a ride. I rented a car. Here is our chariot. Get in, my fair princess."

He makes a deep bow as he signs to Mother, and opens the doors of a black four-door sedan. She is definitely suspicious but Father explains, "What do you know of cars! They are easy to drive." We are all wary, but willing to go along in this adventure. Mother holds Marc tight as she climbs in back. I sit in front, in case I need to hear or tell him something on the way.

He must have got the car to the apartment by sheer luck, for Father has absolutely no idea how to drive. When he steps on the brakes, I fall forward. Turning a corner he doesn't lower his speed, and the car careens wildly until we roll around in our seats. I still get dizzy remembering that ride, and I can feel my tummy turning from the sudden braking and uncontrolled turns. Luckily, the roads weren't crowded that day.

Mother is hysterical, screaming and signing over the back of the seat, into the mirror, pounding him on the shoulders, "Stop! Let us out! You kill us! Who say you drive? You crazy! My baby! My daughter!" He takes his eyes off the road and hands off the wheel as he turns around to answer her in signs. I am sure we are going to crash and cover my eyes, but he turns back, just in time.

He was only trying to make Mother happy, he complains. Father never drove again. He never learned how, either how to use judgment about driving or how to please Mother. Neither one was easy.

The Deaf Club

My parents' fights, carried out in sign, form the background to my life. Augmented by the expressions of their faces, arms and bodies, their signs are angry, tense, and fierce. I watch these signing bouts from early childhood, and while I don't understand their words, their feelings are clear. They do not love each other. They fight when Father comes home late, and for many other reasons. Mother finds reasons not to go out with him, yet she sobs, "You go out, have good times. I stay home with the children." He doesn't know what she wants, and neither does she.

On late nights, my father goes to the Deaf Club. A dingy, smoky room up rickety stairs in the old central neighborhood, off Kilbourn Street. Who goes there? Men like him, off the late shift, tired and lonely after a long day at the linotype machine or the bakery. They play pinochle and poker for money, to forget the dull, daily drag of work.

On special days and holidays, like Christmas, whole families come to the club. Father takes us to the annual Christmas party, with a deaf Santa handing out gifts to the children. Mother comes too, and even enjoys socializing with deaf friends.

Yet those parties have a bitter side, for the Lutheran minister to deaf people is there, to lead prayers and support the community. He targets Father and tries to convert him. Father stands politely, shifting his weight from foot to foot, getting ready to move away. Father does not know Hebrew, and he will not start to pray until many years later, but nonetheless he knows he is Jewish.

Sometimes Father takes me to visit his deaf Jewish friends. Gabriel has two daughters near my age, and I love to visit them. The girls are very friendly, and make me feel at home. Their grandmother lives with them, born deaf like her daughter and son-in-law, so the girls are fluent in sign with both parents and grandmother. I watch, envying them their signing, their free and easy communication with one another.

Mother doesn't come along, and she doesn't invite them to our home. "Born deaf," she sniffs, when we return home to the pall of her gloom and her loneliness.

The New Deal

In 1933, Franklin Delano Roosevelt is elected president. Everybody in our neighborhood votes for him, believes in him, talks of nothing else. We are poor, and so are our neighbors. The Depression is spreading, with long lines at soup kitchens, and people selling apples on the street. Being poor is no shame. Mr. Goldstein, the grocer, doesn't worry when Mama says to charge flour to make the cake. "Things will be better now," he tells everyone, cheerfully, "Roosevelt promised a New Deal."

My father enlists me in his two-man army against the world, giving me the trust he never gives to hearing people. He says I am his smart little sister. He asks me questions about politics, about the Depression, and unburdens himself about everything to me. He even relies on me to make decisions for him.

The Union

One March day I return from school to see Father sitting beside the kitchen table. He is looking hopelessly at a pile of papers, absently running his hands through his hair. He sees me, smiles, and takes a deep breath, "Here is my sweetheart, my clever little girlie. Oh, I am so glad to see you."

That isn't an everyday greeting. What is waiting for me, I wonder, and find out at once. Father points, "See all these papers? Organizers came to the bakery today. They want to start a chapter of the Bakery and Confectionery Workers Union in our bakery. They said President Roosevelt made new laws, so we have a right to organize and join unions."

"I don't like the looks of those men, I say. They are big and tough looking, don't look like bakers. They say a union is good and protects the workers. They promise a lot but you know how hearing people are. I'm not so sure. I'm sure the bakery owners won't like it. I wonder what they'll do to us."

Then he gets to the point, "What should I do? If I join the union I have to pay dues every month. If enough workers vote yes, the union comes in, but the factory becomes a closed shop. You know what that means? Everyone has to join, or lose his job. If I vote no the union officers will fire us if they get in. They gave us these papers, and asked us to fill them in. We will vote on joining the union in two weeks. I can't understand these papers, a lot of big words. Dearie, you are smart. Here are the papers. Help me decide. Just look them over, and then tell me whether to join or not."

I'm eight years old and I have to make this decision for him. I know there is no choice in my father's mind, so I take it on. It doesn't occur to me to tell him I don't know the answers. I am an exceptionally fast reader with a vast vocabulary from my voracious reading, but those papers have a lot of legal words. I start to read, try to understand, to remember everything in the newspapers and newsreels. I know about the Haymarket Riots in nearby Chicago where strikers were killed. Samuel Gompers has organized seamstresses in New York, but Mother never had protection against low pay and long hours. In my mind, unions are good, but also dangerous. I don't know what to tell Father.

That weekend Grandpa Jacob picks me up, and I ask about the union. "Should I tell Father to join, Grandpa?"

He calls me to sit beside him in the living room after dinner. "I'm a business man. Unions aren't good for me. But your father works in a big factory and he's deaf. Many men are out of work, and the factories pay workers less because men without work will take any salary. Yes, he needs protection. Tell him to join."

I tell my father to join the union. I tell him about people waiting to steal his job. He joins the union. In a way I joined the union too, became a "socialist," a defender of the poor, but distrusting organizers, union officers, political appointees who steal power in the guise of being concerned about me. My father and I are not fooled by words. We see what people mean.

Temporary Manager

Belonging to the union has a dark side. Each summer the floor manager takes a two-week vacation, and appoints my father to be the temporary manager. Even though Father can't hear, the manager knows that his lack of hearing makes him more alert, more aware, in case there are problems like stuck machinery. He smells burning before anyone else.

When his manager is promoted to another job, Father, ever optimistic, applies for his job. He is told, "Impossible. This is a manager's job. You belong to the union. You can't be a manager and union member." Another frustration to pile up with all the others. Working conditions in the bakery never improve, and eventually Father loses the tips of three fingers in the roll-cutting machine. As bakeries close unionized plants in Milwaukee, the union finds him new jobs at first, but when the last bakeries in Milwaukee are finally automated, he receives only a very small pension.

Chapter 3. Two Worlds

I'm going on seven. Baby Marc is sleeping nights, so Mother's family decides she can manage alone, that they can take me to Grandpa's house for weekends. Marc scuttles away to the bedroom to hide when Grandpa comes, afraid that they will take him, too.

Father confides, "Your mother's family take you the only night I don't work. That makes me so sad." His dark eyes that sparkle when he plays with me are dull. I long to stay home and visit Father's family with all my cousins.

Still, those Fridays are special. Grandpa takes me to the foundry, where I play in the office, making paper-clip chains or pecking on the typewriter. He takes me home for Sabbath evening, when Grandma blesses the candles and Grandpa sings the blessing over wine. I love to hear his golden voice, like the music in the synagogue.

I'm not just a child of deaf parents anymore. I now have another life, with hearing people and music. After dinner Aunt Mildred plays the piano as we sing old songs like "Bicycle Built for Two." I listen to the radio with Ella, the Metropolitan Opera on Saturday at noon, Sunday, the New York Philharmonic. In the evenings we listen to the scary voice of *The Shadow,* then to comedians like Fibber McGee and Molly. We wait every week for Fibber to open his closet door, so we can hear the crash as everything falls down.

Saturday mornings Grandpa is in synagogue, and I go walking with Grandma to visit her sister Lena and her family. Grandma is happy to have me for company on that two-mile walk. She won't take a streetcar on the Sabbath.

Aunt Lena is really poor. Her husband, Max, lost his leg in an elevator accident where he worked. He did not receive compensation of any kind after the accident, and he is still unable to find work. Religious Jews don't touch money on the Sabbath, so Grandma always brings a handkerchief to be opened afterwards, with money for food for the week for a family of five, Lena and Max and my good-natured, hard-working cousins.

However, whenever I go to lunch and shopping with Ella, she spoils my mood, "Stand up straight. Hold your chin up. You're so homely. Keep up with me. Smile."

Does she expect me to smile while she insults me? I keep my head down not to look at her, drag my feet not to walk with her. I mumble under my breath, "I don't want to walk with you. You're mean."

I want to be with my own family. But Sunday when I go home the worst is still to come. Mama is waiting for me. As the door opens

My mother's family—I am the child, third from the left.

she begins crying, wailing, "Why come home now, so late? Marc and me all alone all day, Sam works, then sleep. Ella take you for a ride, buy ice cream. I know. You loves Ella, not me. Ella talk to you. She talk better, I don't talk good."

I am in the middle of a tug-of-war between Ella, unmarried and childless, and my own mother. As they vent their jealousy of one another on me, misery and unhappiness fester inside me. I feel unwanted in both houses. I don't want to go to Mother's family on Juneau Avenue, and I don't want to come home.

I figure it out: I was adopted. It makes sense to me. Mama doesn't love me, and Ella doesn't love me. Mama sends me away, and gets angry when I come back. Ella invites me and says she doesn't love me. But I don't say I don't want to go to the Schefrins. Don't tell anyone how Ella's words hurt. I can't upset my parents because I am responsible for them.

Gifts

I celebrate my birthdays on Juneau Avenue. During the Depression, Ella gives me clothes, doled out, like charity, with a stern warning, "Don't wear this new coat. Hang it in the closet. Wear out your old clothes first."

Ella reminds me, "Thank us. Be grateful." I hate that word, "grateful." Doesn't Ella do anything for me because she wants to? The dictionary says grateful is "an appreciative response to kindness," but I hear no kindness.

Still, there are occasional pleasant surprises. By my eighth birthday, Roosevelt is president, and we are sure things will be better. So Ella gives me an extraordinary gift, *My Book House*, six volumes of world literature for children. She says, "This is a set so you get only one this year. You'll get the rest, one at a time, for each birthday to come." So that's why she is so generous: no presents to buy for five years.

Those books are my treasure chest: Rabindranath Tagore's stories of childhood in India, poems by Robert Louis Stevenson and Edward Lear. Best of all, with the set of six came another three illustrated books of rhymes and literature from France, Holland, and Japan. My favorite is *Little Pictures from Japan*, charming Japanese woodcut illustrations with poems adapted for children. The poems are translations of haiku, only seventeen syllables. Like snowflakes, they have the same basic shape, but each is different. My favorite is

> Off we go
> to see the snow
> till we tumble down.

This haiku is a children's version of Basho's poem,

> Come let's go out
> snow-viewing
> till we are buried.

I read anything I can. On Juneau Avenue I borrow books from the downstairs tenants, devouring one by one, the volumes of *The Book of Knowledge*, which their children had outgrown. Science entrances me, and I learn about the sun and stars, how things work, and how they began. Better than stories or fairy tales, better even than *My Book House*.

Changes

Slowly, unheralded, my two lives meld into one. I am nine when the doctors discover that Grandma has heart trouble. Ella has to stop working as a bookkeeper to take care of her. Grandma grows weaker

Grandma's family, Anna on the left, Lena in the middle, Ella is third from the right.

and weaker, and soon she can't get out of bed. On my weekend visits I watch Ella feed Grandma strained spinach and cream of wheat.

Grandma dies the winter I am in fifth grade. At the funeral, the rabbi calls her "a woman of valor." I only know her as a plain, quiet little woman, her gray-brown hair pulled back. The grandmother who didn't know much English, but never complained, though she had no friends among the neighbors. Only her sister Lena was close enough to visit.

Walking with Grandma made my Sabbaths good and warm. Her death came to affect my life with my own parents and brother.

Last night I dreamed a huge bear came into my bedroom
and began to suffocate me with a bear hug.

Back to Juneau Avenue

When I complete sixth grade, we leave our apartment to live with Grandpa, Ella, and Mildred, again. That major decision is made in secret, a year after Grandma dies. I don't know why Mother doesn't tell me. Of course, she has nothing to say in decisions involving the family. Ella tells me a lie, "Why move? The junior high you are to attend next year is no good for you. Low-class people go there. Just for you, your family will move back with us on Juneau Avenue."

Mother mourns for her pictures on the walls, decorative items, furniture. All are stored or given away, except for her bedroom furniture and a few boxes stored under the eaves. I am leaving my friends, children of Jewish immigrants like me. We move that summer, shoehorned into a full house. Still I feel at home, here where I spent so many weekends.

Of course, the move isn't for me; it is for Ella. We are clearly there to keep Grandpa company and tend to this warren of rooms. There are ten rooms and alcoves in this "railroad flat," to the left and right of a long central hallway. To the right, the living room opens to the dining room, which opens into the kitchen through the pantry. To the left the front hallway opens onto the little "music room" with barely enough room for an upright piano, and that leads to the porch, which is simply the roof of the downstairs entry area. Three bedrooms march down the hallway on the left, in line with a study alcove.

There is also an attic and basement, back and front stairways, a double garage in the alley, and lines for hanging clothes on the roof of the garage. The house is heated by a coal furnace in the basement that needs stoking twice a day, but the furnace "room" has no concrete floor, just compacted dirt in a walled hole under the stairs. The washing machine stands there as well, so laundry has to be carried down two flights, then up the stairs to the clotheslines, or in winter on lines hung next to the furnace.

My parents will earn our keep. Grandpa is too old to stoke the furnace and my aunts work in offices, outside. All this is now my parents' responsibility. How could they have agreed to this? Is it because of the Depression, when we can't always pay the rent? Is Grandpa tired of bailing us out when Father loses his job, or gambles away his paycheck at the Deaf Club? Or are we paying for Ella's freedom?

Chores

Ella gives orders, "Mildred and I have jobs, so your mother will cook and wash dishes, keep the house clean, and do the laundry."

Mother sinks into despair, saying nothing, not objecting, not even to me. This is a bad sign. I sit with her at the kitchen table, hating Ella, sharing Mother's mood. I, too, say nothing, but choose sides, choose to be Mother's ally and protector. Mother complains, "I give up my own home for you."

As if I am to blame, or that this move is good for me. That's just a lie Ella told so she doesn't have to stay home with Grandpa. I don't argue with Mother. She even suspects me of being against her. I watch Mother at the kitchen sink as she washes dishes, a dour expression on her silent face. She rattles the plates sharply onto the hard marble counter and throws the silverware down. I come over and dry silently.

There is plenty of hot water. Grandpa installed a modern heater when we moved in. Instead of heating water on the stove or going to the basement to light the gas heater, as he did for years, we turn on the timer on the wall near the bathroom fifteen minutes before washing dishes, and thirty minutes before baths. At our old place, the landlord heated the whole apartment. Here the bathroom is so chilly in winter that we bathe less.

Washing dishes, taking baths, we miss our apartment and its instant hot water. In this house, we are seven people using one bathroom. Many a time I jump up and down outside the bathroom door, waiting for someone to come out. If my parents are inside I slide a sheet of paper under the door, wiggle it back and forth so they'll notice.

Father is assigned the heavy chores, shoveling snow off the sidewalk, porch and stairs, with Marc's help and mine. Besides that, he has to mow the lawn in summer and stoke the furnace in cold weather, work he does when he comes home from work in the morning or before he leaves at night.

I love doing chores, physical tasks. Helping Father, I race to help him shovel snow in winter. Mowing the lawn in summer brings waves of energy into my arms and legs. In the slanting afternoon sun, I send the mower easily down the hilly rise in front of the house, follow it down, then give the added push to shove it up again. My muscles still remember every inch of that lawn: the hill, the grass strip between the sidewalk and the street, the shady area along the side of the house, and the square patch of a backyard. I breathe the sweet smell of cut grass as I push and pull the mower. With Father I rake, gather grass into fragrant piles, and carry the clippings to the trash bin in the alley. In October we pile fallen leaves in the gutter in the street, and make a fragrant smoky bonfire.

The changing colors of spring flowers in our yard bring me to the garden day after day. I love the grassy yard, so unlike the gray gravel behind the apartment building. In spring the side yard is lined with purple iris, a deeper violet than the perfumed lilacs drooping over the back garden. Under the lilac tree I stop daily to check the growth of the currant bushes, green gooseberries, and flowers, sucking the nectar in the lilacs, sweeter than honey. I watch milky poisonous berries swell and ripen on the ornamental shrubs out front. Mother grows green plants on the cupboard under the dining room window but never works in the garden. The neighbors downstairs do that.

Flowers, grass, and music accompany each day. We have music with our breakfast from West Division High School, across the alley. The marching band practices in the wooden annex just outside our gate early in the morning, so breakfast has rhythm—snappy Sousa marches, and cheering songs.

Our own little family eats separately most days. Not that we mind. We eat supper at 5:30 P.M. Mildred and Ella eat with Grandpa later, alone.

There are good family times, too, on holidays, when we all eat together. Then Mother and Ella turn out spectacular apple pies, lemon meringue tortes, and peanut butter cookies. I help both of them, in turn. My favorite is Ella's orange cake, soaked with orange-lemon syrup. I whip egg whites or cream, lick bowls, scrape crumbs from baking tins, or make cross-hatchings on Ella's peanut butter cookies with a fork.

Our family spends most of our time in the roomy kitchen, with an oilcloth-covered table in the center. The living room is only for company, except for Grandpa, who sits there in his patent Morris chair to read his Yiddish newspaper. The chair is wide, square, leather-covered, with a matching square leather footstool where I am invited to sit when Grandpa wants to talk to me. Below the wooden arms are wooden pegs to adjust the chair from straight upright to deep recline.

Ella and Mildred's friends come to afternoon bridge parties. They are single, working ladies who dress well, immigrants with no discernible accents or spoken memories of Europe. I call them "auntie," fill and set about little dishes of bridge-mix candy that I pick out with Ella in the Boston Store. She loves to take me shopping, then for a treat at the enamel ice cream counter in the store. Sometimes we dress up and go to lunch at the Schroeder Hotel's formal dining room, with its dimmed crystal chandeliers and uniformed waiters. Ella looks for acquaintances and beckons them over, smiling with pride, "This is my little niece!" But then we return home to the wars.

In Bed

Worst of all, I can no longer get out of Ella's reach, for I share the double bed in her room. I watch her as she gets up in the morning and comes to bed at night, casing the enemy. As she gets ready for work, her dresses, coats, and accessories are perfectly matched. Her hair is curled in a "permanent wave" from the beauty parlor, her nails lacquered, her face made up, with mascara on her lashes. She stands out in her elegance, even among her lady friends.

I go to bed long before Ella, then toss and turn, sleepless, waiting for her. She turns on the night light to undress and put on her night-gown, moving about quietly, straightening her clothes, clicking her beads, earrings, and watch onto a chest. My stomach contracts. I hold my breath, my hands closed into fists, as Ella crawls into bed next to me, settles under the covers, turns, and asks: "Are you awake? Diggle my hair."

I pretend to be asleep, but she repeats, until I respond. With a quiet sigh, I begin to "diggle" her hair, curling strands of her hair around my fingers, twining them around. Her kinky, permanent-waved, dyed-black hair, fixed with hair-setting lotion, is greasy and scratchy in my hands, but she sighs blissfully. As soon as she begins snoring gently, I withdraw my hand and wipe it on the hanky wait-ing under the pillow. I turn to curl up away from her, desperately wanting a bed of my own. I can't get to sleep for a long time, feeling the weight of her body in the bed beside mine.

Diggling. Is it erotic? Maybe she just wants me to touch her. She could hug me, but she is hard. Her voice is hard, too, clipped and staccato, like her purposeful walk. Elegant, cold, distant, her kisses dry, too, her lips pursed like a prune. She always reminds me she doesn't love me.

Two Families under One Roof

A friend painted Mildred's portrait, which hangs over the artifi-cial fireplace in the living room. Her heavy auburn hair, enhanced at the beauty parlor, is the same color as her father's. She is wearing a peach-colored blouse, a soft champagne chiffon scarf draped about her neck and floating down behind her shoulders, and a matching ribbon tied about her wavy hair. Mildred is indeed a beauty.

Mother's youngest sister, Mildred is my favorite aunt and Mother's beloved sibling. Their closeness began when Mildred was a baby. Anna, ten years old, had just learned sign language, and practiced it joyfully, "talking" with her baby sister. Mildred, who was the only sister to learn sign language, translates for Mother at family gatherings.

She tells me stories of mother's childhood, "Those were the days of silent movies, with titles on the screen, so your mother could fol-low the plot. She was working, and had money, so she took me to a movie when I was ten. We were waiting in line, and I was talking without my voice, as I usually did with her, telling her things other people were talking about. The people in line thought we were both deaf. I told her, and she laughed. They were not unpleasant, just curious how we got along."

She talks to me like a big sister. Though she has a college degree as a social worker, she hates social work even more than she hates her job as a secretary at a hospital for the mentally ill. "I went to college, but wasted my education on social work. That was supposed to be a good job for women, but it's awful. Remember that."

She tells me bitterly, "I hate my father. He had to be at the synagogue every Sabbath, because he was the president. Although Jews are forbidden to ride on the Sabbath or spend money, he traveled by trolley since we didn't live near the synagogue. Do you know what he did? He made me walk to the trolley car with him to put the fare in the coin box so he didn't have to do it. I had to desecrate the Sabbath instead of him."

A chorus of unhappy women are living with Grandpa, and they all confide in me, dump their anger and hate and jealousy onto me.

Lessons and Such

Moving away, I lost all my friends. Now, among German-speaking children, I am the only Jewish child in school. It's not a junior high either, just grade school.

I join the Girl Scouts, and after school I go on five-mile Scout hikes. I can barely limp home, the arches of my feet collapsing, misfit orthopedic shoes pinching my toes. There's no point in telling Mother. She will just take me back to the Dr. Locke shoe store where the salesman X-rays my feet and sells me shoes that hurt in a few days. Mother looks puzzled and shrugs her shoulders, and Father gets angry because he's been cheated by hearing people again.

So I limp, and Ella announces, "You are to start elocution lessons next week, because you mumble and are clumsy."

Isn't she encouraging! Yes, I am gawky, as most girls are at twelve. My body is not filling out; my hair is stringy and shapeless. I have wide metal braces on my teeth. Neither ballet nor tap lessons make me graceful or flexible. As for mumbling, I only mumble with Ella.

I go to elocution lessons, reciting set pieces, passionately declaiming "the boy stood on the burning deck." I work hard to develop delivery and poise. During the first lesson, I confess, "I am so clumsy."

The teacher smiles, waves his arm as if to push that idea away, and instructs, "Never mind. Just hold your head erect, and tell yourself that you are graceful. You will be fine."

That's it! Forget Ella and her shaming. Head held high, chin up, eyes aglow, I confidently stride to the door, and knock over the coat rack standing beside the door on that winter day. As coats hats and umbrellas scatter across the room, he turns away to laugh, and I know for certain I'm a lost cause.

Rearrangements

Marc sleeps in Grandma's bed in Grandpa's room. There is little space to move between the beds and dressers, and he has to keep quiet, not disturb Grandpa. So he takes his toys into the attic at the top of the stairs. He and my parents are up there, while I'm below, with my aunts.

Like me, he doesn't have playmates yet, and wanders about in the alley behind the house that separates it from the high school. We play on that stretch of smooth asphalt, roller-skate, or hit a tennis ball against the garage door. Sometimes we play catch with Father.

One afternoon I am sitting in the study reading. Marc is playing in the alley and hits the ball inside the barbed-wire fence around the school yard. He climbs the fence to fetch it, and the barbed wire rips his hand open. When he comes in crying, I run to see what's wrong, see his bloody shirt, then his hand dripping blood. I scream, get Mother, and we rush across the street to Misericordia Hospital, where his hand is stitched up in the emergency room.

"Why weren't you watching him?" Both Ella and Mother blame me! They say I should be keeping an eye on Marc. He is eight years old! Am I supposed to watch him for the rest of my life? When Ella told me I was responsible for my mother and brother, I didn't know she meant forever. I love my brother and my mother, but what about me! Not fair, not fair, I shout inside. I hate my aunt and mother for blaming me, Marc for getting into trouble. Is this my punishment, for the day Marc fell and I didn't get blamed?

Mildred Leaves

In 1939, during the war in Europe, the Depression ends as United States manufacturers sell war equipment. Government offices in Washington increase their hiring, and many women move to Washington for work. Mildred's friends join the migration, get jobs, find apartments. They write to her, describing good times, telling her to come.

Mildred is thinking. Living at home, her fortieth birthday past, she confides in me, "The job in the hospital leads nowhere, nowhere. I've decided to go to Washington."

I will miss her, but her bedroom will be free. Maybe I can have her room. Maybe Ella wants her bed for herself and will give the room to me. No, it's decided. Marc must move out of Grandpa's room. Grandpa is an old man, sixty-seven years old, and needs his quiet. That makes sense to everyone, except me.

Marc, who has already moved himself and his toys upstairs, away from the family, doesn't say anything, but Mother is excited. She can furnish his room as she wishes, for Mildred is taking her furniture with her. A few weeks later, the room is ready. Mother rushes up,

Mildred in her own apartment, after she left home.

takes me by the elbow, and propels me across the hall. "See! I fix the room, everything, like my own house. I sew curtains and bedspread good for a little boy, not from Mildred."

Mother leads me around the room, "See. I buy a new dresser, the best. Look, the bed, shiny maple wood. Feel the mattress, firm. Nice bookcase, fine quality, for toys and for books." She waits for my approval, signs of admiration and I oblige. That is easy, compared to being grateful to Ella. That's fine, for Marc. And I am still in bed with Ella.

Alone on Juneau Avenue

Three years later Ella shocks me. "Grandpa and I are moving to an apartment on the East Side, a much better neighborhood, where the well-do-do German Jews live. We're turning this house over to your mother. I didn't want to tell you before because I knew you'd be upset that I am leaving. Now you have to be responsible for your family, without me. Call me every day, so I can tell you what to do. You'll come on weekends, as you did before."

I stare, wide-eyed, heart pounding wildly. No previous hints? I was cheated. I could have relished freedom coming. How could I not know? Did Mother know all the time and didn't tell me? Did Ella order her to keep this secret? Or did Mother know at all?

I am quietly rejoicing, and also planning. At last I can have my own bed. I can be free of Ella. I can grow up—in every way. A month after Ella moves out I have my first period, but I will never fill out into womanly curves. I believe three years in her bed delayed my physical development.

Exploding with unexpressed joy, I run out to the alley to hit a tennis ball against the garage wall again and again. I run around the block and back through the alleyway. At last, at last!

But Ella isn't finished with me. She shames me again, this time in school. Miss O'Reilly, my homeroom teacher, calls me, "Your aunt told me about your family problems. She said 'Please keep an eye on my niece. She'll be brokenhearted, will have much responsibility, for her parents can't cope alone because they are deaf.'"

I do cry, from shame. Not just shame, but also anger. Why did Ella do it? Miss O'Reilly thought I was brokenhearted.

I am sucked back into Ella's life after she and Grandpa move. I call her daily, trying to cope with the new responsibility of a large two-flat house, and I don't make decisions without consulting her. I do miss having someone to talk to. Father just fools around, and Mother does not understand. Marc is at Cub Scouts or playing ball with his new friends.

Eventually, I find friends and activities of my own, and seldom visit the Schefrins on weekends. When I do come on Sundays, I spend little time with Grandpa. Ella monopolizes me, showing me her new furniture. Only when Grandfather drives over to pick me up do I have a chance to talk with him. He misses my family, as well as Grandma, and spends his evenings reading his Yiddish newspaper or at meetings.

One Sunday evening, as he drives me home, he asks about school and family, his voice quieter than usual. When he lets me off, my unsentimental grandfather surprises me by turning to hug me and kiss my cheek before driving on to a meeting at the synagogue. There he will park and then collapse in the car, dying of a heart attack.

I cry when Ella calls to tell me Grandpa has died. I was the last person to see him alive. That kiss? Did he sense something? I miss him terribly. For more than twenty years I will imagine I see him on the street. I have strong memories of him, singing Sabbath prayers, living together. In summer he drove me to lake resorts. I listened to him talking about how much money he lost in the Depression. Especially after Grandma died, he was close to me in a way he could not be with my deaf mother. Just as I was the daughter Ella never had, I was his deaf daughter with whom he never talked.

Ella in Control

With her father gone, Ella grows more hateful, "No one will want to marry you, because you are homely." Or "You need plastic surgery on your big nose." Or "Who will want to marry you, daughter of deaf parents?"

"I hate you," I curse under my breath, not knowing why she is suddenly attacking me about marriage. Not understanding that she sees me as her mirror, alone and unmarried, with big buck teeth. The most popular girl in my class has a nose larger than mine.

Celia

Deafness lurks beside us always as a social handicap, more than just a physical limitation. As the Depression continues we see it everywhere. Deaf beggars selling sign-language cards in the street send Father into a rage. He shouts, shaking his fist, "You want people to think Deaf must beg! Go find work!" But he would look for work, too. Deaf and other handicapped workers were the first to be fired from their jobs in the Depression. Grandpa was right when he said Father must join the union. Indeed, it found him jobs.

The difficulties of being deaf are woven through our lives, in our own family, and in the community. Many times one of Father's friends, out of work, comes by to ask for money, as a loan or an outright handout. For a while Rose and her husband Fred—friends from the Deaf Club—come to live with us "until I find a job," he says. But he never does find a job, and Mother's family finally comes and throws them out. I watch Mother, her fingers flying, her face red with anger, as Fred pulls his wife's arm, trying to get out fast. It seems the problem wasn't just money, but dark-eyed voluptuous Rose herself. I remember, and cringe.

One day I return from school to find Mother jubilant. "A surprise, deaf couple lives above the grocery. So nice, can talk to deaf neighbor at last, not all the time just housework. I take you to see them. Also they have nice boy, your age."

A block down, Mother found our deaf neighbors, Celia and her husband, and their hearing son, Willy. Mother is delighted to find a deaf neighbor for the first time in her life. She puts her snobbery about born-deaf aside, and regularly drops in to see Celia on her way to the grocery.

A year older than me, Willy is pleasant and likeable, but serious, always working. He delivers newspapers at five in the morning and makes deliveries for the grocery after school. At home he helps his father.

Mother explains, "I must to go there. Celia is afraid to walk alone, even little walk, one block to our house. Willy delivers newspapers, and Celia cannot go out if Willy not home. She doesn't leaves her husband alone. Celia's husband is a weaver. He lose his job because of bad eyes. He is almost blind. So he build a big loom in the attic, under the roof, and work there, makes wool rugs. Celia is afraid when he goes down the attic steps. He can fall. You see how thick his glasses are? The worst thing that can happen to the deaf. Just think, not hear, also not see. Terrible."

One November day Mother drops in to see Celia on her way to the grocery, then rushes home wheezing with asthma. She grasps the door jamb to steady herself, then sits down hard on the kitchen chair and puts her face in her hands.

When she can talk, Mother gasps, "Terrible! This morning Celia wake up, her husband not in bed. So early, she is surprise, go look for him. Doesn't see him. Up the stairs, she find him in the attic. Dead. Hang himself next to his loom. He throw the wool he is weaving over a hook in the roof, tie it around his neck. Poor Celia. Poor Willy."

Without special training in signing for people who are deaf-blind, he could no longer see Celia's signs. Isolated, alone in the attic, deaf and blind and poor, all together, were more than Celia's husband could stand. How will Celia manage? What about Willy? He delivers newspapers, does whatever he can to help his mother. They are so poor. Not like us, with Mother's family helping when we can't manage.

Left alone, Celia's fear of going outside grows worse, and this becomes Willy's greatest burden. It is clearer than ever to me how handicap, especially deafness, makes people both poor and miserable. My gallery of portraits of the poor is growing. The first was my Uncle Max, his leg and his job lost in a work accident before Roosevelt's New Deal created Social Security. I worship Roosevelt, thinking of Uncle Max.

New Friends

Milwaukee has a high rate of skeletal and thyroid problems. I am thirteen when school X-rays show a pronounced slant in my spine. The school nurse gives me a note to a doctor, but Ella decides, "I told you, you don't stand straight!"

Nothing is done. Gym is a disaster. I'm embarrassed in the showers with my undeveloped breasts. Inept and uncoordinated, I also have astigmatism with its accompanying poor depth perception. Catching the baseball flying toward me is difficult. A baseball slams me in the chest, taking away my breath and leaving a sore black-and-blue area. The school nurse says not to worry.

Mother also has a bruise on her chest from a work accident when she was young. Neither bruise heals properly.

I am obsessed with my tiny breasts. The next time Mother's friend Mona comes to visit, her daughter Evelyn rescues me. Skinny like her mother, she has round breasts. I complain, "See my flat chest. I hate to have people look at me."

She smiles. "I'm flat, too," reaches into her bra, and pulls. "See! I cut Kotex pads in half and put them in my bra. Lots of girls do."

What a relief! I can look okay in my clothes, feel better about myself. I join the drama club and find new friends.

Life Is Good

Europe and Asia are at war, but the United States is sure it is safe, protected by two oceans. Supplying warring countries with food and weapons ends the Depression. Father is working steadily. The foundry makes a lot of money as farm-equipment factories turn to war vehicles and supplies. Ella and Uncle Sam work harder than ever.

Our private lives take a good turn as well. Mother finds new friends at the Deaf Club's Christmas party, the Yolleses. Leon's wealthy parents, owners of a lock-manufacturing plant, sought the best education to prepare their deaf son for a position in the firm, and sent Leon to Gallaudet College for the Deaf. There Leon met his pretty and intelligent wife, Betsy. Much younger than Mother, they still develop a close friendship, for they too hunger for stimulating Jewish friends and company, like my uneducated but artistic mother and clever father.

I, too, thrive on that friendship, for they bring their three young children, who sign, with them. I read them stories or we play card games while Mother enjoys their parents' company using signs. So does Father. Their signing is "educated," a real language, not what Mother picked up when she was young. She is excited to be learning proper signing from them! I cannot figure out her logic.

Stimulated by new friends, Mother is happy and energetic. One day she shows me the *Ladies Home Journal*. "Look. Is this good to buy?" The Elizabeth Arden cosmetics company is promoting a beauty package, from makeup tips to an exercise regimen. We order the kit, exercise together, and experiment with makeup. We are brought together through movement and touch. I am closer to both my parents in our own home.

I need to help Father, too. He was elected secretary of the Deaf Club, and has to type reports for the club on the typewriter that came with his job, but neither of us knows how to type. At school, I fight for permission to take typing, a "commercial course," designated for below-par, nonacademic students. I convince my advisor and take the course, but I do just as poorly at "blind" typing as I do in gym, lacking coordination. At least I know where the letters are on the keyboard. Assistant to the secretary of the Deaf Club, that's me.

Pearl Harbor As Sam Tells It

This is what Father tells me on Sunday morning, December 7, 1941, "I don't miss anything. I watch, look around. I make up for being deaf with my eyes. I am coming home from the bakery after I finish making hamburger buns all night for delicatessens on Sunday morning. I see newsboys, waving newspapers with giant red letters, their mouths open wide, their chests moving up and down like loud breaths. I hurry to look, buy this paper. Look! Look what it says: December 7, 1941. Japs bomb Pearl Harbor. Roosevelt declares WAR with Japan!"

He ponders, "How can it be? Doesn't President Roosevelt have spies who know what was going on? I hurry home to find you, my clever daughter, to ask you: What is happening?"

I answer, "I was awake. I heard the newsboys. Show me the paper!"

I read, "The Jap planes bombed all our warships." Hard to believe! They were just sitting in the harbor in Hawaii. As if someone threw a burning bowling ball down the alley and crisped all the pins, and the pinsetters too.

I continue reading, "No one can think how many sailors were killed." I stop, just stare at the paper. The phone rings. Ella, of course.

Father watches my lips, "Yes, Father brought me the paper. Turn on the radio? Okay. Thank you."

Mother gets up, looks at the paper, sees the headline, and starts to scream. Father thinks, "Anna acts always without thinking, suspicious, excitable."

Where is Marc? Still asleep, a growing boy of twelve, already taller than me. Father wakes him and tells him the news, says, "Come, children. We sit down together for breakfast this terrible day. Though I prefer to eat a heavy meal, the food Anna saves me from supper, after a long night's work. But this special day maybe you, my children can help me understand."

Who can understand? Children? If the generals and the president don't, how can I? But I'll do my best, leave the radio on all day, report every bit of news I hear. Ella calls again and again, as she hears more news. Death and destruction. Father does not go to bed, waits for me to tell him further news.

Family Wars

Fifty years old and alone after her father dies, Ella's anger festers. She phones, "You're so selfish, don't phone to ask how I am, if I'm lonely."

What does she want from me? I don't know that she resents the burden of managing her sisters' inheritances. My uncle, her co-trustee, is overwhelmed with the rush of war business. He tells her, "Ella, I don't have a free moment for the trust. The workload is killing me!"

So Ella complains to me. "My father saddled me with my sisters and their money." Six months pass this way. Then, certain her buck teeth have kept her from marriage, Ella has them pulled and replaced with a perfect set of false teeth. She drops by on her way home from the dentist, shows me, "See! My new teeth are perfect, small and even. It's so important to have nice teeth. I didn't have an orthodontist to fix my teeth when I was young, like you. You know I paid for your orthodontist."

Ella Marries

Whether it is the teeth or the money she inherited, she does meet a man after her brother phones: "I want to introduce you to Jake, a nice looking man who owns a men's store. He's recently widowed, looking for a wife. He came to America alone at nine, uneducated, but his children are doctors."

Jake, on the right, and our family at a family celebration.

Jake proposes, and they marry. Maybe she'll let me alone, I fervently hope, but she phones a month later, "Jake's got a high fever that won't come down. I'm bringing him to Misericordia Hospital across the street from you, so I can stay with you."

After Jake has been in the hospital for a month his older son, a doctor, comes from Florida to be at his father's side. The next day Ella rushes in. "His son diagnosed Jake's illness, prescribed medication, and Jake is recovering! Lucky my stepson is a doctor."

But the son sold the store, certain Jake was dying. The sons will keep the money, according to a legal agreement made before his marriage to Ella. When Jake recovers she realizes, "I've got a husband, but I'll have to support him the rest of my life."

As Jake recovers Ella complains bitterly, "I have to do everything for him, even buy his cigars. Marriage! It's not so wonderful."

It's a repeated theme in our lives, Ella and Mother, both disappointed with marriage.

To College

I am finishing high school. Ella talks as if life goes on as usual after Pearl Harbor. "When you go to college I will pay the expenses with the money from Grandfather. So I decide where you will go and choose your living accommodations."

We have been living alone more than two years, and I thought I was free of her meddling. I tell her, "I'm preparing for the statewide Latin scholarship exam. I listed the university in Madison first, then Marquette. I won't need money."

The problem isn't money, but control, and a secret. It is Mother's money, but Ella hangs on to it, managing the money and our family, especially me. Ella deceives me, tells me that my parents are poor. Yet Mother's trust is worth well over $150,000, a small fortune in 1941. But Mother isn't allowed to touch it, because she is deaf.

A Visit to the Dorm

Ella hammers in another insult, "Scholarship or not, you are going to the University of Wisconsin, to separate from your family so you can meet people who won't know you have deaf parents. How else can you find a man to marry you?"

I keep quiet, absorbing another emotional kick in the stomach. Ella continues, "The university has a new dormitory that is cheaper than the others. Jake's cousin-the-lawyer's daughter lives there, and I've arranged to take you to see her room."

She drives me to Madison a few weeks later, saying, "When you go to school just pay attention to your studies. Who will want to marry you, homely, bent over, a big nose, deaf parents?"

Old witch, I rage, silently. Shut up! I slouch down in her classy new car, the one she bought after Grandpa died. I feel her take my measure, from the orthopedic shoes to still slightly buck teeth that orthodontics had not conquered, topped by my shapeless hairdo.

At the end of a miserable two-hour drive we pull up in front of the enormous spanking-new dorm, denuded of green, with bridging walks connecting identical five-story wings. We enter the massive building where Fay, the pretty and well-dressed daughter of Jake's cousin-the-lawyer, meets us. "Hi, Auntie Ella. Come to our dorm room. Dee, we are so fond of your auntie."

Ella and I settle down on the chairs, Fay and her roommate on the beds. Then Ella strikes, before two strangers, in the dorm where I am to live. Like the wicked wolf savaging Red Riding Hood with her new perfect teeth, she asks, "Will they let my niece stay in this dorm? Her parents are deaf, so her father can't afford to send her to college. I am paying the dorm fee and tuition with her grandfather's money."

No one spoke. Like a punctured balloon, I can't breathe. Trapped in the dorm where I don't want to live, at a school I didn't choose. Rockefellers go to school on their grandfather's money and it's no shame. Why don't I shout that out?

Why does Ella always attack me? It is a question I have puzzled over all my life. Life is like a dammed river, turning back on itself, going nowhere. My aunt keeps me on a string, controlling money and schooling. I will be in a dorm where I have to hide from Jake's cousin-the-lawyer's daughter and her roommate, and who knows how many girls she will tell about me. Mother looks hard at me when I come home: "What happen? So jumpy, nervous?"

I can't eat, say Ella took me to lunch, and run to curl up alone in the study.

Chapter 4. Leaving Home

There is another surprise in store. Ella can be helpful, or so it seems at first glance. The summer between high school and college she arranges for me to be a summer camp counselor. On returning home, I have a shock. I'd been sent away while Ella and Mother sold the house on Juneau, and bought a single family house on the West Side so Marc could have a better social life. Didn't anyone think about that for me? Going to college now seems like banishment. My little brother is now their darling, as he grows up tall, handsome, and charming.

University

I enter the university in September 1942, in wartime. Inspired by an exceptional teaching staff, I sponge up liberalism and economics, brilliant discussions, and chamber music. I apply for tuition scholarships for the next year, and work setting up bowling pins in the gym. I write almost daily to my parents, and get weekly letters from Father with funny spellings and grammar: "Hi, dotter dearie, I am soooo-oooooo loooo-oooonesome for you, my little girlie."

When I come home Mother proudly shows me the new uncomfortable French Empire style couch. "I do all shopping myself, without you, without Ella. This house close to North Avenue, good for fast trolley buses. Now the butcher and baker from old neighborhood move near, Sherman Boulevard. Easier. Sam's family live near to visit. Also Jewish neighbors, good for Marc."

Father's Accident

One day that spring I wake to find a dark sticky discharge coming out of my right breast. I rush to the health clinic, afraid it is cancer. The doctor discovers a cyst where blood from a blow from a baseball bat in high school had coagulated. Neither Mother nor I followed up that blow—or, for that matter, the scar on Mother's chest, which unknown to me was changing color and spreading. She doesn't go to the doctor, and Father has no time for her problems. The wartime shortage of workers means working long hours at the bakery.

Marc writes, "Father's exhausted, working fourteen hours at a time. Yesterday he had one of his terrible headaches, but went to work anyway. He was slicing dough and got dizzy. He didn't move his hands in time, and the roll-slicer cut off the tips of three fingers. I was in school. The school secretary called me. Dad's supervisor was calling. Dad was in the hospital.

"I ran home to tell Mother. She started to cry and wail. I calmed her down and we took a cab to the hospital. She started wheezing with an asthma attack when she saw dad. It is ugly! The doctors stitched up the remaining ends of the fingers."

My heart sinks. His fingers, tools for language, the signs he uses with Mother and his friends. I rush home that weekend to visit Father in the hospital with Marc. Mother doesn't come along, explaining, "It makes me sick to see his hand."

Father sees me, looks miserable, asks me, "How can I sign?"

Father, do you always expect me to have answers for you? I tell Marc, "I don't have to worry about being away. You handle everything so well, and only fifteen."

I don't know that the family circle is closing, with me left outside. Mother loves and trusts him. As does Ella. Did I have anything to do with it as I "raised him?"

Father has sick leave, thanks to the union, but no compensation, although the dangerous machinery had no safety switches or protection. The union steward tells Father to get a lawyer to fight for compensation, but he refuses, "No. Lawyers only cheat the deaf."

That theme will play itself throughout his life.

Education For Life

The Second World War continues, and my schoolmates are just beginning to join the army. We begin to feel changes in our lives. My roommate is Ginnie, tall and skinny, with an auburn braid down her back. She's wearing a green skirt and a loud pink sweater.

I have never heard anyone talk so fast. "Hi! Great to see you! We'll have a ball! My Mom gave me a cookie jar, and promised to keep it filled with her almond cookies. Take some whenever you want, you don't have to ask."

Ginnie keeps me up late at night, uses my pens and paper, making up for the cookies I gobble as I stay in the room and hide. I put on twenty pounds. My clothes no longer fit.

At Saturday suppers we sing ballads about a girl left behind, pregnant. "I've got sixpence," and "Around . . . the block she wheeled a baby carriage." We walk on the lakeshore below the dorm, even in rain and snowstorms, watching the wind attack the trees and roil the water. I wonder about the little rubber tubes lying all over the walks. "They're condoms," Ginnie says, but I don't understand what they're there for. That has nothing to do with my life. I'm a good girl. In fact, I'm scared of men.

Remembering Mildred, I decide I will not study "women's work," be a teacher, or social worker. I choose to study international relations with Spanish-speaking countries, my coursework an amalgam of economics, business, Spanish, international law, and journalism. Latin gave me a good base for learning languages.

Boyfriend

Ginnie informs me, "I'm going to teach you to play bridge. You sit in the room alone too often. You have to get out, and we need a fourth. Come downstairs right away." I go along obediently, and she coaches me briefly, enough to play a mediocre game.

When my partner tells a high school friend that Ginnie's roommate is Dee Becker, he asks to meet me. Larry, medium-tall, slim, nice looking, with thick wire-frame glasses, calls on me the next afternoon, but his face drops, "I thought you were somebody else . . . uh, from my high school."

I know the girl he means, a buxom blonde who is nothing like me except for the name, but Larry takes me out anyway. We see each other often, because I accept his terms. "I don't have money for dates. I'm working my way through college." I think I'm poor, too. Evenings we study together in the dorm lounge, listening to his Count Basie records, and "necking," a gentle buildup of warmth as we study, listen to jazz, and kiss—until the housemother comes by. She makes the rounds every few minutes, tapping couples briskly on the shoulders with a ruler, measuring, "Too close, less than twelve inches!"

Mother dislikes Larry intensely. "No good, too much like your father, makes jokes, not nice." I pay no attention, for she is criticizing my beloved father.

One afternoon, after a slap on the face and a stormy confrontation, I tell Larry we're through. My roommate, my takeaway Ella, sees I'm upset. "You are nervous. When I get nervous I smoke a cigarette. Come. Learn to smoke instead of eating cookies." I start smoking that day, though I hate the smell of cigarette smoke and the burning sensation in my throat.

The Army

In June Larry announces, "The army found a way to keep the colleges open, to provide engineers and officers. I'm joining ASTP, the Army Specialized Training Program. I'll continue studying physics and engineering at a college in Iowa. I'll write regularly. Don't worry." Why would I worry? It's wartime, but in school he will be safe.

When I visit home I call Del, my best friend from high school. She bubbles right through the phone, "I got a secret. I'm pregnant, gonna have a baby in six months. My boyfriend Jeff was sent overseas, so we got married before he left. I got this little apartment and painted used furniture, so it's nice and homey."

I am delighted and rush over at once, hug her and gush, "That's so exciting. And you fixed up the place so sweet and sunny. You've got magic in your hands, like my mother."

When Del's baby boy is born in November, she lives frugally on her allotment as an army wife. On visits home I go to see her first. Domestic Del with her baby is the island of peace in my life, along with our friend, Helen, who is losing her hearing as did her mother. Helen copes, and accepts. She, too, is married and pregnant. Her husband, an engineer, has discovered new technology aids for deaf parents. He brings home a radio-receiver to mount on the crib rail, with an amplifier that Helen can carry around. The baby's cries will light a bulb on the amplifier wherever she is. The label on the receiver carries the legend, "Developed at the Rochester Institute of Technology."

"Sisters"

After two years in the dormitory, I move to a sorority house on "fraternity row" to live with my twenty-two "sisters" and a slightly alcoholic housemother in a rundown mansion, a stark contrast to life in the dorm. Two of us are assigned to an attic room under the eaves. My roommate Annie is pleasant, easygoing, an art student, a painter like my mother. We are a veritable family in this homey old mansion. Everyone has a steady in the army, and expects to get married when the soldiers came home, except me. I enjoy Larry's letters, but that's all.

I get a liberal education, living in intimacy with twenty-two girls. "Watch how I twirl my nipples," says one, "It makes them stand up real perky. I do it before I go out on a date, especially if I'm wearing a tight sweater . . ." She embarrasses me and makes me even more conscious of my flat chest.

One evening two roommates return from a double date, laughing loudly, "It's so funny to watch men get hot. We flirt, and kiss and pet, really get them excited, but we're safe on a double date."

They scare me: What if they run into two men who overpower and rape them? How do they take chances like that? All things I read in an article in Mother's dresser drawer but never discussed with anyone. Then my art-student roommate wins first prize in the winter carnival. She carves Lady Godiva, riding naked on her horse, out of a large block of ice on our front lawn. The lady embarrasses me every time I walk past her.

A year later Larry writes, "My ASTP unit was sent overseas, to the Signal Corps. We're based at Chinese headquarters in western China, sending wireless messages to the front. From India we traversed the Burma road in trucks without springs. Now I know what a Burma road is, mud and rocks and holes. Here we're treated like royalty, invited to official eight-course banquets."

We all wait anxiously for the daily mail from soldiers overseas in the war. We sing "They're Either Too Young or Too Old" and "Dear John."

Peacetime?

The next fall, with office skills I learned at night school, I work at Hillel, the Jewish student center. The fighting is over in Europe, and those soldiers are back in school. Al, who hangs out at the student center with other army returnees, flirts with me, but nothing more. Only at the end of the school year does he invite me out for a drink. We sit in the hotel bar, and he shocks me, "I want to say goodbye, because me and my friends are leaving next week. We are joining volunteer fighters in Palestine! We've been training all year!"

I never shared my dreams with Al. I gasp, "Why didn't you tell me? I would have gone with you! I want to fight for Israel too!"

He is taken aback, says he will look into the possibility, but do I have boat fare? No! The money I saved is gone. Larry wrote his mother that he was thinking of marriage. She told Ella, who took me shopping, to buy the one thing she said a woman needs: a fur coat. I have a coat, and no money to do what I really want to do. Will I never do what I want? Will I have Ella controlling me forever?

So, of course, Larry and I get married when he comes home from China. Ella had been laying the groundwork all along. Larry had kept his virginity for me, and I had kept mine, so there was no thought of anything but proper marriage. Love? Like my parents? All the girls had been waiting for all the men, and all of us got married. Then we go to work to support our husbands while they go back to school.

Los Alamos

Larry completes his master's degree and is offered a job at Los Alamos Atomic Laboratories. We wait for security clearance, staying with my parents while Larry drives a cab. I am pregnant, and Mother is ecstatic. "At last, at last, my grandchild."

We sew together, clothes for a mother-to-be. We fashion a smart wool suit, and Mother lets me help her for the first time. I have made her happy, finally, because I am pregnant.

When the security clearance arrives, we have teary farewells and drive away to Los Alamos. At the border of New Mexico, heading into the mountains, the sun paints the bare peaks a breathtaking bloody red. Larry reads the map. "They're called the Sangre de Cristo range—Blood of Christ. Dry and bare, not like Wisconsin."

We drive upward on a narrow road, winding around arid foothills, up to the plateau where we will live, 7,200 feet high. We are assigned to barracks-like apartments close to the laboratories. No one will hire a pregnant woman, so I get acquainted with Hispanic neighbors and the close-knit cluster of Jewish families who have created a community. No one here is deaf.

Our next-door neighbors, a young couple with a little boy, are native New Mexicans. That implies Spanish and Mexican roots, and the native Indians from the pueblos (mud-brick towns) who maintain the laboratories and town. In that raw new community, social castes are instantaneously created according to the language spoken (Spanish or English), college degree, and university attended. I hear a story that children on the base taunt each other: "My daddy went to Harvard and yours didn't!"

Our Baby

The Los Alamos "hospital," really a set of old Quonset huts, is run army-style, with minimum contact between doctor and patient. I have brought with me Dr. Grantly Dick Read's book, *Childbirth Without Fear*, on natural childbirth. I do his preparatory exercises, follow instructions for nutrition and diet. No one tells me that the thin atmosphere at 7,200 feet above sea level affects the development of the fetus, that babies here are born below normal weight. Nor does anyone tell me that the martinis I drink with our new social circle may affect the growing baby's development.

In May labor begins. Larry rushes me to the hospital building. "My wife's in labor. Hurry! Sign her in." He is ordering the nurses around!

Sam and Anna with their first grandchild.

"There's no rush. Contractions are just beginning," the nurses tell him. "Calm down, and get out of the way. We're taking your wife for preparation." An enema and shaving. That wasn't in the book. Larry paces frantically in the hallway. "Can't I sit with her?" he asks the nurses rushing by. "We want to do natural birth."

"We?" The staff has never heard of husbands wanting to be involved. "Out," says the head nurse. "Back to the reception room." There is no possibility that Larry can be present to share in the birth. He feels left out, his child an intruder. And he will always feel that way.

I may have read the book, but I had never had a baby before. Delivery is twelve hours of work and discomfort, alone, without my husband to sit with me. In the end it is an easy delivery, no medication or tearing, but how much of that had to do with Dr. Read? Baby Aliza weighs less than six and a half pounds, and her head is small.

I am fully awake as the baby comes out shrieking and screaming. But at feeding time, the nurse doesn't bring Aliza. "She's in an isolette. Children born in this thin atmosphere go into incubators for twenty-four hours." If I don't get my infant, she won't stimulate my flow of milk! "Please," I beg, and wait.

Visitors

The birth announcement reaches Milwaukee a few days later as Father is cleaning up the yard. He sees the mailman bring the envelope, then hurries to Mother, waving the announcement and doing a jig. Mother opens the envelope and a photo of our tiny newborn falls out. I wrote "Meet your granddaughter Aliza, who weighs six pounds, five ounces. Aliza means joyful."

Mother is worried. "The baby too thin. Terrible." She doesn't like the looks of that baby. "No good. Too far away. Needs grandma to help." Isn't that what her family said to her?

A few weeks later, Father's brother Morry, returning to his home in Arizona after a trip to Milwaukee, brings my parents to see their first grandchild. As six overnight guests overflow the two-bedroom apartment—my parents, Morry, his wife and two sons—our warm-hearted Hispanic neighbors invite Morry's family to sleep in their apartment. My father sleeps on the living room couch.

When Morry's eight-year-old son wakes up, he comes into my living room, straight to *my* father on the couch, and calls, "Daddy, wake up!" He can't tell his father from mine, they look so much alike. Everyone laughs, a typical Becker family gathering.

Grandma

Mother is happy to have her first grandchild—at last. She holds Aliza, chanting "Aah-Aah Baby," croons to her, walks with her, and tells me, "Four hours don't need to pay attention, when baby cry you give milk, like I do for you." She puts the baby down to open the load of gifts she has made: a white crocheted poodle, a soft ball with a bell inside, an assortment of embroidered bibs, a sweater, cap, and six sets of booties. The clothes are yellow and green, since she didn't know what sex the baby would be.

She recalls, "You are big baby, over eight pounds. Always hungry, always crying for milk. Good I have much milk. But my sister and mother watch me always. I can't take care of baby alone, they think. All the time talk to you, take you downstairs. They think I'm not good mother because of deaf." Her thoughts turn back twenty-five years, replaying scenes of my infancy.

She sleeps in the baby's room, where I hear her, checking to make sure Aliza is all right, as she pads back and forth to the crib. She closes the window tight, "Night air, bad for baby. Also keep baby close, to see." As if I were deaf. Alarm bells should be ringing.

Everything I do, she doesn't like: the way I nurse, hold the baby, diaper her. She feels responsible for my baby. "Let me. I do it better," she says, just as she did when I was little and wanted to help her. When my parents return home, Mother happy, at last, with a grandchild to think about, I relax. My milk flows plentifully.

Mother's Letters

Dreams of a grandchild fulfilled, Mother's creative side flowers. She writes us letters in a poetic stream of consciousness, with comic mistakes. The first letter describes their trip home, "As we traveled under the wheels of the train . . ." Like a hobo riding the rails.

The next letter describes the movie she saw with Charlton Heston playing Moses. She calls it *The Ten Condiments* not *The Ten Commandments*. The third letter is unforgettable. Writing about a luncheon she attended, she sends a tuna casserole recipe: "Mash the tuna. Close the window. Add salt. Stir all together" A warning in the middle of the recipe! During her visit she kept warning me that night air isn't healthy. In the letters, everything runs together—this is the way she thinks. In the middle of another thought, her mind goes back to me as an infant.

Anna's Grandchild

Mother worries in her letters, "You have small breasts, not enough milk. Poor baby, too thin. Also alone in bedroom, window open at night, bad." Mother builds her worries, like ABC blocks, one on the other, into a Tower of Babel. When we plan to come to Milwaukee for Thanksgiving she writes, "Foolish to come so far with small baby. But good I can see how much she grows."

Aliza is five months old. On the trip I wrap her in a blanket in the heated car, for there isn't a snowsuit to be had in snowless Los Alamos. We plan to go shopping in Milwaukee right away. That's why Mother gasps when we come in with Aliza. "No snowsuit. Terrible! She'll freeze! Also still small and thin. You must give the baby to me. Now. You don't know how to take care of your baby."

Ghosts from my infancy are wailing in her head, assembling to strike me down. Mother's unspoken thoughts have been waiting, forming all my life! Looking back, I know that scene began when I was born, when Mother was told, "You must come back to live with us. You cannot take care of a child."

This time it's her turn, as if she is saying, "They took you away from me. Now it's my turn. I want your child. You owe her to me." Now is the hour of judgment, the final condemnation: No good, failure. "You must give the baby to me."

Mother's words cut, slicing into my heart. Cut. That's the idea. I lay Aliza in Mother's arms, and head for the washroom. I'll cut my wrists. Mother can have my child, to raise without interference from her sisters and her nasty little girl who thinks she's the mother in the house. I am the surrogate mother to give her a child all her own. Retribution for a child torn in half between her and Ella.

I find Father's razor and hold it to my wrist, make tentative scratches. No! Aliza is mine, not hers. I will not cut. I hesitate, put the razor back, wash the shallow scratches, and come out of the bathroom. I walk to Mother to take Aliza back. But she has lost touch with reality. She thinks she's holding her own baby. She shouts, "No! Mine!"

Larry rushes to my aid, twists Mother's arms from behind to make her let go. Mother and I wail in our Greek chorus, our tragedy. Not a Thanksgiving, not a holiday.

Raising Baby

I am insecure about my capacity to be a mother. I ease up gradually since my friends are on their own like me, away from family, and we learn from one another. I enjoy Aliza, who is clearly destined to be a painter like her grandmother. She always throws her strained beets at the wall, smiles, and claps, admiring the colored splatter.

On a visit to Los Alamos a year later, Mother makes peace with me when she sees that Aliza is growing. She buys an Indian drum for Aliza her grandchild, the first of many musical gifts to come. She

---

Mother's Music

The drum she gave to my firstborn / Was followed by a xylophone,
A concertina, horns and pipes / Record player, records.
Mother gave my children / music she could not hear.

Deaf at two, she still sensed sound,
Its synchronies and rhythmic beats / Singing as she ironed
Or chanting lullabies: / "Aah-aah baay-by."

And she was a dancer, / Moved to inner music,
Unencumbered as she danced.
Undisturbed by worldly noise.

---

brings other noisy toys too, like a battery-powered machine gun that makes a frightful racket. Maybe she enjoys the vibrations.

"No!" Larry shouts when he hears Aliza energetically pounding the drum and shrieking with laughter. "Such a racket. The drum goes in the closet," and there it stays—until I go away for a weekend six months later, leaving Larry with Aliza. When I return to the house, I hear Aliza banging away happily on the drum! "Why not," Larry mumbles, and buries his head in the newspaper.

I am suspicious as I take a load of diapers to the washing machine, and open the cupboard under the sink, reaching for the soap flakes. Larry could be overenthusiastic about order, but this is going pretty far. "Larry!" I call: "Why are the soap flakes in a jar? Were you housecleaning?"

"No," he says sheepishly. "I was running water for Aliza's bath, and she started screaming in the bedroom. I ran to see what was wrong, but forgot the water. It overflowed, and all the boxes under the sink got soaked. I gave the drum to Liz to keep her from screaming!"

Aliza keeps the drum, and Mother's love of music, all her life. She will grow up to have a career in ethnic music, with drums!

Back to Madison

Larry has been working at Los Alamos for nearly three years. More and more frequently he returns from work tired, rubbing his eyes. "My eyes hurt from the computer's flashing lights. I need a Ph.D. to get a better job."

I agree. We are frugal, accumulate savings, but I am pregnant again as we return to Madison. We leave close friends, our community. Rootless, ever since childhood. In a housing complex for faculty and graduate students at the University of Wisconsin we are assigned a two-floor apartment with a garden and sunny rooms. We are lucky, for other students with families are living in trailers parked in a muddy lot thirty miles away.

Our second child, Ben, is born in Milwaukee, at Mount Sinai Hospital, while Aliza stays with Larry. When Ella drives me home with baby Ben eight days later, after the circumcision ceremony, I enter the apartment calling, "Mommy's home, Liz. Come see your baby brother," but Aliza is nowhere to be seen.

I find her upstairs, sitting on her blanket, thumb in mouth. Under the blanket she has piled all her belongings, toys and clothes. She's only twenty-seven months old, doesn't understand our leaving Los Alamos, followed so soon by my disappearance. I don't know how to comfort her. Both of us are insecure, uprooted, as I look forward to Larry studying with little income.

I type theses at home. Our parents, now grandparents, are delighted to have us nearby. Larry's parents or Ella drive up on the weekends that we don't come "home." On Saturdays, Father's day off, they bring my parents, laden with food and presents. Mother continues to crochet white poodle dogs and sews bibs, shirts, and jackets. We wish we could always stay together. It is a good time for all of us, as the children grow close to their grandparents.

But Mother stays home most of the time, sewing exquisite clothes for the children. "My toe always hurt, you remember, broke before your wedding."

I remember. Beside the narrow walkway around the house was an old well, with a wooden cover. I didn't like the looks of it. The wood looked rotten, and I said so, but no one listened. Just before my wedding Mother went out to throw away some garbage. She stepped on that well cover and it broke. Her foot fell through the rotten wood, breaking her little toe. It isn't healing, eight years later. That doesn't sound good. She says she goes to the doctor, but no one is with her to translate.

Father comes to visit often, riding with Ella and Jake, or Larry's parents. He and the children play together, laughing and loving. He teaches the children signs, and they shape words carefully on their lips, or find other ways to show what they want. They laugh, jumping up and down when they see him get out of the car. It is a fullness of mutual love.

We exchange babysitting with our neighbors, and join the Hillel Married Students Club. In a neighborhood women's faculty group I read all nine volumes of Proust's *Swann's Way*. Sadly, we are to move far from our families again.

To Seattle

Two years later, Larry bursts in, "I failed the exams for advanced studies. My brother says I need to take basic physics again since the ASTP courses were poor, but I'm looking for a job. Not in Los Alamos again. I should find better work now with my experience."

He is hired at the Boeing Airplane Company in Seattle, Washington, part of an army of engineers creating weapons for war. Again, war work. Moving is hard on the children. Aliza again collects and hoards her belongings. Ben, not yet two, wakens from his nap in Seattle shrieking and screaming every afternoon. I am sure he misses my father, as I do.

Yet in our damp rainy new milieu, again we build a community, people like us, away from family. We help found the neighborhood synagogue, and buy our first house. We drive or fly home cross-country over the Rockies once a year, even going as far as Washington D.C., where my brother's family now lives.

My family comes to visit regularly. Then one day Mother writes, "I don't come this time. So hard to travel. My toe bothers more, the one broke before you marry. Doctor doesn't understand my talk. Asthma also bad, and pains in chest." That deep scar on her chest is metastasizing.

Father can't tell me more. He is worrying about work, for the bakery is closing and moving south to Georgia, where workers have no unions. The union has a job for him, farther away, three buses to take, and a new supervisor who must learn to communicate with him, and will not let him take over in the summer.

Still, on visits to Seattle he forgets his troubles and becomes a happy, loving grandfather, full of mischief and laughter. The children sign and gesture, skip and jump, learning ways to get his attention, happy to be with him. He mows the lawn, and visits people in the local deaf community. He contacted them through the *Frat,* a monthly newsletter for the Jewish deaf community throughout the United States. He keeps up with doings in Chicago and in general in the world of deafness, through this beloved newsletter, and now he uses it to find friends in Seattle. I don't know any of these people from the local deaf community. I am out of touch with my other half, my other world.

Father enjoys visiting our friends too. One Sunday one couple, Tom and Betty, invite us to their house for brunch. The dining table stretches into the living room beside a back hallway, where the phone sits on a shelf. As we sit at the table the phone rings and Tom jumps up to answer, heading into the hallway, where the phone is out of sight. Father calls out, "If it's for me, tell them to call back later. I don't want the food to get cold."

Tom is puzzled, "How did he know the phone was ringing?"

"It was simple deduction," Father explains, "I saw him look toward the hall, and jump up."

What a funny smart man! He has developed acute powers of observation to compensate for deafness. He knows what's going on around him, without hearing.

Mother Ill

Mother sends me two exquisite aprons, but I worry about the note she encloses. "My toe never get better, hurt all the time, and doctor doesn't fix. I stay home, make pretty organdy half-aprons, appliqué, chintz flowers. Also crotchet poodle dogs for Becker family grandchildren, like Aliza was a baby. Your aunt Sylvia Becker comes to see me. She likes very much the white poodles."

I am shocked when Ella writes, "I had to pay an expensive hospital bill for your mother. Remember that scar on her chest. She didn't pay attention when it changed color and spread. It turned into cancer that spread to her bones. That's why her toe was hurting. Cancer, all over."

Next is a painful letter from Father, "Dearest Dotter, things are bad, hard for me. I come from work, have to cook supper. Mother can't get out of bed. She can't move without screaming, just lays in bed. I sleep a little, get up, clean the house, mow the grass, go shopping for food, pay bills with money she gives me. She still takes all my money for work, doesn't trust me. Terrible!"

I am tormented: Maybe there should be a law that children of deaf parents can't move far from them. I should be there to help them, but I am thousands of miles away. Mother's deafness brings her a frightful isolation. Distrust of others, fear, waiting for bad things to happen, her active life over. Even letters about craftwork stop. She tells Father the slightest motion feels like hot knives ripping through her body.

Father writes a month later, "Your Mother feels worse, weak. The less she moves the weaker she gets. Sometimes we only have crackers and tinned tuna. I am sooo-oooo tired, work a long shift six days, then take care of your Mother. Too much."

Ella's next letter is worrying. "It's impossible for me to visit your mother. I can't get in, because she doesn't get out of bed to answer the door. If she does let me in, all she does is cry and shout at me about things that happened years ago, things she imagines I did to her. She won't give me a key, says she doesn't want anyone to come in and steal. She thinks I'll steal the money I bring her! I have to manage her money alone, and that's the thanks I get. I'm not young either, have Jake on my hands. I can't take care of her alone, even if she's my sister."

The two women are like Siamese twins, bound together by Grandfather's trust. Since Ella controls her finances, Mother's suspicions grow along with the illness. Cancer is eating her body and her mind.

Her isolation breeds depression, filling loneliness with anger. Father too is the butt of her angry complaints. In her empty days she goes over everything Ella, or anyone, ever said or did, and what she thought they did against her, again and again.

More than halfway across the country, now with three young children, how can I help? I come with the children as soon as possible, but we wait on the porch half an hour until she gets up to let us in. Hobbling, wincing with pain, she starts off, not even welcoming us.

"Don't trust Ella! I ask how much money I have. She says too hard to explain. Anyway the money not for you, she says, for the children. That's a lie. My father want to take care of me. Maybe your father lose his job again."

I need to stop that dirge. "Mother," I ask, "Don't you have medicine for pain?" Morphine is all she has. "No good," she says, "only makes me weak. Better I don't move, lie quiet." She asks over and over, "What do I have in life? You and your brother take my grandchildren away." Am I supposed to stay in Milwaukee, to lead her through life, as I did when I was small?

Then she lets up complaining, happy to see the children. She finds energy to dress and cook. Isolation or pain, which is worse? Her deafness isolates her in illness in a silent world. Her friends no longer keep up contact, because they can't get in. She is too weak, or miserable, to get up when she sees the doorbell-light flashing. When Ella visits, she writes ahead of time to make sure Mother will know to let her in, but often leaves, frustrated. Mother writes her a note that she didn't see the light. The Beckers come by, but can't get in if Father isn't home.

I return home with a heavy heart. Ella writes, "Today I brought money and medicine to your mother. I was hungry, wanted to make a sandwich, but there was nothing in the house. What's the matter with your father?"

What is the matter with her? Can't she cross the street to pick up the makings for that sandwich, and one for Mother? Has she no concern or pity? Has hate festering made the sisters more hateful to one another? No longer can I take sides. I can sympathize, but I live my life in Seattle, without my head full of Mother's pain and complaints. Ella can't. Clearly Ella, five years older, is not to blame. She has her own burden, her husband to support and care for.

Every letter from Milwaukee shakes me. I feel helpless, useless, when Ella writes, "Your Mother is such a burden for me, and I have other troubles. Jake is losing his sight and hearing. It's hard for him to get out of a chair, and I have to pull him up though he's much heavier and bigger than me. I can't drive any more, sold my car, so I depend on rides from friends to play bridge. I take buses, can't waste money on cabs."

Marc, me, and his daughter, visiting Mother.

I consult with my brother and his wife, arranging to bring both our families to Milwaukee at the same time, to see what we can do. But I worry, rightly so. Again, when we arrive we ring the bell, and wait a long time. When Mother opens the door she is dressed, much thinner, but surprisingly full of life. She gives us a fleeting smile, hugs the children and takes them to the kitchen for milk and cookies.

Then she returns, takes my arm, and says, "You know what Ella do when you get married? She doesn't let me say how I want the wedding." Fifteen years later! My brother pities me, watching that scene, so he calls me aside. His family will stay with her while we go to a nearby motel to sleep, to spend daytimes together for a few days.

Before we leave we go with Ella to buy Mother a television set—using Mother's money. She has to guess at most of what she sees, but it is company. She watches reruns of old musicals, hour after hour. When the movie features Dolores del Rio she gets out of bed, moving about. Television relieves Mother's loneliness.

Farewell to Mother

Ella calls, "Come right away. The cancer attacked your mother's liver. She's dying, in Mt. Sinai Hospital."

I arrange for friends to care for the children, and arrive at the hospital within three days. Ella is keeping vigil, knitting to keep from smoking. Mother, drugged against the pain, is sleeping, motionless and gray. Still she feels my presence and opens her eyes. She looks at me, expressionless, and closes her eyes again. Is that only because of the drugs? Does she even care that I am there?

Ella takes a deep breath. "Thank the Lord you got here," then stops. "Quick, take your mother's watch out of the drawer in her bedstand, so the nurses won't steal it. She's dying; we might forget."

That's her greeting? I walk to Mother's bedside, open the drawer. As I take out her watch she opens her eyes, looks at me in horror, her eyes telling me I am stealing her watch. At that moment she dies. Again, I disappointed my mother. I wonder, did she die of a broken heart because she saw me take her watch?

WALKMAN

As I pass walkers floating down the street /
Walkman sound clouds cradling their heads

I remember Father.
Deaf at seven, / He lost the sounds that filled the outer world.
Yet a song cloud hovered in his memory. / He loved to sing to me,
Inner rhythm bore the lyrics' / Cantillation monotone.

When Mother died / The music played in Father's head.
Returning from the funeral he went to nap.
I heard wailing sounds, / Loud, then louder.
Grieving in his sleep?

 When he woke, I asked: / "Father, were you crying in your sleep?"
He smiled: "I dreamed. / I was courting your mother long ago.
I watched her dancing, / Like a beam of light.
Our love for music bound us to each other. / I wooed her with my songs."

Love remained on an internal Walkman tape.
The sound of music fills his brain,
With inner melody.

When the doctors verify Mother's death, Ella is neither sad nor sympathetic. "Stay here. I'll phone the newspaper with the obituary. I don't want her correct age to appear; people will know how old I am."

The curtain falls, the play is done. The years of difficulty between two sisters finally end. I'm stunned.

Money

Marc arrives the next day, and we remain seven days for the shiva, the traditional mourning period. Sitting on low stools according to tradition, we go over Mother's papers. I call Marc, "I found a box in her bedroom closet, with every letter I wrote from the day I left for college." She did love me, after all!

Marc is worried. "What about the money? We can't find bank books or records. We know Mother didn't trust Father, always made him turn over his paycheck to her. What did she do with the money if she couldn't get out of bed and wouldn't let him go to the bank? Father doesn't even know her account number. I found some bank deposit books, but the balances are from nearly ten years ago, about the time when she got sick. I've looked everywhere, except her top dresser drawer, It's locked and no key anywhere. Should I force it open?"

We struggle with screwdrivers, files, and picks, until the lock turns, the drawer opens, and Marc gasps, "There's a big wad of money here." He counts, "Ten thousand dollars in cash!" This was a considerable sum in 1968. "Is it from Father's paychecks over the years? Why was she hiding it?"

Marc contemplates, "She didn't trust anyone! She wouldn't ask Father, Ella, or us when we came on visits, to take care of money matters. Maybe the bank books are correct. She stopped putting money in the bank when she took to bed."

That's when Father comes into the room, sees Marc holding the wad of $100 bills, and shouts, "Where did you get that?" We show him the broken lock, and his face turns red: "I worked hard for that money. I gave Mother my pay and she put it in the drawer. It's mine! Give it to me! I'm deaf and my children want to steal my money!"

We assure him, "We aren't going to take it. We just found it, this minute."

Father has good reason to worry, for neither Mother's money nor the house was willed to him. The house is registered in her name only, her children the beneficiaries. The trust from Grandfather is not his to touch. The bakery where he is working is closing down, and the union won't find him another job after his accident at work. His bakery pension will not even provide minimum requirements for food and shelter.

My brother calls me aside, and we decide to give Father the cash on the spot. He doesn't thank us. Why should he? It is his money. We don't need it—Marc has a successful business selling hearing aids, and Larry has a decent job at Boeing. We will do more when Mother's estate is settled, dividing the trust three ways instead of two, providing for Father out of our shares. Of course we would never turn him out of his home, so we turn that over too.

Closure

During the mourning period Ella sits with us, and sighs, "At last! It's over. You and Marc got your trust. I hope you understand that I took care of that money, guarded it for you all these years. I didn't get another trustee when my brother died from a heart attack from overwork during the War. I didn't want to spend your money for a lawyer. Besides, don't ever forget, I was responsible for your mother when you went away. You left her alone!

"I've been taking care of her all her life. When we left Russia I had to hold her hand all the way so she wouldn't get lost, until we got to America. In Milwaukee Ma and Pa couldn't talk to her, because she didn't understand them and they didn't understand her. Ma always asked me in Yiddish, '*Vos zagst er*'—what is she saying. She was spoiled. Ma never made her do anything, so I had to help with cleaning, everything. Your mother went to dances, to parties, had lots of beaus, and those deaf men were not nice to me. I saw her laughing with them and looking at me.

"Even after she married! When you were born we had to take your parents and you back into the house. I had to teach you to talk. Then, when I married, Jake got sick and I had two people to take care of.

"Did you ever think how hard it's been for me? When your mother got sick it was impossible. She didn't answer the door. She wouldn't give me a key. I got a cleaning woman, but she wouldn't let the woman in. No one came to visit her except me. Then all she did was complain. I did my best. At last I can rest."

We are all off Ella's hands along with the trust, not just Mother. I don't hear sorrow from Ella, just relief. I can feel sympathy for the aunt I always criticized, seeing only the bad in her, but I can't feel affection for her, not after that attack at the dorm.

Chapter 5. Changes

There is something to be said for generations living together. Father is widowed and out of work, but he is happy, spending long vacations with Marc and his family. Marc sends cheery reports of Father raking leaves in the yard and playing with the children.

Father stays with us for two months, right before Ben's bar mitzvah. "Let me do the baking," he says. "I'll make you the best cookies you ever had."

He never baked at home! Now he is baking a variety of perfectly shaped cookies and pastries. He is a master baker, but no one knew. "I watched all the time I worked. Your mother didn't need my cookies, and I was too tired when I was working. This is the first time I ever baked."

We are happy while Father stays with us. He helps in the yard, romps and plays cards with our children. Still, when he hints that he wants to move in permanently, we don't encourage him. I remember living with Mother's family. He leaves to stay with Marc.

Marc writes, "When you went to college my job began, responsible for our parents. When Dad had that dreadful work accident you weren't there. When you married you moved far away, and left me with our parents. When Mother was ill you had your own problems, off in Seattle. Dad feels you drove him out. Now he is with us, and we don't object. Living with us is not an ideal solution for him but we are offering him a home and our loving children who care about him." Was he letting me know something new, showing anger at me for not continuing to be his little mother?

Some months later Father writes, "I hope you won't be angry, but I am getting married again. I posted Mother's obituary in the magazine of the Hebrew Fraternity of the Deaf, and every widow who

Sam chopping wood in Marc's yard.

read the notice wrote to me. Those women were driving me crazy. I have to escape those ladies. So I already picked my bride. Her name is Selma; she lives near Chicago with her daughter. She is eight years younger than me, a widow, with a deaf twin sister in California. They were born deaf, so I'm practicing signing. She can't lipread."

He chose another twin, like Mother! He sends us a photograph of an attractive woman, with a sweet smile. I write back to him sincerely, "We're very happy. You're still young, and deserve to enjoy yourself. We hope to meet Selma soon."

Marc brings me up to date. "Selma's family all use sign. Father is learning proper signing, the formal system that Selma learned in school, with new signs. Mimi and I signed up for a course in signing,

---

MIME

Master mime Marceau / Moves expressive, wordless,
Paints images in motion. / Catches butterflies.

Can I learn sign language?
Are my hands too old / To trap fluttering thoughts,
That dart like dragonflies, seeking food for thought
Within a pool of meaning.

Like the bird / Sucking honey at my window
From the heart of spring's pink blossoms,
Can my hands draw meanings from my heart?

---

and we're teaching our children to sign. Otherwise we can't talk with Selma."

I don't learn to sign. How would I find a course in signing in Seattle? I have no idea where to look. Even if I could, we are so far away. There is no way I can be close to Father's new wife.

When Father and Selma are married in Chicago, we all come to the wedding and meet Selma's children and grandchildren, all of them signing. Selma is as pretty as her picture, her children warm and welcoming. I barely remember the few signs I learned, just smile politely, with my husband and children. Outsiders. Again.

To New York

After the wedding Marc writes, "Dad's been asking me for advice. Selma was living with her daughter, so Father can't move there. Selma doesn't want to live in Milwaukee, so he wants to sell the house. New York City is building subsidized housing for deaf and other handicapped residents. I've learned about a housing project where Dad and Selma can live comfortably, called Tanya Towers. The headquarters of the New York Society for the Deaf are nearby, in the Emanuel Y on Fourteenth Street. Their office provides social services and translators.

Sam and Selma, newly married.

"I registered Dad and Selma with Tanya Towers. Now I'm arranging for them to move to New York because they need to be residents of the city for a year to be eligible for Tanya Towers. Mrs. Green, the mother-in-law of our deaf cousin Miriam Schwam, will rent them a room. After a year they will be residents with first priority, since they have no home of their own. I'm helping Father sell the house." Now I realize that my cousin from the Schefrin family, Miriam, is also related to Father's deaf cousin, the one his grandfather brought to America.

It sounds like a good plan, but letters from Father are full of complaints after they move. "This is a hard life, a bad time. Terrible. We have all the time to worry that we don't bother Mrs. Green. It's not a home. We don't have a kitchen, so Selma can't cook meals. We look for a cheap restaurant. Even if it's raining or snowing or any bad weather we have to go out to eat. Selma all the time complains. I thought to marry, at last be happy, but that's not the way it is."

Selma's Accident

During that waiting time, Father and Selma visit her children and Marc often. Father writes, "Thank goodness Marc doesn't live far away. The bus from New York takes five hours. Not bad. We are visiting now Marc for a whole month. Selma has a good time with Marc's children signing. My signing is better, too. Marc teaches me signs he learns.

"I keep busy, and Selma takes long walks while I work in the yard. Mimi cooks kosher, and teaches Selma. She learned nothing about Jewish at the state school, away from home."

Then Marc phones, his voice high and distressed. "Selma went for a walk this morning. There are no sidewalks in this neighborhood. A car came up behind her. The driver tooted, didn't realize she couldn't hear, then ran her over, across her knees! A neighbor saw the accident, and ran to tell us. Selma's in the hospital, and Father's frantic."

The callousness of hearing people! As Selma lies in the hospital, with broken kneecaps, Marc tells Father to hire a lawyer to sue the driver but Father refuses. "Lawyers cheat deaf people. We will get nothing. Only the lawyer will get money."

The same refrain he sang after his work accident. The driver's insurance only pays for medical bills. Deafness is definitely a legal handicap. And Father's dream of traveling with Selma is over. Her injuries leave her with crippled knees, surgical pins that don't hold, and pain. She develops arthritis in her hands from holding a cane to walk.

At least the waiting in Brooklyn pays off. They move to Tanya Towers, to their own one-bedroom apartment. But I don't like what Father writes. "We moved into a nice apartment but the neighborhood on Thirteenth Street is terrible. We can't go out at night because of drunks and drug sellers. They live in burned-out apartments on the corner and across the street."

The city plan to build Tanya Towers turns out to be part of a neighborhood rehabilitation, the rest yet to come. Father and Selma are to suffer years of living across from rubble and among derelicts and drug dealers. Still, the tone of the letters changes as he meets his neighbors, "I know many neighbors, Jewish Deaf, from conventions. The New York Society for the Deaf is only four blocks away so I went there right away. They have meetings, parties, something every day. Selma joined the ladies' auxiliary. I am secretary again. They know I was secretary of the club in Milwaukee.

"The building is for all handicapped people. The office has a social worker who understands sign. We have a club room, where we play cards on Monday. She has new friends here. I take the dirty clothes to the laundry room for Selma. We bought furniture, so we are settling in to be a happy married couple, at last."

Praying

Later Father writes, "Can you believe? The Reform Jewish send a student rabbi to lead prayers once a month on Sabbath and on holidays. Imagine—prayer services for the Jewish Deaf. I can pray the first time, the dream of my whole life. I never believed it would happen. It's good to live here."

Larry and I to Israel

Larry bursts in from work, shouting, "Boeing laid off 70,000 workers today! I may be out of work soon." He slumps into the chair before the television, as the phone rings. He answers, "Fred! You, too! I'm sorry."

A friend was fired, the first of many. Larry is still working, but he comes home fatigued, says the atmosphere depresses him. A few months later a delegation from Israel Aircraft Company arrives to recruit workers, offering a three-year contract with all moving expenses paid. Larry is open to changes, decides, "When Ben finishes high school in two years, we'll go to Israel."

I can realize my dream, and return to studying Hebrew. I will be the family spokesman. My role as a child, again! An Israeli friend tells me, "We need native English speakers in the high schools. Get a teaching degree."

I can get a degree as a foreign language teacher in a year, taking linguistics courses in "English as a Foreign Language." Rose, a professor of education, arranges for me to sit in on an advanced Spanish course as a refresher.

I realize how burdened Marc feels, for he and Selma's children will be responsible for Father. Still he writes, "I know you've always wanted to go to Israel, but it will be hard without you here. Anyway, you may be able to do something valuable for the deaf community with your linguistic studies. The audiologists' association is holding a conference on teaching language to deaf children. Can you write a paper from the point of view of foreign language teaching and linguistics? There's so much disagreement."

I write the paper, arguing not only for teaching signing, but incorporating any and all ways to acquire language—acting, movement, audiovisual aids. (Later in life, this will become my own path. I will create "Energetics," a movement program for the elderly that combines movement, storytelling, and a practice called kinesiology, which connects specific movements to brain activities.) In the paper, I emphasize teaching grammar, remembering Mother's "unconstructed" thinking.

I will have no inkling of the response to the paper after I move. Nor will I discover a connection to deafness in Israel for some years. Perhaps the paper does make a difference, but for a time, first in Seattle and then in Israel, I forget I am a child of deaf parents.

Betty

In Israel we rent a garden apartment in Holon, a suburb of Tel Aviv with few English speakers. Aliza stays behind in college, while Ben goes to school on a kibbutz, which accepts new immigrants. I help our youngest son Eddie with his lessons. I can read and explain the nature, Bible, and grammar texts. He needs no help with math.

We are blessed with our neighbor, Betty, who immigrated to Israel from Bulgaria in 1948. Every afternoon she invites Eddie over to play with her daughter, just a year younger. Language is not a barrier as they play board games or romp in the small backyard.

Betty is our "absorption ministry." She invites me for coffee in the afternoon, and helps me with my Hebrew lessons in the language class for new immigrants. She arranges for me to give English lessons in the afternoons, collecting her daughter's friends as private pupils. This isn't purely altruistic. She wants her daughter to learn English.

Over coffee we struggle to bridge the language gap. She teaches me to make *bourrekas*, the rich Mediterranean pastries filled with mashed potatoes or cheese. I teach her to make pie crust for an apple pie. She shows me how to mop the stone floors with a rag and a stick with a rubber squeegee on the end, standard housekeeping tools. Her daughter is taking piano lessons, and I sit with her as she practices, helping with simple techniques, as I did in Seattle with my own children.

Father Visits

Father enjoys traveling, for he has the money we gave him, and his wife is well off, but Selma no longer comes along after the accident that left her lame. Now he comes to visit us after an organized tour to the Basketball Tournament of the Deaf in Europe. Betty, my neighbor, invites him for coffee! Although she doesn't speak English, Father's humor is a magic tool, compensating for lack of a common language.

Betty's daughter is practicing the piano when we walk in. "Don't stop," Father tells her, smiling and waving his hand. "I am enjoying the music. You play very well."

Betty grins, knowing he can't hear the music, and Father winks at her. That's a warning I don't catch. Father merrily leading the way, he and Betty take turns insulting me, and I sit between them translating those insults! Father begins, turning to me, "Tell her she has a nice house, nicer than yours." I translate and Betty catches on to his game, replies in Hebrew, "Tell him I know."

Off they go. "Tell her that her daughter is nicer than your children." I translate, she answers, "I know." "Her daughter plays piano better than your children." He compares my coffee and hers, cake, furniture, children. I repeat each insult, each confirmation, and pass it along. His humor is twice as funny, since it's happening in two languages, bridged by their mutual victim, me. They had a wonderful time, without knowing each other's language! I was their hapless but willing victim, and wished he'd never leave.

"Sound and Silence"

My mother loved to dance. Now Deaf dancers are actually on stage in Israel! In 1974 we are living near my friend Ora, in Petah Tikvah, an eastern suburb. She calls, "Come over. There's an article in today's paper about a dance troupe, 'Sound and Silence.'"

This is my introduction to choreographer Moshe Ephrati's dancers. They work in pairs, Deaf dancers paired with hearing, and the hearing dancer leads. Ora and I make a date, go to a performance. We can't tell which dancers hear, as they all flow together on the stage with the music. I watch, pleased and sad, for my mother, the dancer, who never had this opportunity. I imagine her dancing, as she danced for me.

My path will cross with these dancers again. In 1977 I see them rehearsing behind the flat I buy in Tel Aviv, especially a tall, dark, handsome young man—to die for, as the young girls say. He is Amnon Damti, the lead deaf dancer. I will learn he is the son-in-law of an acquaintance. The connection grows between me and deafness again.

Amnon goes on to dance in New York at Lincoln Center, and at the White House. Naomi, his mother-in-law, updates me at the Tel Aviv Community Theatre.

Father Visits Again

In 1980, my father comes to the International Convention of the Jewish Deaf in Israel then stays with me for a month. Selma doesn't come, complaining of the pain in her knees and hands. While I am at work Father sits on the seashore, watching children at play. He returns each day happy and sunburned, wanting to stay in Israel forever, with me, the deaf community, and the sea. But Selma won't come, he knows.

One evening we go to a movie. Since movies in Israel have English translations at the bottom of the screen, Father has no trouble following the plot. "Wonderful! The words on the screen! Let's go to movies every night!"

We leave the theater in the black darkness of a semitropical night, to stand under a streetlight waiting for Father to get his balance. A young woman walks up, and asks Father for the time in Hebrew.

He answers her, "Nine o'clock."

I don't believe it. "How did you know what she wanted?"

He smiles: "It was simple. She was looking at my watch."

I always knew he was sharp! When his visit ends I will miss that too, seeing his cleverness anew.

The Deaf Community

Father takes me to Helen Keller House, the Community Center for the Deaf in Tel Aviv, for a party to mark the end of the convention. The whole community is there. I don't know Hebrew signs— they are even less familiar to me than the American signs—but many of the people here speak English. They are very welcoming to me, ask why I don't come more often.

Why would I do that, I think. I don't know their sign language. The sign language they use in Israel is not the same as American sign, just as the spoken languages differ. I am "deaf" to myself, though I do really belong and do miss their friendliness. Now that I am divorced and my children have returned to Seattle, I am alone in Israel. I miss the opportunity to establish roots in Israel's deaf community. I am cut off, at least for now.

Money

My washing machine breaks down during the visit, and Father offers to buy a new one. I accept, recalling that the money for the machine comes from what Marc and I gave him. He doesn't remember, and I wonder if his memory is failing. I don't worry. Certainly his wife and my brother would know such things.

He's going back soon. Both of us are sad, he at leaving me and Israel, I at being left without family, especially my beloved Father.

Deaf Culture and Music

Deafness does not preclude enjoying and creating music. I've seen the "Sound and Silence" troupe, dancers paired in perfect symbiosis. Suddenly the world seems to be filled with deaf musicians. Why not! Beethoven, the great composer, wrote music after he became deaf.

The ear is an antenna that collects energy vibrations, not only sound. I see a cellist on television who feels the vibrations of her bow and instrument through her feet on the floor. Deaf actresses even star in movies now. Watching *Children of a Lesser God*, I watch deaf children singing and dancing, feeling the music. I pause, remembering Father singing, Mother dancing, alone.

I attend a concert in Tel Aviv by Evelyn Glennie, a stunning young woman from Scotland. She dresses for optimal exposure to vibrations from her instruments, wearing slacks laced together at the sides with lots of skin showing. Glennie is a percussionist, extraordinary, and completely deaf from the age of eleven. Her drumming teacher had her stand outside the room where the drums were playing in order to feel their subtle rhythms and vibrations in and through the walls. She performs on a stage lined with percussion instruments, racing between them, barefoot, to play music composed specifically for her.

Learning Hebrew Sign Language

Storytelling friends in New York are interpreting the stories they tell with signing. I dream of telling stories in sign language and promise myself I'll learn Hebrew signing. I register for a three-month course in signing at Helen Keller House, the community center for the Deaf in Tel Aviv.

Once a week I join a dozen classmates, social workers, and community workers dealing with deaf community services. I'm the oldest student, so several classmates adopt me, touched by my late attempt to acquire signing. We use Hava Savir's textbook of modern sign.

Our born-deaf teacher, Ruthie, conducts the lessons in sign, delightfully and clearly. The best way to learn! I do my homework, feel my fingers wake. I enjoy myself thoroughly. The alphabet is easy, based on the English letter signs. These are the same signs which Father taught me, the signs on the card I still keep with me.

I come to lessons, study, and go with members to gatherings and talks, joining in the deaf world in Israel! It's not easy. I can't freely communicate with limited signs and I am not the ideal age to learn a new language. Still, I am inspired.

After two months of lessons, I can sign *Red Riding Hood*! Food in her basket, wolf, grandma, red, phrases I know! I tell the story, my hands on my head for ears, tripping along with the basket, asking the wolf why he has such big eyes! I have a great time. It's easy, but the students are puzzled. Why did you do that?

My fellow classmates invite me to parties and other gatherings, activities in outlying locations. But the course doesn't give me the tools to become fluent. I need daily practice, and I don't have a car to get out to the deaf community centers regularly. Nor do I know how to find activities closer to my home. Nor do I ask.

Encountering Deafness in Israel

Without a car, I lose that connection to the deaf community, but in 1983 it reappears. I become aware of religious issues around deafness when Miriam, a social worker with broad horizons, calls, "I have an invitation for two to hear a brilliant rabbi who is an expert on medicine and *Halacha*, religious law. You're involved in alternative medicine, so I'm sure the subject will interest you. You know Israel has two legal systems. One is religious, dealing with legal matters from the point of view of ancient sages. The rabbinical judges are meant to interpret those opinions as they relate to present-day life."

She reminds me that I demonstrated the "Touch for Health" system, originally developed by Dr. John Thie, to her and her social work fellows. It is a technique of working directly with our bodies, checking muscle response for health and other issues. It's a relative of sign language, but free of formal language! It comes naturally to me, a way to communicate without words.

Of course I want to go! I thank Miriam, and join her. I don't know that the lecture will be my introduction to the way Jewish law viewed deaf people. A coincidence?

As the rabbi begins, he mentions deafness in Jewish law. "We will study a case involving a mentally defective bridegroom and the question of divorce. However, it focuses more generally, on the general classification of handicapped people, as to whether they are capable of being full members of the Jewish community.

"First, the terminology. A man who is mentally limited in any way is classified as 'handicapped' in *Halacha*. Handicap covers three groups, all limited in understanding: the toddler, the deaf-mute, and the mentally defective."

Clearly the rabbis consider my deaf parents mentally defective. Father was right! I am livid. I will spend years researching the subject, to better understand what "deaf-mute" means in this context. Eventually I find the work of two researchers doing doctoral theses on the subject, stating that the judgment is not clear. The deciding factor is knowledge, which in this case means language. It is clear to me that sign language is language, and raises the religious status of the deaf Jew.

Ella Ill

Larry's brother keeps in touch with Ella. In 1977 he writes, "Ella has cancer on her spine. I take her shopping with me once a week. She comes, carrying pills for her heart, holding onto a cart for support. Now she is dying and wants you. Come at once."

I use my limited funds to buy a ticket, and arrive within a week. Ella is home, lying in bed, motionless and gray. She has gone down to seventy pounds. I'm not sure she is conscious. As I sit beside her, I can tell from my work with body responses that she is not dying of cancer, but malnutrition, caused by the appetite loss from chemotherapy. I give her a tablespoon or two of warm milk with honey every hour. Within two weeks she recovers her strength, gets out of bed, dresses and returns to her daily activities.

The cancer is still painful, but she explains, "So many of my friends have died who played bridge together. I have to get to the games. I'll take a pillow so I can sit without intense pain."

Ella, Jake, and Mildred.

She has responsibilities, her husband and her bridge-playing friends, to get going again. I am amazed at this strong aunt of mine. But, before I return home, she says, "Dee, it was nice of you to come. Here's money toward your plane fare. Twenty-five dollars."

That's all! Twenty-five dollars for the plane trip! (I didn't know at the time that Ella was running out of money.) I don't say a word. Why don't I react like a normal person? Just as my hands can't sign, I'm frozen when I should be furious. Frozen emotions, frozen reactions.

Ella holds out another four years, until she secures a place for her husband in the Jewish nursing home. She lays down and dies, three weeks later. Counting back from my mother's age, I know that she is ninety-one when she dies. I don't grieve. The twenty-five dollar check had been the last straw.

Ella and Jake, getting old.

I admit that Ella did a lot for me. Today I can grieve, knowing I had two mothers in two parallel lives, one in the world of deaf people, and another in the hearing world. After Mother died things were peaceful between Ella and me. She was my children's favorite aunt, and we were a close-knit family.

After I return to Israel, Mildred writes, "I stayed after the funeral to close up the house. In her desk I found Ella's diary, so I'm sending you this Xerox copy."

Now I understand what happened the day in the dorm. And more.

Ella's Diary

Anna ruined my life. I never was freed of my little sister. All the way to America I had to watch her. The time Anna got lost in the forest comes back in nightmares.

They said America would be a Melting Pot, everyone equal, but I was a Jewish immigrant from Eastern Europe, Anna's handicap my handicap too, "Ella with the deaf sister." All my life I was Number Two, right hand to Ma and to Pa. I went to business school, but my younger sisters went to college! When Dee went to college I remembered them going to college, the opportunity I never had. Besides Dee didn't appreciate my planning for her to go away to school. I was sure, if she left home maybe she could get married. The boys there won't see her deaf parents.

But Dee wanted to live at home and go to Marquette nearby on scholarship. She had a boyfriend there too but he wasn't much, short and fat, even if he was studying law. Besides, she couldn't have walked to school—one of the points she made—because we were selling the house! That neighborhood wasn't good enough for Marc, handsome and gifted. No Jewish social life there. It didn't matter for Dee, homely and disagreeable.

I am responsible for everyone and get nothing in return. Dee isn't even grateful, didn't thank me for anything I did for her, even when I sacrificed my privacy, had her family move back in with us so she could go to a better school. She seemed to know the real reason was that her mother could take care of Grandpa and the house since my mother died. She didn't know there was another reason, that Pa was sick of bailing her family out when they had no money for rent.

We had to double up bedrooms, so Dee slept with me in Pa's old double bed. A chance to cuddle my niece, but she slept with her back turned to me, and jumped if I got close. Daytime Dee sat near her mother, guarding her against me. Even when she was an infant her Mother glowered at me, as I taught the child to talk: "No need. I talk fine. Now I feed her. Out!"

Dee never was grateful, even when I took her to lunch and concerts. The money for college was Anna's, but it was in my charge, my responsibility. I saw to it that Dee had a chance to marry, by getting friendly with Larry's parents. I was amazed that they didn't object to her because her parents were deaf, probably because they liked me.

Then she got married and moved far away, so I was left responsible for her mother. When Anna got cancer Sam would not go to the doctor with her. He insisted doctors don't listen to deaf people, and I had to take her. I don't believe she took the pain pills the doctor prescribed but I had no way to find out. She kept the door locked, and wouldn't give me a key. Did she think I wanted to steal something? I could steal money from her trust if I wanted.

I wrote her notes for appointments with the doctor, but she didn't let me in when I came to pick her up. She'd write me a note, that she fell asleep, didn't see the doorbell ring. Then give me a key, I asked, and she never answered. I could have gotten a key by making myself her legal guardian, but she still has a husband, and children. Dee lives on the West Coast, her brother on the East Coast, but both have enough money to come more often. Do they expect me to take care of their mother because I hold her money?

Anna didn't read or sew or crochet when she got sick. She just lay there, having delusions: "Maybe you steal my money." I couldn't even ask how she was before she opened an attack, crazy accusations from the distant past like: "When I bring Emmanuel to visit you flirt with him. That's why he don't marry me." I put the diary away to resume my life.

Turning Around

This announcement in the newspaper sounds interesting. "The Adler Psychoanalytic Institute in Tel Aviv runs a summer program for psychologists from all over the world. English speakers are invited to join them, using Adler's approach to human issues."

I sign up, joining seven other Israelis and eight overseas visitors, all psychologists and social workers except for me. When we introduce ourselves, Naomi says her daughter is married to Amnon Damti, a deaf dancer from Ephrati's "Sound and Silence" dance troupe—the handsome dancer I met on the street! I tell Naomi, "My parents were deaf!"

Zelda, a social worker, asks me, "Do you know Israel Sela? His wife is a teacher of the deaf, who runs Helen Keller House. I'll give you his phone number."

I visited Helen Keller House with Father when he came to Israel, but never returned. I call the Selas, who immediately invite me to their home. Hyper-energetic, pacing the floor, Israel begins, "My parents were deaf. Father was born here. Mother came from Germany, using German sign language. There was no Hebrew sign language, just languages immigrants were bringing from all over the world. Mother created a Hebrew sign language out of all those languages. It has elements of German, the Latin alphabet, Spanish, and juicy phrases. The first sign language was created in Spain, by a Jew!"

He continues, "With her firm convictions and strong will, my mother, and my father, raised the money for Helen Keller House, the center for the deaf in Israel. With their inspiration I studied social work and compiled the first Hebrew sign dictionary. I continue their work, running Helen Keller House.

"Do you know about CODA, Children of Deaf Adults? It's the organization of people like you and me, based in the United States. You should join." He hands me a brochure: "Take this newsletter."

So the Adler Institute brought me to the Selas, back into the world of deaf people, signing up as a member of CODA. A year later Israel calls, rejoicing, "I have a grant to study for a Ph.D. at Gallaudet University in Washington, D.C. My spoken English is weak, but I know American sign. Come visit us in America." He gives me his Washington address.

This connection with deafness in Israel and CODA becomes my bridge between Israel and the deaf community in America.

Going Back

I attend a very different Adler Institute workshop the next summer, with a crop of visitors more inclined to get involved with our lives. When I say my children are in the United States, an Irish psychologist gasps, and turns to me, her green eyes wide in her round freckled face, "How can you stand to be here? Aren't you lonely? Don't you miss your children? Why don't you go back?"

I reply, angry at her nerve, "I do miss my family with a terrible aching, but there's no way I can afford to go back." I go home from the meetings to bad dreams. I cry, angry at the Irish psychologist.

When the Adler group leaves, I am also having money problems, like everyone in Israel. Inflation is spiraling out of control. Business is good, but I have to run to the bank with payments the minute I receive them, for the lira might be devaluated as much as 20 or 40 percent overnight. Then the government threw the money out! Overnight we were presented with a new currency, the shekel, worth ten lira. The value of my money was 10 percent of what it was the night before.

Several months later I wake up grinding my teeth, my fists clenched. The day before I lost 10 percent on a contract because of overnight devaluation. My competitors in English services cut their prices in half since business is bad. This is no way to live.

Then my friend, Roberta, asked the same question as the Irish psychologist, "Why don't you go back? My mother is seventy-eight years old, and she's working part-time as a legal secretary in California for good pay. Employment agencies are desperately looking for word processors, especially legal secretaries. You can easily get work."

Maybe the Irish psychologist was right. I am an expert word processor, a legal secretary. But who will hire a sixty-year-old woman who has never worked in the United States? Still, I have been practicing Transcendental Meditation for ten years, ever since my divorce. It has changed me, given me nerve and courage. I am entitled only to a tiny Israeli pension. Perhaps I should go to the United States for a while. I close my business, lease my apartment to tenants, and buy a one-way plane ticket. In the worst case, I can return to Tel Aviv.

Like the Selas, I set out toward a new life, not knowing it will be in New York, near my father, in the amazing Deaf community of New York City.

America's Deaf World

My first stop in the United States is to see my brother and his family, and then the Selas, who are living near my brother in Washington, D.C. Israel is still excited. "I'm not only studying at Gallaudet. I'm also involved in a synagogue for the deaf nearby—it is a full-time synagogue, meeting every Sabbath and holidays, and holding bar mitzvah ceremonies. This is the opportunity of my lifetime, to learn and to work."

I will say that too, soon.

New York

1985

I write letters to my brother, my children, and Roberta, who sent me to America.

Dear Roberta,

I went no farther than New York City, where my Father lives with Selma, his second wife. My brother gave me a book on signing but it doesn't help much in talking with Selma. My hands feel numb when I try to learn. I think I should take a course, not try to learn from a book, but I don't know where to do that.

Father is eighty-two years old, with a huge stomach. I asked, "How did you get so fat?"

HANDS

1. I saw a film, a blind girl / Touching plants with her hands.
Her hands spoke to her, / Of colors, shapes and textures.
Her hands grasp form, Carry sense, sensation, /
Feel colors for the blind.

The word-dance of the hands,
Sign language, conveys content,
Probes into silence.
Hands toss out the form / Of what they want to say.

2. When I learned to talk I was forbidden to use hand signs.
"They'll see your mother's deaf," / Said Mother's sisters.

Limited to lip-talk, soundless oral speech,
My mouth shaped emptied words,
Formed outlines around sounds which
My parents struggled, probed.

I struggled to convey.
Straining to put feelings / into lip-shaped shells of thought
I EXAGGERATED, grimaced,
    S t r a i n e d and s t r e t c h e d my face
To **MAGNIFY**, to **amplify!** the words they could not hear,
Danced meaning with my mouth / instead of hands.

Now my hands dance—on computer keys
As I remember loneliness, deafness internalized,
A soundless blind spot / Darkening my mind.

"We go out for coffee when we are out walking."

"Just coffee?"

"With a doughnut, just a little something sweet."

"A little, every day? Those doughnuts can kill you," I warn him. His parents died of heart problems. His father was ninety-two, but still it was a heart attack.

I stayed for a few days with a friend. His street-smart girlfriend told me: "Look in *The Village Voice* for digs under 'shares.' They're usually illegal subleases."

Within a week I moved into a sublease, a furnished fifth-floor walkup at the edge of Central Park and Spanish Harlem, on the bus line to Tanya Towers. I speak Spanish to the tenants who are friendly, even protective of me. I commit myself to staying here for three months. Life is making decisions!

You were right. I did find work in New York! Helen, an employment agency interviewer, grew up with the lawyer I worked for in Tel Aviv. She is sending me to temporary jobs.

I'll keep you updated.

Next I report to Roberta:

Connections are making a difference. An old friend suggested, "If you're looking for a regular job try the Jewish Theological Seminary. You are active in their movement and you know Hebrew."

A tangent I never considered—a regular job, staying on in New York. I contacted the seminary personnel manager, who gave me that "look," seeing an elderly lady. Then she said, "We do need someone with skills in Hebrew and English, and you know computer word processing. You'd be a valuable addition to our staff, since none of us knows anything about computers. Besides, you can set up a research center for our professors and guest professors from Israel. We'd like to hire you."

I accepted the job, on the condition that I am equipped with a computer. Yet I found only a typewriter when I report to work. I began nudging until my new friend, the librarian, suggests, "I have an unused computer with a Hebrew-English program. You can come in to use it whenever you want."

Such a warmhearted welcome, and such chutzpah I show! I am out of my office, in the library half days with a note on my door, "Using the computer in the library." I am getting my own computer next week. Did meditation make me so feisty?

One of the job benefits is that I can take courses free, even during working hours! So I am continuing my masters degree in education.

With love,

I write to my children after a year in New York:

Sorry I haven't found time to visit you. Here is a change of address, a studio apartment near the seminary with a legal lease. I am making friends among faculty and staff. Visiting professors from Israel make my office their home. Joe Lukinsky, a professor of education, has become my good friend and mentor, sending me to workshops in alternative ways of teaching, like storytelling, journaling, and psychodrama. I never heard of these methods before. Being in New York is a revelation!

I'm also taking courses with famous professors, psychologists, nurses, and physicians, a continuation of the "Touch for Health" work I learned in 1982. With a good position, friends, and learning opportunities, I'm not going back yet. Especially, being close to my father, I see signs of aging that concern me. He can't take the bus to visit me because he has to urinate frequently, even as often as twenty minutes. I am arranging to take him to the doctor as he doesn't trust interpreters.

At least you and I can talk by telephone within the country, so stay in touch.

Love, Mother

I write to Roberta the next summer,

It's over a year since I came to New York. I learned my way around the city, from the Lower East Side where Father lives to the area around the Seminary on the Upper West Side where I live and work. In Central Park I'm learning racewalking with a new friend, Linda, a sunny native New Yorker who lives near me. When I said I was here from Israel she was excited, "I love Israel, and am glad I met you. I have relatives and friends who come from there. We can be good friends. I'll show you around and take you places."

Linda is showing me the ins and outs of New York, like what days museum visits are free. Most important! Because of Linda I'm writing again. She called one evening, "There's a notice in the newspaper from the International Women's Writing Guild. They're looking for candidates to be their Woman of the Year. You're such a hero, living in Israel, coming here at sixty, your deaf parents, everything. Call them. I'm sure you'll win."

I didn't see myself as their woman, but joined the guild, which encourages women writers. I'm writing poems, short stories, and memoirs on my office computer, with official permission, coming in early and staying late. Back from the guild's summer workshop at Skidmore College I am continuing in a writing group in the city called "Writing Out of Your Life." The teacher is a Holocaust survivor who wrote a book about her years hidden in Holland during the war. She had to stay in bed for nearly two years, so no one would hear her footsteps in the attic room. She was eight when she got out of bed at the end of the war, and had to learn to walk all over again.

Last night a story I call "Shame" exploded out of my pen, memories from my childhood. I didn't intend to write it! So strange, like reentering my life.

With love,

Years later, in Israel, I meet the workshop teacher's niece, who turns out to be a relative of an elderly friend of mine, also a survivor from Holland.

In 1988 I write to Marc:

With the help of Seminary staff I found a pleasant apartment in walking distance of work, and the rent is reasonable. It's a long-term lease, so I'm staying on in New York. For Father's sake. His health is worrisome, and he is quite dependent on me. After all these years of separation!

Note the new address and phone number

Love, your sister

Chapter 6. New York

In my life there has been an empty space, the world of deafness. I am now finding my place in that world.

I write to Roberta and my brother about Deaf society in New York.

Dear Roberta,

This move to New York seems heaven-sent, because of the good job and its benefits, and being with my father. I spend Saturdays with him. His wife Selma is in constant pain, her face drawn and gray, since she was run over by a driver who thought she could hear! As her hand that holds the cane grows more arthritic she leaves vacuuming and cleaning for Father. So Father is caring for an invalid wife again! After all his dreams.

Today Father took me for a walk near his apartment. "See," he said, "how bad the neighborhood is now, even worse than we moved in. We can't go out at night, and you can't come after dark. The empty lots across the street are where people burned down buildings in the summer riots. See those bums on the corner—drug dealers. They use that burned-out building for business, sit here all day on broken furniture, drinking beer and liquor. Terrible. How can they ask the Deaf to live here?"

The state of the area is shocking. Clearly motives other than concern for the handicapped led the city to build Tanya Towers on Thirteenth

Sam's extended family at his eightieth birthday celebration. Sam standing center, surrounded.

Street. Who else would agree to live there? That old refrain, "not as good, don't need as good," Deaf and physically handicapped lumped together!

I react like that every time I see injustice against deaf people, especially my father and his wife.

I write my brother that winter,

Father needs me so often. How did he manage before I came to New York? He writes me notes every week to make and change meeting times and doctor appointments, to take care of matters that were waiting. I settled a double billing from *Readers' Digest*, and called Sears' service department to repair the air conditioner that had not worked for three years. Why did it wait for me?

Phoning from Tanya Towers is impossible. The superintendent removed the pay phone in the lobby of Tanya Towers because someone was making long distance calls and charging them to Tanya Towers. Father grimaced when I asked about leaving messages, "No. The supervisor doesn't like to be bothered."

I've been making phone calls for Father from the payphone in the street, dialing with frozen hands, in wind and snow. I didn't know that the New York Society for the Deaf provides TTY service until Nelly, Father's next-door neighbor, asked me to come see her phone. She has a TTY Telex typewriter, which sends and receives messages through a telephone line. When the phone rings a signal lights up, and the machine types both incoming and outgoing messages.

Nelly, a second-generation born-deaf woman, lives with her mother next to Father and Selma, and teaches sign language to deaf immigrants at the Emanuel YMHA nearby. She told me, "Call me to give your parents a message." But I need a teletype machine too to do that. I suggested I buy one for Father but Selma said no.

Will keep you posted, with love,

Dear Marc,

Last week Father suggested, "Meet me at the Ambrosia Restaurant near our apartment. Selma won't mind if she doesn't have to cook for you." I visit Father regularly at the restaurant, our second home on Fifteenth Street, close to the Emanuel Y, the meeting place of the Deaf Club. It's the perfect Greek restaurant, serving huge portions of delicious food cheap. Since the Deaf community eats there, the waiters picked up sign language. Pete, a chubby young waiter, knows everyone's name, and knows sign as well. Father always sits at his table and tips him well.

Most important, there is something new! At the Emanuel Y, the Reform Rabbinical Seminary now conducts Sabbath morning services for the Deaf. I love to attend these monthly prayer services with Father and Selma. Picture Father joyfully singing in the "choir." He lamented for years, never dreamed he would have a place to pray.

As I watch the signing of the prayers I'm learning to read—but still not use—more signs, and feel a part of the community. Moshe, an elderly resident whose parents gave him a bar mitzvah and a Jewish education, is an invaluable aide to the student rabbi. Although the rabbi makes an effort to learn sign, he insults his elderly congregation, talking to them as if they are incapable of understanding. But it is he who doesn't understand them.

This fledging congregation doesn't always understand the prayers either. I was watching the choir, tracking the psalms in my book, and stopped short. What a gaffe! The English translation was "You shall smite my foes," but the choir leader had never seen the word "smite." So, since it looked like a familiar word it became: "Smile at my foes." I had a hard time keeping a straight face. Well, there is power in a smile!

Love, your sister.

Daughters of Deaf Parents

In November, I write to Roberta.

Just returned from a trip to Illinois for Selma's birthday celebration. Her daughter is welcoming to all of us, warm, and knows so much about the world of the Deaf. Their birthday gift was a new device—a "caption channel" control. It's a TV set-top box which imposes subtitles on programs marked "CC" in the TV schedule.

Selma is now following soap operas and educational programs with the caption channel, on the large black-and-white set, while Father watches his beloved baseball uncaptioned on the small color set in the corner. Selma prefers educational programs, to learn more than basic skills taught at the state school. I remember my mother lying ill in bed with no company except a silent-to-her television set. The world is expanding for deaf people.

Yours, D.

That winter I report,

Dear Roberta,

I'm becoming WHOLE, being an active CODA. That stands for "Children of Deaf Adults." Awareness of the deaf community is growing. JoAnne Greenberg's book *In This Sign*—about the little girl whose brother was killed—was the Hallmark Theater Christmas production on television. I videotaped that performance, but I can't look at the part where Brad falls. It's too close to my own memories.

I joined the New York chapter of CODA, and discovered the camaraderie of "brothers" proud of their identity. Daughters of deaf parents, many of them Jewish, are writing autobiographies about their lives with deaf parents. All of them used sign language with their parents. Not like me.

Lou Ann Walker came to a CODA meeting to promote her autobiography, *A Loss for Words*. Just as I was expanding "Shame" into a book! I stopped writing because I don't believe there is a market for me if she has already published a book about life with deaf parents. My identity isn't that clear. It's like I'm half a child of deaf parents, half a child of mother's family. Anyway, writing is an interesting experience.

It's midnight, so that's it for tonight. I'm using my new skill, "journaling," in writing, to create, and record, *imaginary* dialogues with people in my life, "letting them speak." It opens up completely different viewpoints.

Yours,

A letter to Roberta from 1988

Did you read about the student rebellion at Gallaudet University of the Deaf in Washington, D.C.? The students went on strike when the college board installed a new president with no knowledge of sign language, unaware of the issues of deaf students.

What an exciting time for the Deaf community! The strike is succeeding, for King Jordan of the teaching staff was appointed the first deaf president of the university! More than one hundred years after sign language was banned by hearing teachers in Milan, it is receiving legitimacy in teaching and communication at Gallaudet.

I met Jordan at our last CODA meeting. He's young, athletic, good-looking, poised. His speech is clear, his tone and diction pleasant and easy on the ear, and he easily lipreads. Gone is the stereotype of deaf/dumb born-deaf who cannot be understood nor understand.

Closing, in a very UP mood,

Dee

Around the same time, I write my brother.

It must be an exciting time for you living near Washington with the Gallaudet revolution. Do your audiology acquaintances follow what is happening?

In New York City too, things are happening. It seems that the renaissance of the deaf community is everywhere! At the Museum of Natural History I saw Simon Carmel, a deaf-mute professor, lecture with an interpreter on "Deafness as Culture." Carmel teaches at the Rochester Institute of Technology (RIT), in Rochester, New York, which complements Gallaudet's focus on liberal arts, teaching, and a liberal education. RIT is the only college of technological education for deaf students, their MIT.

The museum recognizes deafness as "culture" since it invited Carmel to speak. The lecture took place in the framework of "The Anthropology of the Deaf Community." It is fashionable now for sociologists and anthropologists to redefine deafness as a sociolinguistic subgroup. That's going a bit far, but new ideas are often extreme. I've seen the museum's exhibits of African tribes, Buddhist monks sculpturing butter, and Japanese tea ceremonies. Deafness a foreign culture, like an African tribe? Well, that's better than being looked down on, I guess.

I read Carmel's signs as the interpreter translated. Carmel was describing his work setting up a definitive American Sign Language and an international sign language. Afterwards, when I spoke to him through his interpreter, I learned he worked with Israel Sela, creating a definitive Israeli sign language, and that he did graduate work at Tel Aviv University!

Carmel is informative and entertaining. He tells jokes, like the one about differences in Israeli, German, and American sign. Holding his hands up, palms facing, he stood the first finger on each hand up, "facing" one another. That is "face to face" in English. He then held up the first two fingers on each hand, for the same phrase in German—showing two eyes on each hand. He capped that by holding up the first finger on one hand and two on the one facing it, Moshe Dayan, with his eye patch!

Later a friend called, back from a visit to Ethiopia, "I had a funny experience. I knew there was a deaf community in Addis Ababa and sought them out, wondering whether I could communicate with them, at least through an interpreter. In a very pleasant meeting with the group the interpreter told them I was from Israel. I asked them if they had a sign for Israel, and they grinned, then put a hand over the eye where Dayan wears a patch!"

Carmel interlaced "deaf jokes" through the speech, some of them true stories. He told of two deaf boys on a bus conversing in sign. The man sitting behind them stared, watched, and finally passed them a note asking if they could read. The boys read the note and scribbled an answer, "No, but I can write." Carmel guesses he confused deafness with deaf and blind, knowing only of Helen Keller.

My favorite stories of those he told are about a true encounter of young people in a restaurant, and a "legend" of a woodcutter who cuts deaf trees!

How did I find out about this talk? I happened to pick up a flyer in the museum. I didn't see any notice in the newspaper. Some of his former students and college-age members of the community heard directly from Carmel, and contacted a few friends. They stood out in the smallish audience, signing to one another across the hall. "How did you know about this?" "My brother at RIT wrote to me." "Good you came."

The museum staff had not notified any Deaf organizations or schools of the event, so I contacted their office, recommending organizations for the Deaf to contact, and suggesting making an interpreter available for future lectures of all kinds. Nothing was done. There is so much to do to develop awareness and understanding.

Love,

I write my brother shortly after.

I attended a talk by a lecturer from RIT. She lost her hearing as an adult, and still speaks in a clear, modulated voice. Monitoring her tone through feedback, she sets up a closed-loop audio system which creates a "field" about the audience. As questions and comments come through her combination microphone-hearing aid terminal, she can hear us and herself, conducting a dialogue. Awesome!

Computers, teletype telephones, so many devices that can be adapted and used for and by the Deaf! I know you too are developing programming and related materials for teaching teachers and professionals in the field.

I'm also reading books in the public library about deafness and by deaf authors. I love the "deaf poetry" quoted in such books. It's visual in its descriptions. I am blessed to be here, in this time of breakthrough.

Father's Illness

Worried about Father, I write to my brother:

Joe Lukinsky, my mentor at the seminary, is opening new ways in teaching and learning to me. I am studying towards certification in Dr. Ira Progoff's Intensive Journal Method® of transpersonal journaling. His staff director is entranced with the idea that I will teach these workshops in Israel, so they give me the courses without charge.

This way of writing, by listening to my inner voice, is a powerful tool for self-understanding and development. The three months I planned to be in New York have become three years of work, learning, and responsibility.

I continually worry about Father. His health is deteriorating, his illness exacerbated because he is unable to make himself understood in the health service. I worry even more after he told me, 'You know I fell out of bed when I was seven. Now I jump in my sleep and fall out of bed again."

It sounds to me like possible small strokes, like the ones his mother suffered. He clearly needs a medical checkup. The Society for the Deaf provides a translator for visits to doctors, but Father doesn't have patience for that. In fact, he doesn't seem to have patience for anything, or anyone. I am arranging to go to the doctor with him.

When I pick him up at his apartment I am shocked. He suddenly lost weight, but the doctor says it's nothing! I come up with a temporary solution: "Father, put chairs next to the bed so you won't fall and hurt yourself."

Medical care for the elderly is poor altogether, worse for deaf people! I asked the doctor about Father's trouble holding urine, for he no longer can take a bus trip longer than twenty minutes. The urologist recommends a prostate operation, but warns: "Any operation presents some danger for men your father's age. There may be complications, so consider that."

Selma is not capable of (nor interested in) dealing with Father's medical problems, so I am consulting with you. You have so much good sense. What do you advise?

Love, Your sister

I don't know yet that Father's extreme impatience is a symptom of strokes. Father has always complained that doctors don't listen to the Deaf. I am learning that he was right.

Marc decides: "Possible danger is outweighed by Father's discomfort. Arrange for the operation."

The operation goes off without immediate problems, but a few months later, Father is showing signs of aging. The notes he writes me are hard to read. He has fits of anger, attacks his neighbors. Selma can't tolerate these rages, and does not understand what is going on. I do research and tell my brother, "Fits of temper are a symptom of electrical disturbances in the brain, like strokes. So are his headaches."

"You're not a doctor," he retorts. My brother doesn't take my competence seriously, though I have been studying alternative approaches for nearly ten years. But a month later he calls me, frantic, "The superintendent at Tanya Towers called me to say: 'Your father is shaking and trembling. He looks terrible.' He called me because Selma doesn't have your phone number, and Father is shaking so much he is unable to give it to her. Please check it out now. I'm coming as fast as I can."

I rush over. Father is lying in bed, moaning and crying, shaking all over, his legs cramping. He weeps, "My legs won't hold me up."

A neighbor with a teletype phone calls a taxi, and I carry my father down the stairs. I can do that because he has lost so much weight. We ride the mile to Beth Israel Hospital's emergency room, where the attendant checks Father at once, and says, "His heart is in fibrillation, and he may die within the hour without shock therapy, though I must warn you that he may not recover from the damage he's sustained, and the shock. Shall we shock him or let him go?"

I cannot make such a decision alone. When Marc arrives an hour later we agree to have Father's heart jumpstarted. Father is wheeled away, Marc leaves me with him and goes home! Father may not live, but he goes off! I promise to call him every night. Since I have three days' vacation from work for *Shevuoth,* the Feast of Weeks, I sit beside Father, watching the irregular, weak lines on the monitors.

Selma doesn't come to the hospital. "What good to sit," she says. "He's asleep." She doesn't seem to care. I know she is worn out from her own pain, from Father's tempers and constant falling out of bed.

As Father lies in his coma, I sit in his room alone. I consider alternative techniques I know, and wonder: Why not do some simple healing? I try using reflexology, a technique that stimulates the feet in order to trigger electrical impulses in the nervous system. I begin to stroke his feet gently, and it seems to me he stirs. Stroking his cold feet, though I am barely touching him, the monitors show a stabilization of his heart beat. Like a violinist sensitive to his instrument, I am tuning into my father. The silent communication we built all our lives is a healing tool.

The next day I use a technique called polarity, working with the body as a "battery." Cupping my hands near his ears, I move my hands closer and away, gently, in a pulsing movement. Then—Father opens his eyes and asks, in a clear voice: "What am I doing here?"

Father "heard" me! Energy absorbed through the natural antenna, the ears, brought him back.

Breakthrough

I am studying the Jewish mystics with a professor from Israel, learning about techniques of connecting to cosmic power. At home, practicing Transcendental Meditation, I think of the Kabbalistic ways of meditation. Jeshurun Synagogue has a stained glass window with the Star of David. I can meditate on that, rather than the Sanskrit mantra that I don't understand.

I close my eyes and see that star, but I have forgotten that the letters of the "unpronounceable name," the four-letter name of God that Jews are forbidden from speaking, are printed across the star. A bolt of light hits me, seeming to penetrate my skull. It is a cold blue light, the color of electric sparks, the cosmic force called *hashmal* that the prophet Elijah saw as "fire from heaven." I try to scream as my body jumps, shakes, vibrates. Electricity is running through my body, into my arms and legs. I am being electrocuted. Is it punishment from beyond for using the holy Name?

I don't know how long I struggle and pray. When I open my eyes everything feels the same! No changes in my body, nothing. Medical literature describes this feeling as a symptom of a massive stroke, but I suffer no after-effects. Now I realize that there is something beyond our daily ken, and that I have awakened it in my meditation. I no longer "believe" in the possibility of something more, something Beyond. I KNOW.

Terrified, I phone the professor of Kabbala, who isn't skeptical, but instead is sympathetic, "A friend of mine is here who is creating an image of the legendary golem for the Jewish Museum. He understands dreams and unexplainable experiences. I'll send him to your office in the morning."

"Happens to be here?" It's more than coincidence that this man is in New York.

The next morning his friend, tall, heavy, and reassuring, comes to my office. He puts me at ease as he explains: "What happened to you is not unusual. Many people experience unexplainable events and don't talk about them, since our society considers it lunacy. But it's not, not unless it happens daily—or one thinks it makes him or her a super-being. Most of these experiences are ecstatic. Perhaps yours was frightful since you made the connection in the way you perceive things. Our own perspective may determine what we see."

The way I perceive things? Fear, fright? Of course.

He explains that I have formed a possibly lasting connection beyond the ordinary. In the future I may have occasions, even extended periods, when things "happen," but it is not a sign of insanity. "You emptied your energy into your father while healing him. Like the Kabbala legend of the beginning of time, you were a vacuum, so the cosmic Light entered freely, not held to the usual limits of our physical systems.

"How it happens, in my experience, has to do with deep love transcending one's "reasoning" with intuition. You loved your Father 'with all your heart, soul, and might,' like the prayer. In your love and concern you forgot the limits that we are forbidden to use our own energy, only to pass energy through for healing to take place."

I live with fear of that Light for two years, staying away from anything to do with healing, until a Chinese Master of Chi Kung (a Chinese system of yoga and meditation) comes to New York. I practice and learn a technique called "moving meditation," which creates a protective shell around me, relieving my fear. Ever since then I continue to do Chi Kung nearly every morning.

Waking Father

Father remains conscious and lucid, so he and I begin to work with gentle Alexander and kinesiology movements. The Alexander Method is a system for correcting problems in his posture, and kinesiology relates specific movements to brain activity. While I guide his hands, to touch his left knee with his right hand, then right knee with left, the nurse peeks in and asks what I am doing.

I explain: "I am reconnecting his neural network, teaching him natural walking motions, guiding him gently. Though he's still weak, he concentrates on what I'm teaching him. He can already sit in a chair and stand. Maybe he remembers that he re-educated his body to walk when he lost his hearing. Now I need a walker, so he can practice walking."

She says: "That's not allowed without doctor's orders," but watches, amazed, as he begins the exercise without my help.

Father grins and says: "What's next?"

She relents: "I'll see what I can do." A walker is waiting beside his bed the next day.

Within ten days he is on his feet, with assistance. When Marc comes to pick us up, and Father walks out of the hospital with the walker, the nursing staff runs after me, shouting: "What did you do? Stay here and teach us!"

I reply: "I have five tools—two eyes, two ears, and a heart. Love and caring are the strongest components of healing. Dr. Dolores

Krieger does this work at New York University Hospital. Contact their School of Nursing." I don't realize that I can indeed teach them. I think that what I did was only for my own father.

Farewell to Tanya Towers

I tell Marc: "Father is still very weak from the pounding his body's taken. Now I understand what was happening, so I can help him recover. We can arrange for a nursing aide, and I'll come after work."

When Marc conveys my request to Selma she glares, signing to Marc: "No room for more people, only one bedroom. I have pain, can't take care of sick. I go to my daughter now."

I've already heard these threats to leave him. I know that she has stopped cooking, and that Father has to do the laundry and the cleaning. Is she really walking out on her husband of eighteen years when he is so ill? It seems that she is. She will leave in just two days, giving us only a polite goodbye when her granddaughter comes to take her to the airport.

I try another angle. "While Selma is gone I'll stay in the apartment, hire a day attendant, and keep you informed."

Marc is clearly upset by the nurses' reaction to me at the hospital. He mutters something that sounds like "witch," turns sharply and answers, "Healing? Are you a doctor? I'm taking Father home with me. If he stays here he's all your responsibility. Yours. Totally. I will have nothing to do with his care."

Do I understand him? Maybe he thinks it's my turn, considering the years I lived in Israel, leaving him the burden of our Father. Stunned, I answer, "I can't continue healing Father if he is so far away. You know I'm barely making ends meet, and in two more years I will be sixty-five and pensioned off to return to Israel. I can't assume full responsibility."

Marc glares at me. "Responsibility? Why did the supervisor have to call me when Father was sick? Where were you?"

We will finish that conversation much later.

After brief farewells to the neighbors, Marc takes Father to his home in the countryside. There Father sits alone in his bedroom, while Marc and his wife are at work. He cries, grieving for Selma, who writes him a postcard now and then. Marc and the doctors say he is crying because he is senile. Then Marc sends Father to a daycare center, where there are no other deaf people and no one knows how to communicate with him.

I take the train to visit Father on his first weekend at Marc's, the first of many such trips that will come to replace visits to my own children. Father's bedroom is in the back, down the hallway, past the kitchen and living room. As I step through the front door, Father senses my presence at the other end of the house. "Dee, it's you," he calls out happily. Marc stares, then runs out of the room, as if he sees a witch.

Father is overjoyed to see me. He talks and talks, about loneliness in the countryside, about Selma leaving him, about being sick. He cries, and so do I, when the weekend is over and I return to work. I promise to come next weekend.

On my next visit my brother announces: "I took over legal guardianship for Father, to handle his finances, and make decisions. I canceled his apartment lease."

I ask: "Without consulting with me? Why? Now Father has no home to return to. Don't you have any faith that he may recover?"

The unspoken answer is clear from the way he glares at me, as he begins: "Now you show up! From the time you left for university you left all the responsibility for our parents for me, and that meant fighting with Ella about money too. When you arrived in New York you asked me why you had to take care of so many things undone.

"I did my best but I live in Washington, and I have my family and work too. There is a professional staff at Tanya Towers and one at the Association for the Deaf in the Y. I contacted them for help, and they asked Father to come in. He refused. He said he doesn't trust hearing people, or that Selma wouldn't let anyone interfere, one excuse after another.

"You have some nerve, showing up when you're sixty years old. You wander from one rental to another, and we don't know how long you'll manage to keep your job. You tell me you don't have money, so how can you take care of Father's needs? You make me laugh, with your hocus-pocus 'healing.' It didn't prevent Dad's stroke. You are out of touch with reality!"

He takes a deep breath: "Where were you when Selma had her accident? When have you ever come to visit to be helpful, not just as a tourist? It's been very difficult for us, me and all my family, with you away. Everything on my shoulders. Don't complain. Be grateful I took charge."

Grateful? This is just like Ella, all over again!

Further Light

The Light left a connection, like a wall outlet, waiting for something to plug itself in. It's not constant, and it happens unannounced. "Coincidences," like a friend calling as I lift the phone to call her. It seems Father and I are connected. Sometimes I feel a sharp tap on my left upper arm, as if he is calling. We always communicated without words. Maybe it's built-in.

My journal work seems to be about rewriting my life! Ideas surface during meditative writing, knowledge that seems to come from my depths. Things happen. Writing is bringing people back to life!

In November a poster across from the seminary advertises "Instant Enlightenment by Master from Viet Nam, at Teachers College." I won't miss that, even though I don't believe the claim.

The lecture hall is filled, with a large contingent from Columbia's department of Buddhist studies. "Master" is a tiny woman who is sitting on a wooden table on the stage, legs folded. She tells of her synthesis of the religions she learned from one set of Buddhist grandparents and one set of Catholic grandparents.

Then she instructs: "Instant Enlightenment? It's so simple. Just stop eating animal flesh and go on a vegetarian diet. Start now, and return to the next lecture in twenty-four hours."

Sounds too easy, but I eat salad, nuts and vegetable soup, and return the second day.

"Now we begin," Master instructs: "Just close your eyes as I speak. If you see or hear something write it down to share when we finish."

I'm relaxed, facing the stage, eyes closed. As in a dream, I see a flying carpet coming in from the left backstage wing of the stage, and on it sits my mother! She turns, smiles at me, and the carpet flies off into the right wing!

Time for comments and questions: A religious Jew saw Jesus. A Catholic saw the Buddha. One after another tells of sounds, sensations, and visions. I ask, "What does it mean, that vision of my mother?" and Master smiles: "You have released your mother's spirit from her unhappiness."

That would fulfill a dream—Mother happy at last.

The Path to Stories

While Father is in the nursing home, I am writing stories from my life and sharing them with a writing group. "Baby Cry," a bitter memory, bursts onto paper.

I also attend Paula Oleska's "Brain Gym" movement course, using specific exercises to accomplish personal goals. It becomes a framework to bring together Chi Kung, "Therapeutic Touch," "Touch for Health," writing, journaling, and studying for my master's degree.

When my friend Joe invites me to a lecture at the Jewish Story-telling Center, I discover a program to develop the newly reborn ancient art of storytelling. I hear traditional folktales and meet people telling stories about their lives. I join the New York City Storytelling Center, in a loft on Union Square, ornamented with origami foldings. Our inspirational hostess, Lillian Oppenheimer, nearly ninety years old, refurbished this loft when she was eighty-six, as a workshop for origami, puppetry, and storytelling.

Here, with supportive critique and training from veteran story-tellers, I am ready to tell my own story, which I call "Can You Hear Me?" But I'm not ready emotionally. It's a story I wrote, but I never "felt." Facing an audience I am thrown backwards in time, reliving my childhood. Shaking and sweating, my voice trembles, weak and wavering, as I begin: "I want to invite you into my home, to meet my deaf parents."

I incorporate my poem, "Hands:"

> " . . . forbidden to use hand signs
> . . . I strained and stretched my face . . .
> danced words upon my lips instead of hands."

As I tell the story, everything breaks loose inside. No longer dumb, I speak out, proudly, about my deaf parents, bringing fifty people into my story. Everything comes together in my storytelling, in me, and for the audience. I am no longer dumb, no longer ashamed.

Rae, a veteran storyteller, asks: "You end with your Father signing the prayer 'Hear O Israel.' Can you sign that prayer? That would be very moving."

I can't, but I will. On my next visit to Father I ask him to teach me the prayer in sign. I take photographs. They are my last photographs of Father, happy and smiling, his eyes alight as he sings at the top of his lungs, signing: "Hear O Israel, the Lord our God the Lord is one. Praised be His glorious name for ever and ever."

Sam reciting the prayer "Hear O Israel."

Those photographs hang on my wall, as if we continue to pray together. I can sign the prayer now.

Stories As Our Own Life

After I have been in New York nearly five years, Father's health begins rapidly declining. My job at the seminary is completed, since the professors now have their own computers. My brother is traveling, and he transfers Father to a nursing home inaccessible for me by train.

Time to go home. I resign my job, give up my apartment lease, and tell my tenants in Israel to vacate. Back home I can collect a little Social Security to augment my small income, and use my new skills, Journaling, writing, and Storytelling, to teach tell and write. I book a flight home.

Storydrama

I round out my New York life attending Mimesis leadership training with Sam Lauechli, professor of religion at Temple University, and his wife, Dr. Evelyn Rothschild-Lauechli, a family therapist. They integrate psychodrama with traditional myths, fairy tales, and legends, by adapting them to our contemporary lives.

I travel to the first session near Philadelphia by train. Lauechli picks me up at the station, where he introduces me to a tall, thin, sandy-haired young man: "Dee, meet Hans, who came from Germany to study with us." He turns to Hans: "Dee is returning to Israel soon after we complete the course."

Hans stares hard at me, turns, and begins an animated conversation with Sam in German, closing me out. When we arrive at the workshop center Hans stares at me, again turns away. I'm uncomfortable.

Babel

We meet for the first of nine sessions, taking time to get acquainted. Hans has been studying for the Protestant ministry. Other participants work in social services or psychology. Lauechli explains that this Mimesis "playing" comes from hidden inner truth. As we "play" with legends, they reverberate with our lives and dreams. Then, not necessarily now, things become clear.

In our first session we relate the Tower of Babel story to communication problems. We set up a scenario—two passengers who do not speak the same language seated together in a plane. Sam says: "Let's make it real. Who speaks a language no one else in the room understands?"

Since I speak Hebrew, and another participant, Steve, speaks Japanese, we are chosen to communicate without using English. We try out several languages, find we both speak French, though mine is rusty. Steve sits rigidly, and begins a polite conversation about weather and other trivial matters. After a struggle to keep going, I feel: This is empty talk, a *lack* of communication.

I say in French: "Excuse me. I want to sleep," and end the playing.

Bedlam, a real Tower of Babel! Shouts, bitter reactions; loudest of all is Hans, shouting, "Don't stop! You'll spoil everything."

Spoil what? There was no communication, I answer. We are playing out of our lives, unconsciously, but I don't get it yet. That WAS my communication in childhood, no understanding, no communication.

Thanksgiving Dinner

In the second session, we enact a family Thanksgiving dinner. Sam warns that lack of structure will have consequences in our playing, even create havoc. Everyone chooses roles; I choose to be grandmother after most other roles are already chosen. Hans gleefully jumps in: "Then I am the grandfather. I am hard of hearing."

He knows my parents were deaf! He spends this skit annoying me, pretending not to hear me. Is he acting, or re-acting to me? I'm uncomfortable, don't know what to make of it. Do I have any memories of Thanksgiving? Not yet.

Medea

In the next session a woman psychologist plays a modern Medea. She says she is playing herself, an Italian toughie from Philadelphia's south side, real Mafia. As a psychologist her Medea murders her children's souls, not killing them outright.

In the session after that, Medea's children are now adults. I remember an earlier session when Sam's wife Evelyn told a story of a suicidal girl, feel it fits, and ask to play the daughter. Hans immediately chooses to play my brother. Again, choosing to react with me?

In my role, I dolefully proclaim: "Medea wished I were dead, so I am lying in the hospital. I cut my wrists to sacrifice myself, to fulfill Mother's wish that I were dead." It's based on the story Evelyn told, but I don't remember that it was once *my* Thanksgiving story, when Mother wanted my firstborn.

In turn Hans describes himself: "I'm a cold-blooded Italian Mafia gangster from the inner city, like my mother. I've killed a lot of people. Killing means nothing to me." Murmurs of "Of course, yes. Mafia."

German Hans a Mafioso? I wonder aloud: "Hans, are you Mafia, or a Nazi?"

He looks at me, hard, but no one reacts. Instead they turn to me, one after another, to "reason me" out of the suicidal mood. Their words sound false, superficial. I was feeling that young woman inside me from years ago. No one could reach me until Evelyn asked, "Are you willing to talk to your brother?"

"I am always willing to talk to my brother," I reply, thinking of the situation in Israel, of Jews and Arabs who don't talk to one another. I turn to Hans.

He looks at me, and speaks, his voice quiet, slow and loaded with pain: "I've been watching you, my sister. Whenever the nurses leave, you run to the bathroom to reopen your wounds. You've been doing it for years, to continue to get sympathy." He lowered his eyes and continued. "You cannot imagine the terrible agony your suffering causes me, because I could not prevent it."

Now I know what is happening between us! At the seminary I have met young Germans seeking spiritual expiation for the sins of their fathers. I am, for Hans, the Jewish People. Is he making expiation to me for the Holocaust? My heart goes out to his suffering. I hear Evelyn's voice, asking me: "Do you still feel suicidal?"

I have forgotten my role, my suffering so small against Hans's. "I'm fine, I have no problems," I answer.

That night I dream of King Solomon's judgment; two women pulling at one child, tearing his soul from limb to limb. Awakening is happening deep within, though I still do not recall my own Thanksgiving thoughts of suicide when Mother wanted my child!

Closing a Circle

The workshop ends. I head home, to war. The playing, storytelling, and writing close a circle, and I am beginning to understand Mother. I released her unhappiness at Master's workshop. I reached freedom to love her, from playing, then remembering, and then writing. Writing with love, writing free. It took time, but it did happen.

Chapter 7. New Worlds

I return to Israel at the end of 1990, although my friends worry: "You can't go back. The Mideast is heading into war. Wait until things are better."

Things don't get better in Israel, I tell them. When I return to my apartment in Tel Aviv, life is at a standstill. Three weeks later Scud missiles fall. War begins. Radio and television are broadcasting the warning *sound* of the siren, without visible messages! The deaf community is in a state of panic, with no way of knowing what is happening. It takes over a week until a signing interpreter gives warning instructions in a corner of the television screen.

Teaching in Wartime

Israelis are fleeing Tel Aviv, leaving the country. The roads are deserted except for buses heading away from Tel Aviv. In my building only three of us remain. Stubborn or foolish, craving my computer, I stay to unpack my lift, delivered the day before. Through plastic sheeting on the window—supposedly to protect me from poison gas—I see the glare of exploding missiles less than three miles away, on Abba Hillel Street.

Day after day, for two dread-filled weeks, the Scuds don't let up. At every warning I run to my bedroom, my "sealed room." I sit on the floor with the bed between me and the windows for protection, writing furiously in my journal. Meditations, poems, stories, deep thoughts. And nightmarish dreams. The journal keeps me sane.

Schools have been closed for a war we assumed would be brief, like previous wars. They are to reopen next week, since parents are home with their children and can't go to work. I remember substitute teaching during the last war, and call my former supervisor to volunteer. She is delighted. "Can you teach English—and art—in an elementary school in Ramat Gan? Their teacher went to her parents in America."

As a storyteller I can use stories to elicit expression in art. Mugabu, a West African storyteller, realized storytelling was a better way to teach. I can bring in my stories and my sensitivity, sharpened by connections with Father.

The night before schools are scheduled to reopen, missiles rain on Israel. One strikes just a kilometer from *my* school, but I don't know that since the government censors don't broadcast specific information. I am unprepared the next morning, when I alight from the bus to find a crowd of people scurrying about with armloads of clothes, loading them into vans, calling out to one another, "You're alive. Thank the Lord!"

Dumbstruck, I hurry to "my" school, where the principal, a disheveled and weary woman in her fifties, greets me. She explains, "We've all been up all night. After the Scud hit just down the road I set up an evacuation center, and we spent the night moving bombed-out families to temporary lodgings. Half of your first-hour students were evacuated, and will arrive late on minibuses from their hotels. This is not our first hit. Ours is a magnet school, with children from all over the city. Many live on Abba Hillel Street, where Scuds demolished rows of apartments."

The same missiles I saw from my window! She continues, "My head aches from lack of sleep, but the school day is beginning. So it's back to work. You will teach four classes of English to bright students, and art to fourteen classes of bright and very slow learners, from first through eighth grade. Thanks for helping out."

What have I taken on? The principal leads me to a half-empty room, where twenty seventh-graders are sitting quietly, almost numb. I have no idea what I am to teach. I quickly glance at the lesson plan and the class list. I begin calling out names to see who is there, and who is missing. I ask the students what they were studying at home during their forced recess. As they show me the workbooks they took home, we get to know one another.

The lesson is nearly over when the missing half of the class arrives in a van, tired after a sleepless night. These are evacuees whose apartments were demolished. Yair, a tiny, dark-eyed seventh-grader, stumbles in carrying a plastic sandwich bag. He's never seen me before, yet he comes to me, and says, "My father told me to show this to the class."

Yair's father knows something about trauma release. The boy turns to the class, opens the bag, and pulls out one item at a time. He holds up a brownish inch-and-a-half square, "My father told me to tell you. This was my favorite book."

Silently, he puts it back, and then takes out a strip of twisted metal about three inches long, "This was the corner of my bedroom." That goes back into the bag, to be replaced with a bluish burnt strip, "My bed. And the blue bedcover."

Yair walks back to his seat. We are silent. I was not prepared for a room full of bombed-out children. I didn't help him, didn't know how. A few days later I will find my way to work. I show my eighth-grade students a book, *The Creative Journal* by Lucia Cappachione, full of drawings people made expressing fear and the need for security. They begin drawing silently, furiously.

Lina brings me a black-on-white sketch of a face frozen in a scream, hair standing on end. "That's me," she says. "Our brand-new home disappeared under my feet, right after we moved in." She begins to cry.

Spontaneously I ask, "Do you want me to put my arm around you?"

She nods yes, and I hold her quietly. It's closeness we need, not just learning. In every lesson, in each class, I walk from desk to desk, patting shoulders, comforting, as the children draw pictures of fear, destruction, and huddling in sealed rooms. Formal lessons are secondary to my role as an anchor.

The Goat in the Sealed Room

Storytelling works magic in the classroom. I revise a story called "The Crowded House," a European folktale about a poor man with many children who lives in a tiny, very crowded hut. The problem is solved by bringing in more and more animals. I create a version related to the war:

In Ramat Gan lives a near-penniless man with his wife and four children in a tiny two-bedroom apartment. One room has been sealed against missiles and poison gas, and everyone has a gas mask. The first Scud falls, and all six huddle into the sealed room, so they are even more crowded than before. The man asks advice from his rabbi, who asks: "Is there someone worse off than you?" So the man invites the elderly couple next door to come into the sealed room with them because they are afraid to be alone.

The man reports to the rabbi that it's worse now, and again the question is who is worse off. The man remembers the young woman with twin babies whose husband has been called to the army, and brings them into the sealed room, too. The babies are in special sealed cribs since they don't have gas masks, which takes all the remaining space in the room.

The man returns to the rabbi to complain of being more crowded than ever.

The rabbi sighs, "I'll come myself, to see what to do. But, as you know, I'm allergic to dairy products, and have a goat that I milk. I need to bring her, too." When the rabbi brings his goat, everyone discovers that a gas mask is useless against the smell of a goat!

The students ask for that tale again and again.

A New Mars Invasion

I recall hearing Orson Welles's radio dramatization of H. G. Wells's *War of the Worlds* when I was eleven. People who listened panicked and fled their homes, believing little green men from Mars had invaded New Jersey. I tell that story to replace fear with fantasy in the classroom. Instead of Scuds, the children draw little green people coming down from space, along with green puppies and kittens, dolls and toys.

Father's Spirit

Four weeks later the war ends, and teachers are told to go back to teaching "as normal." A complete lack of sense and sensitivity, for many of my students are still living in hotel rooms! Disciplinary and emotional problems are increasing in schools and society. The number of heart attacks and emotional breakdowns zooms. I stop teaching, for the teachers' pay has eroded seriously, and I care too much about my students to pretend nothing has changed. It may be time to follow new paths.

Excerpts from my journals from 1991–1992.

July. A helpful feeling, being in Israel and knowing Father is going downhill. His letters are infrequent, hen-scratch lines, accusing me of anything. Marc writes that Father is weak and incoherent.

Today everything is going wrong. The bank lost a check. The grocer overcharged. The milk I bought was sour, and the bank clerk and store salesmen wouldn't listen to my complaints.

That's what I write. But the problem is not in Israel. The channel in my head from the Light is open again, open to my father.

The next day, I write,

Though I scheduled a lecture on journaling, "something" told me to cancel it. But I got logical—which shuts off intuition.

Practicing Chi Kung in preparation for the lecture, I felt a sharp blow on my left shoulder! Carlos Castaneda's Don Juan says our Death walks behind our left shoulder. I shouted, "Father died!"

I told myself I probably pulled a muscle. Forty minutes later the phone rings. My nephew is calling. "Grandpa died forty minutes ago. He had a bad stroke yesterday, and was struggling for his life for twenty-four hours. Dad is on his way home from Maine."

The blow happened the moment my father died! Did his spirit come to me in Israel? Are we so attached? Or did the Angel of Death give me a blow to shake our heartstrings apart? Is it because of Father's struggle for life yesterday that everything went wrong?

Strange ideas, but it's time to stop being rational. When Marc calls two hours later to tell me not to come to the funeral the connection is fading. My phone is dead and I don't know when the funeral is scheduled.

Two days later.

11:30 at night in Israel, 3:30 P.M. in Milwaukee, I wake suddenly, jerked out of my sleep. I feel that my feet are being pulled into the ground! Maybe Father is being buried and we are *literally* bound together. I call out in my imagination, silently: Father, let go. It's time for you to leave. I promise to watch over you, say the Kaddish memorial prayer three times every day. The pulling ended.

Two days after that.

When the telephone repairman shows up, he reports that someone cut the wires! My friend Merry, who uses energy healing, explains: "Sometimes our connection to cosmic energy waves is so strong that it overwhelms the lower energy waves. Your phone was interfering with contact with your father."

The phone is reconnected. I call my brother and learn that the "pulling" feeling did happen at the time of the burial. Marc says, "We won't be observing the mourning period because I'll be at sea. We have a long-standing date with our sailing partners."

Someone, preferably a male relative, has to say the requisite mourning prayers for eleven months. I promised Father. I will do it. I don't accept limitations against women in Judaism ever since I learned how deafness is considered in religious law. I pray for Father morning, noon, and night, and soon praying becomes integral to my life.

I am in continuous contact with Father in my inner thoughts. I write in the Journal of a process, a, fantasy, seeing his spirit slowly separating from his earthly self. So that's why we mourn for eleven months, to accompany the spirit through a process of separation, as wisps of the physical side drift away. Praying and meditating and writing blend and flow. The process of writing in the Journal brings me into depths of wisdom and dreams.

At the end of the mourning period, I write a "Twilight Image" in my Journal, of Father reaching the gates of heaven.

Eleven months later.

Oh no! Mother is standing there, waiting for him, just as she waited for him through the years, never knowing when he was coming home. She's shouting: 'Where have you been? I've been waiting. You are always late.' She died in 1968, twenty-three years before!

That is too much! Imaging has gone beyond my control! I'll 'talk to her,' writing imaginary dialog: 'You are in heaven, no longer deaf. Just enjoy the afterlife in peace with Father now that he is with you.' The scene fades away as they walk off together.

Of course, I never tell any of this to my brother. Nor does it matter what anyone thinks of this funny unspiritual farewell to my parents.

Things beyond the so-called normal don't have to be serious, do they?

To Hell and Back

I continue practicing Chi Kung in Israel with Joe, a local teacher. That autumn Merry and I join his five-day retreat in northern Israel. The view from the mountain stretches to the Lake of Galilee, glimmering crystal blue, reflecting strong sunlight. The food is plain, and I gorge myself on the juicy mulberries growing wild on the mountain. White ones, oozing sweetness, and purple ones, exploding their juice over my hands and underfoot. Like delicious finger paint, from these trees, the source of silk.

Joe announces, "We will go into the fields every day at 4:00 A.M. and 6:00 P.M. to practice Chi Kung. Please observe three days of silence, except during our afternoon meetings, when we study Chinese philosophy. We'll begin with a tradition: An infant in China receives a secret name from his father when he is two months old. What's the importance of a secret name?"

From Native American lore I reply, "The father thinks about his child as if he were that name—say Running Deer—and the child absorbs the message in his father's eyes, of lightness and speed. When I was born my mother chose the name Dolores for me, but her parents changed it."

Joe doesn't give me time to explain about Dolores del Rio, the dancer whom Mother worshipped. He makes a deceptively simple request, "May I use your example to develop the subject?" Because I agree, I learn why tradition forbids saying the name aloud.

The next afternoon Joe begins, "Dolores means 'sorrow' in Spanish. Dee's secret name is her life of sorrows. She carries a cross of sorrows, like Jesus on the Via Dolorosa, the Stations of the Cross."

Joe relates, one for each "station," secrets about my life that I told him in confidence. I don't confront him in the dedicated silence of the retreat.

Into Hell

The next morning I stumble in the predawn dark and scratch my arm on rusty barbed wire. When we start home, my arm is itching badly. I am sure it is only an allergy, but the itching grows worse, no matter how many antihistamine pills I swallow and how much calamine I apply. Burdened by Joe's cross, I write in my journal of that Via Dolorosa, becoming more and more depressed. The next day, before the Day of Atonement, when we wait for the divine decree whether we will live or die, I write a lamentation, asking to die.

Something clearly miraculous happens. I find an audiotape in my mailbox from Ira Progoff. I did not order that tape, but it speaks directly to me, as Progoff emphasizes "In difficult times we do not work alone. We seek help from others."

I make a date with Merry for the next morning, who will listen, without judgment. By morning red lines are running down my upper arm, blood poisoning from the rusty wire. Maybe my prayer to die is being answered! Still, I run to my doctor for a heavy dose of antibiotics before visiting Merry.

Reading the lamentation aloud, crying bitterly, I sit facing her. Merry rests the soles of my feet on the palms of her hands, to keep us connected, she says.

She instructs, "Now close your eyes, breathe gently, and tell me what you see. Let your imagination flow."

I report "I see blue sky, and God, seated on his throne, looking down at me—and laughing! Does he see me as a speck, a marionette acting a show for his entertainment? Is that all? Is my pain meaningless in the greatness of the cosmos? To Him I am no more than a grain of sand. Is that why he is laughing?"

Merry gently encourages me to continue, and I close my eyes again. "Wait. At his side, I see my father sitting on a stool. He is laughing, too. But they're not laughing at me. My father is teaching God to laugh! Laughter is the elevator out of hell."

I begin to laugh, harder and harder, and continue to describe the images flowing one after the other. "My tears and my laughter are washing out a stream of figures, people in my past, floating away on the water of my tears. Now a little door is opening at the side, in the space they left empty. Like Alice in Wonderland, a little girl is peering out. Now she is coming out, growing like Alice did, filling my emptied inner space. She's about six years old."

Have I been hiding in there ever since my brother fell down the stairs? At last I have found the way back to life, let the frightened little girl out, to be a part of me.

Father taught me to live, again, through laughter. I am blessed with his love and laughter, during his life, and forever. We never needed words.

Memorial

I travel to Milwaukee to represent our family at the "unveiling" ceremony for Father's tombstone. I also attend a Becker family reunion, and write to my brother,

> I am at Aunt Sarah and Uncle Max's sixtieth wedding anniversary. Family stories are flowing like ocean waves, one after another! This is my chance to catch up on family history. Cousin Mac remembers a high-school party, where everyone admired his pretty girl friend, Aunt Pearl, only six years older than me.
>
> Love, your sister.

That evening Sarah reminisces, "Long years, hard work, and now it's time to celebrate. Ma worked when we were little, so I was responsible for Sam after he lost his hearing, even though he's older than me. I always took care of everyone, brought my parents to live with us when they got old. I had to put Ma in a nursing home when she started to wander, but Pa was with me until he died at ninety-two. My grandfather came to live with us, too, when he came from Europe. He lived to be eighty-five, and I took care of him, especially his ulcerated legs. I did my duty."

Sarah cared for her parents and grandfather, with nary a complaint. She wiped her eyes, as we remembered her as the Becker's wingless angel.

Uncle Al's children are the comedians, with their stories about my grandparents! Mickey, Al's eldest, recalled, "Grandpa Harry didn't stop working until he was over eighty years old. I remember him making deliveries, an enormous cloth sack over his shoulder filled with coal, delivering a ton of coal one hundred pounds at a time.

"Grandpa was righteous, too, a founder of the synagogue. He never got paid for a lot of the coal he 'sold' in the Depression, you know. Religious and charitable, everyone knew him, and everyone owed him money.

"But sometimes he got carried away in his pursuit of justice. Grandpa went to jail when he was eighty-five years old! My father got a call from the district attorney, saying that Grandpa was in jail for assault and battery because he beat up the *shamash,* the synagogue custodian. He caught him stealing out of the charity box! The *shamash* was bigger and younger, but Grandpa's rage gave him strength."

My father probably would have done the same thing. The Bible says, "Justice, justice, you shall pursue," and Father, too, was concerned with justice, furious about people taking advantage of him because of his deafness.

Family Mischief

Al's son-in-law Jack regaled us with stories of the years when Sarah and Al had both retired and were helping Jack in his odd-lot store. "One day a man came in to buy the advertised special, light-bulbs. Al said I asked: 'where are the trade-ins? Didn't you bring the used bulbs?' I couldn't believe what he did! Went out and returned with used bulbs!

"I remembered that story when my daughter was engaged to a young man studying science at university. I'm self-educated, didn't warm up to this educated boyfriend, and fate played into my hands. When she brought him home for the weekend, the lightbulb in the guest bathroom burned out. Our fancy guest asked me for a new bulb, and I remembered my father-in-law's prank. I asked for the burnt-out bulb. Why? asked the scientist, and I answered: 'I'm making a darkroom!'"

We applaud his genius! Maybe it's hereditary.

To the Cemetery

Because Sylvia's daughters are quarreling during the party, I see other Beckers communicate beyond the limits of this world! The next day the younger sister visits her father's grave, tells him her sister was picking on her, and then phones her sister: "Daddy is mad at you for picking on me. He says Mama told you to take care of me but not boss me around."

The following day, at the unveiling ceremony in the cemetery, Betty is in a huff. She goes to her parents' graves nearby, to ask her father if he really was mad at her. She reports loudly that her father denied it. No one seems surprised at these conversations.

At Father's Grave

The next winter Marc comes with me for his first visit to Father's grave. There has recently been heavy snows, but we find his grave at once. I wonder: is Father's spirit guiding us? I tell Marc: "I brought my camera, to photograph the gravestones, because I get here so seldom that I want a visual record."

I point the camera, push the button, but nothing happens. Odd. It worked fine yesterday. Maybe the batteries leaked, or it's the cold. I try again and again, six times in all. Then—a whirring, and the camera is running like a movie camera, releasing for all the times I clicked. I try photographing Mother's stone another half dozen times, at first with no results, then the same release, the camera whirring away.

Returning to the car, slogging through the snow, I kid Marc: "Maybe it wasn't the camera! Is Father playing jokes with the camera, letting us know he is here?"

We look at one another, and I see a brother I have never known. We both "know." Father must have been there—still playing practical jokes! Father definitely remains with us, in spirit, and laughter. I reconsider. Maybe the slap on my back when Father died wasn't what I thought, a heart-breaking separation. Maybe Father, ever the joker, smacked me on the shoulder, exit laughing: "So long, dotter dear!" Proof that humor was part of his soul. It's still my connection with Father, like stage directions: exit laughing.

CODAs in Israel

To learn to read what silent love hath writ:
To hear with eyes belongs to love's fine wit.

—Shakespeare, Sonnet 23

When Israel Sela completed his doctorate at Gallaudet and returned to Israel, there was no funding for deaf community service. He left the country to organize the Jewish community in Budapest, yet he returns to Israel frequently. When he organizes the first meeting of CODA, to promote the organization of Children of Deaf Adults in Israel, he invites me.

I am the only participant without parents in attendance! When we introduce ourselves, I learn that I am an outsider, not "one of them," an immigrant among children who grew up with deaf parents in Israel. Besides, my parents were not born deaf. Always the outsider, in both the deaf and hearing worlds? Neither spoken nor signed Hebrew is my native language.

Sela opens the conference: "People understand Deaf as Blind, like Helen Keller. They assume children of the Deaf have a difficult childhood, different experiences. True, we can't explain certain things to our families, like—a fart makes noise! Or, just because people are turned away from you they are not talking about you. We have our role, as CODAs, our connection.

"CODAs also have a special relation to grandparents, who see us as substitutes for the child they could not relate to. Siblings too are sometimes unaccepting. So we grow up with much anger!"

So it's not just me, nor my mother nor her family! It's a given! It took all this time to find out!

Sela continues, "As children we were not listened to. We were ears and mouth, and our own personal opinions and questions were not of concern. We didn't have a 'normal' childhood."

Is that why I became a storyteller! Do I seek an audience, someone to listen to me, a magical way?

He warns, "The eldest child, especially if that child is a daughter, is the translator and connection to the world. We live our lives as *translators* between two worlds. We may behave as manipulators. There is also a question of personal identity, 'Who am I,' a person or a CODA?"

I've questioned all along, where do I belong, in which world? Like schizophrenia. Or the infant in Solomon's judgment, with the false mother ready to tear him apart. Yes, I am different, though it's not visible. My way of speech is emphatic, almost aggressive, as if I'm always trying to explain something to my parents.

And the lack of self-esteem, from being low on the social scale. Everything Sela brings up rings a bell, sets off alarms.

He continues, "Then, as we grow up, come the problems of children leaving their deaf parents, with no phone access. Guilt, especially living far away."

I was far away as Mother lay dying of cancer. Then I came to New York, where I had never lived, and stayed, for my father.

Other participants offer their own observations and personal experience.

Peter says, "I had a life experience that others don't understand, but it was a rich life."

Hava Savir, a deaf professor, spoke from the viewpoint of a deaf parent. She was determined to be an independent parent and person. Still a neighbor was concerned that the baby might cry and Hava wouldn't hear her. So the kind woman devised a scheme, a string through the keyhole that she could pull to let Hava know the baby was crying. (I meet Hava again, some years later, after her retirement. She was instrumental in developing a powerful program for training deaf people to become storytellers.)

Estie Barak, a participant, says deaf people are indeed the children of a lesser god. We CODAs had two choices: to curl up inside or go outward aggressively, and nothing in between, unhealthy choices unless we synthesize them.

Throughout my life I curled up, and I still have periods when I need to curl up alone. I know my writing sometimes is void of emotions, but that's the way it was for me, feelings locked up inside, and only a minimal vocabulary for affection.

The good news is that since 1988, because of the Gallaudet uprising, more people consider deafness to be a culture, not something pathological, not just a handicap. Deaf people in the community are gaining respect, and their status is acknowledged. In films, television, the media, we see talented deaf actresses, dancers, even musicians.

Only when I stood up at the New York Storytelling Center and invited the audience to meet my parents did I finally overcome my shame and set out to share stories of my life, embroidering memories with imagination.

The 1995 International Conference on Deaf Education

The International Conference is to take place in Israel, at a hotel within walking distance from my apartment. Friends who know the organizers at Tel Aviv University suggest that I submit a proposal on using storytelling in teaching deaf children. I'm not in academia or deaf education, but their personal introduction opens doors, and I am invited to submit two papers and make a presentation on storytelling.

Two young women from South Africa share the room for the presentation with me. They have brought a video and a booklet of their work using storytelling with deaf children in kindergartens. Costumes, movement, rhythm, words, all blend with classic children's stories. I am delighted, and dream of doing such work.

During the conference I observe how each country handles the dichotomy between sign and lipreading, using new techniques. I discover that deaf people connect worldwide through the Internet, their world expanding beyond old borders and barriers. I can chat minimally in sign with professionals, and approach the principal of Balfour School for deaf children. But she is leaving elementary education.

Then, nothing. My brief signing course was not sufficient. I don't have the proper credentials, so no one takes me seriously–AND I am seventy years old! Good-bye again to the deaf world, I think.

In Touch

I live mostly apart from deafness, touching it now and then. On my weekly visit to the produce market I buy greens and squash from Shoshana Golan, a deaf woman who runs her stall with the help of her children. Her speech is excellent although she is totally deaf. When an unfamiliar customer tries to get her attention, I explain that she needs to see our lips to know what we want. Other produce stalls have deaf salesmen too, a decent way to make a living.

Deaf Education

Oliver Sacks's research with the Salk Institute, published in the book *Seeing Voices*, determined that the brain of a deaf learner reprograms itself to use the areas regularly assigned to hearing for other perceptions and learning. Vibrations and rhythm are also basic instincts that stimulate learning. I know from my experience in waking Father, stimulating energy absorption in his ears, that the vestibular system (the vision/hearing/balance integration area of the brain) can absorb auditory wave-signals, although it cannot translate them to sound.

Now and then deafness beckons to me in whatever I am doing. In my work with Brain Gym exercises for learning, an eleven-year-old deaf boy named Benjie comes to me for help with his reading problems. After our first meeting his mother calls me, excited, "When we came home my husband looked at Benjie, and asked 'Who is this smiling kid? What did you do with our grouchy grumbling child?'"

Benjie becomes a fluent reader after only four meetings because I know how to reach him. He bangs on the metal door knocker to feel vibrations. He jumps on a trampoline outdoors to awaken energy movement, reorganizing his mind for maximum usage. He is motivated to read by the funny stories I give him.

Deaf Storytellers

In 2003, the community center director in Tel Aviv sets up a storytelling program for Deaf adults. He invites me to the last meeting of the course, where I watch young deaf people in a moving performance. They use a shorthand of gestures and movements that they all understand. Just like all teenagers! I get permission to tell one story I heard, and that story, called "A Different Little Girl," is now being told in Singapore through the National Storytellers' e-mail network, under the auspices of the National Storytelling Network in the United States.

The deaf storytellers' groups are "making it" professionally today in Israel. Two years ago they were given an evening on an outdoor stage of the annual Storytelling Festival in the Tel Aviv area. The next year they were upgraded to a performance in the theater itself. Now they perform in many venues with their own company. Leah Sela, Israel's widow, is one of their "angels."

MICHA

MICHA, the foundation for early childhood work with deaf children, is very active in Israel. This remarkable program works with infants and parents, teaching them to communicate in sign as well as providing hearing testing and technology. SHEMA, and similar organizations for the nearly deaf or hard of hearing, are developing beside it.

In spite of these resources, the public school system seems unaware of the physical limitations of deafness. Teachers assume that deaf students have at least partial hearing, and that mainstreaming is the best way to teach them. (Even now, as I write this, newspapers still publish editorials demanding that all children be mainstreamed.) Sign language is only used in one elementary school in Tel Aviv and its suburbs.

At the liberal synagogue, the rabbi announces a deaf boy will celebrate his bar mitzvah coming-of-age ceremony on the Sabbath. I attend even though I don't know him personally, but I experience intense disappointment. Moshe stands on the platform, "speaking," but he is profoundly deaf and his voice is unintelligible. There is a sign-language translator, signing his words for the deaf members of the audience, but what about the rest of us?

Moshe found a way to resolve the ridiculous situation. He wrote and then printed out his speech on his computer, and he distributes it to the audience. He encapsulates the whole problem of his education in that speech, tells of nursery school and public school where he didn't understand anything because only lipreading was taught. He had tantrums until the third grade, when his parents transferred him to Bialik School where sign language is taught and used. There his learning took a great leap forward. Today he attends high school with the help of a private tutor in some of the classes, merging the standard and "handicapped" programs.

Afterward, I talk with Moshe. He wants to go to Gallaudet College, certain that Hebrew sign language is similar enough to American sign that he will be able to manage.

Then I meet his parents, attractive, clearly prosperous. They cannot accept that they have a handicapped child. He has to speak, even if he can't. He has to be like a hearing child, even if he isn't. Are they going through my old trauma, Shame? Can that be, even in these enlightened times? Is it so terrible to have a child with a handicap? Maybe they see their handicapped child as their own handicap. Like my parents' families, nearly a century later? At least their son is moving beyond his parents' limitations, so I see hope in him, and the new generation, worldwide, after the Gallaudet rebellion.

Rediscovering Identity

In 1973, my brother's daughter brought me a copy of Joanne Greenberg's book *In This Sign*. My reconnection to the world of deafness began with that book. Writing and telling these stories, I have found my connection, not only to my parents, but to the world of the Deaf.

I know who I am. Though I live with one foot in the hearing world, I carry my other world within me. I look for connections, joyfully greet Shoshana in the Carmel produce market. I thrill with Amnon Damti's success as a dancer. Now I am whole, daughter of the Deaf!

MY HANDS

Who cut off my hands?
I come here to grieve
The loss of my hands.

To shape my thoughts
In my hands, on my hands, with my hands.

Who stole my hands?
On the piano, fingering is labored,
My hands heavy, clumsy.

Who stole my childhood,
My communication, satisfaction?
Mother? Her family? Teachers? Provolo. The world.

Can I do it now? Take back my hands,
Re-connect to heart and brain,
Eyes and ears, and mind.

Through stories, telling, writing,
Bring my soul into a path of story dancing
Through my hands.

Afterword

Now that I have completed this book I can look back on me and deafness and life. Someone recently asked if the subject wasn't an obsession with me, and I smiled. Do you think Einstein was obsessed? I have researched, discovered so much material, had articles printed, given a presentation at the International Conference of Educators of the Deaf, and am telling stories out of the book. I met Simon Carmel. A friend fluent in Italian translated material on Antonio Provolo. I am happy, and funny, Father's legacy.

Maybe it's time to make a movie. So I've only begun.

Imagine with me. Maybe the Light hit me again, not electrocuting, but shaking me up, leaving the connection open. So the writing itself was indeed a healing, for me and for the memories, and maybe, just maybe, for the souls of my parents and, yes, my aunt.

Appendix

Excerpted from my article "Antonio Provolo: Hero or Villain? *Journal of Deaf Studies and Deaf Education* 4(1): 69.

A friend was driving through Italy, photographed a plaque reading: "In this building Fra. Antonio Provolo developed his system of teaching deaf children to sing."

Thus I discovered Provolo, his accomplishments, and how his disciples caused the banning of teaching of sign language to deaf children.

In the 1820s, Father Antonio Provolo (1801–1842), of Verona, Italy, was "inspired" to teach deaf children to sing, giving them the gift of speech through music. Provolo's passion was to transform mute children, who seemed stupid and retarded, into human beings with a soul capable of worshipping God.

He developed his own oral methods in Verona, abandoning the domestic signing system altogether. He worked from the premise that deaf children respond to rhythm, to beauty, and to the love of man and God. He began teaching deaf students who had residual hearing, and soon they were able to sing as well as hearing children. He achieved great success, and wrote manuals setting forth the first formal system for teaching oral speech to deaf children. (Provolo's *Manuale* is available on rare-book microfilm at the Gallaudet University Library.) . . .

Provolo related to his students as intelligent human beings, not just as people who were deaf and dumb. He called his method *armonica*, harmony. Using a set of graduated springs like tuning forks, on a scale of seven musical notes, he taught the students to feel, through the vibrations, the different sounds they could not hear. . . .

But Provolo, carried away by his success, banned any use of signing, and his disciples became even more fanatic. Thus, in 1880, at the Milan Conference on the Education of Deaf Children, his successor Giulio Giori brought about a complete ban of the use of sign language in teaching deaf children. Politics were involved. The conference was a battleground of hearing teachers against deaf teachers! Deaf teachers would not be able to teach a purely oral approach! Until the revolution at Gallaudet University in 1988, signing was not accepted by the great majority of *hearing* teachers of deaf children.

Notes

1. Golda Meir, who came to Milwaukee from Russia as a child, went to school with Anna's oldest sister. She later was to become prime minister of Israel.

2. Two of these immigrants, Harry Soref and Sam Stahl, invented the steel padlock, the portable lock and key. Larry Yolles, Soref's deaf grandson, attended the new Gallaudet College for the Deaf in Washington, D.C., and later entered the family business, the Master Lock Factory.

3. In 1827, Czar Nicholas I instituted a law that called for conscripting Jewish men into the army for a period of twenty-five years. In fact, it was kidnapping rather than conscripting, and the soldiers would never see their families again.

Bibliography

Books

Capacchione, Lucia. *The Creative Journal.* North Hollywood, Calif.: Newcastle, 1989.

Cohen, Leah Hager. *Train Go Sorry.* Boston: Houghton Mifflin, 1994.

Dennison, Paul. *Switching On.* Ventura, Calif. Edu-Kinesthetics, 1981.

Giora, Tzvi. *The Unconscious and Its Narrative.* Budapest: T-Twins, Budapest, 1991.

Greenberg, Joanne. *In This Sign.* New York: Holt Paperbacks, 1984.

Herman, Judith. *Trauma and Recovery.* New York: HarperCollins, 1992.

Jamison, Kay Redfield. *Exuberance*. New York: Vintage, 2005.

Keller, Helen. *The Story of My Life*. New York: Bantam Classics, 1990.

Kisor, Henry. *What's That Pig Outdoors?* New York: Hill and Wang, 1990.

Nin, Anais. *Diaries*. Vol. 1. New York: Harcourt Brace, 1966.

Padden, Carol, and Tom Humphries. *Deaf in America: Voices from a Culture*. Cambridge, Mass.: Harvard University Press, 1988.

Progoff, Ira. *At a Journal Workshop*. Los Angeles: Tarcher, 1975.

————. *Life Study: Experiencing Creative Lives by the Intensive Journal Method*. New York: Dialogue House Library, 1983.

Sacks, Oliver. *Awakenings*. New York: HarperCollins, 1990.

————. *Seeing Voices*. Berkeley: University of California Press, 1989.

Shakespeare, Rosemary. *The Psychology of Handicap*. Essential Psychology series. London: Methuen, 1975.

Sidransky, Ruth. *In Silence*. New York: Ballantine, 1990.

Walker, Lou Ann. *A Loss for Words*. New York: Harper and Row, 1986.

Zvi, Giora. *The Unconscious and Its Narrative*. Budapest: T-Twins, 1991

Doctoral Dissertations

Abrams, Judith Z. "Disabled Persons and Disabilities in Jewish Sources from the Tanach through the Bavli." PhD diss., Baltimore Hebrew College, 1993.

Hartman, Tzvi. "Halacha and Handicap." PhD diss., Hartman Institute, Jerusalem, 1993.

Articles

Catholic Herald, "Immigrants Played Essential Role in Catholic, Jewish Life," Jan. 27, 2004.

Dolnick, Edward. "Deafness as Culture. " *The Atlantic* (September 1993): 34ff.

Hyams, Hanna. "Shame: The Enemy Within." *Transactional Analysis Journal* 24 (October 1994).

Shurman, Dvorah. "Antonio Provolo, Hero or Villain?" *Journal of Deaf Studies and Deaf Education* (Winter 1999).

Wolkomire, R. "The Quiet Revolution in Hand Talk." *Smithsonian Magazine* (July 1992): 30–44.